Stuff that you find at the fron

- Any of the maps used in this book were copied from the CIA website; you just wouldn't believe the goodies you can find there. Goes some way to making up for the hard time they gave Jason Bourne.
- https://www.cia.gov/

Copyright stuff

In the highly unlikely event you end up using any of the pictures or content, just tell folks where you got it.

Other stuff

- Sorry about all the cussing, swearing, sexual innuendo and for anything else that you might find offensive.
- If you have Princess Leia's phone number, can you send it onto Oisin.m.hughes@gmail.com

Thanks to the following folks

Dathy, Bar, Eamo, Dar, Figgs, Mole, Jay, Jamsie, Eamo, Seany, Jane, H, Pablo E, Jolly Green Jim, Geoff, John, Josh, Joe, Erns Juice, Shannon, Mick, Mike, John, Mary, Uisce, twisted robot, Maccer, SusieJoe, Heidles Schnidles, Benny, Tri, Half-moon Frenchy, Claudio, Ewan, Charlie, Sam Gamgee, Mr Fluffykins, The two Swedes, Miriam, Vanessa, Sam and the guy who cooked me ham in Prudhoe bay.

Published by Oisin Hughes.

I never learned anything listening to myself

Robert Mitchum

How the fuck?

In November 2009, I stood looking down a road at a bridge full of heavily armed soldiers. The bridge traversed the border between the two Central American countries of Honduras and Nicaragua. I was in Honduras desperately hoping to cross into Nicaragua, but as the day wore on it was looking increasingly unlikely. It was time to face reality; I was in deep shit. The "dumb smiling Irish paddy" routine wasn't going to avail me this time round.

I had no immigration entry stamps in my passport for Honduras and was thus in the country unlawfully and judging by the pitch of the shouting coming from the customs folks; my motorbike was here illegally too. There were gangs of people standing around shouting at me for one reason or another and no one spoke English, not to mention the fact that I couldn't speak Spanish.

Politically, Honduras seemed close to melting down. The recently ousted President Zelaya was due back in the country at any time; it was only a couple of weeks since a coup removed him and the atmosphere in the country felt like things could get nasty at any moment. I could not wait to get the hell out of there.

Without the proper paperwork, It looked like there was going to be no way through. The only option was to go back to the border with El Salvador and try to explain to the migration centre that they forgot to stamp me in. All this would have to be accomplished with a smaller grasp of Spanish than the typical mongoose; it was going to be a nightmare to get this mess sorted out.

I asked myself "How the fuck did I end up in this situation?" "How do I always, always, always end up in these fucking situations?"

That I may die roaming...

Prologue

My name is Oisin and I'm from Dublin, Ireland.

In July 2008, I undertook riding a motorbike 34,000 miles through North, Central and South America. The route that I intended to take would see me leaving Toronto, driving initially east to Nova Scotia, and then riding thousands of miles across Canada until I got to Anchorage in Alaska.

Once there, I would continue my journey north to Prudhoe Bay in Alaska, the most northerly town there is a road to in North America. From there I would ride south for months, back down through Alaska, Canada, mainland USA, Mexico, Central America and South America until I got to Ushuaia, near Cape Horn, the most southern tip of South America.

The final leg of the journey would be riding back north to Buenos Aires in Argentina, where I'd fly both myself and my bike back home; all going well in time for Christmas 2008.

In total, I planned to go through 14 countries, namely Canada, USA, Mexico, Guatemala, El Salvador, Honduras, Nicaragua, Costa Rica, Panama, Ecuador, Peru, Bolivia, Chile and Argentina. I hadn't made my mind up about Colombia yet.

I had an adventure filled with thrills, spills and some unbelievable situations. In my wildest dreams, I could never have imagined all the stuff that would happen to me. This book is my account of the journey.

I went on this trip to put some excitement in my life. Every kid I knew growing up, wanted to be Luke Skywalker or Han Solo. In my head, going on this trip represented my chance to blow up the death star and snog Princess Leia.

When I started I knew the outcome was uncertain but that the days ahead would be filled with adventure and fingers crossed, sex would be around every corner

Most people would love to do something like this; I'm just one of the people who did. Hopefully, after reading this book maybe you'll think about setting your sail and having an adventure of your own.

Thanks for reading, and May the Force be with you.

Oisin

Chapter 1

On a cold and wet Friday in September 2005, while out shopping I was enticed over to a DVD stand in HMV. The banner said, "Buy 3 DVD's for 30 Euro"; I picked up two movies I really liked and because I couldn't see another movie that caught my fancy, I grabbed a DVD called the Long way Round.

It was a documentary series with Ewan McGregor and Charlie Boorman detailing their trip around the world on two BMW motorcycles from London to New York, heading east. I had seen ads for the series but never watched it and to be honest wasn't even remotely interested in motorbikes or in the two lads heading off to foreign shores. That said, it was as appealing as anything else on the stand so I picked it up and went home.

The relentlessly crappy Irish weather continued for the entire weekend and with Liverpool losing on the Saturday the weekend was turning into a complete washout. I picked up the Long way round DVD and stared at the black and white cover photo of Ewan and Charlie with their motorbikes and said "fuck it, nothing else to do" so I threw on the DVD.

To my complete surprise I watched it straight through, episode after episode, finishing up the following morning at around 2am. I was hooked. I wanted to do something like this; No I simply had to!

There were however a couple of minor obstacles to overcome, like I didn't own a motorcycle, nor was I able to ride one.

At the time I was married. Things weren't going well primarily down to the fact that I was a bad husband, about as emotionally available as a tin of processed peas and I was spending far too much time in work. As the winter wore on, my enthusiasm to do a trip started to wane, what with on-going marital problems and being up to my tonsils in work, I put it to the back of my mind.

Around November 2005 one of my best mates, Dave, asked me along to the annual motorcycle show in the RDS arena in Dublin. As I was walking around the displays looking at all the bikes I came across a stand for Globebusters, a husband and wife motorcycle tour company in England who run overland trips. After exchanging a couple of pleasantries, I walked away with one of their brochures.

I looked at the back page and there it was, the Pan-American motorcycle trip stretching from Prudhoe Bay, the most northerly town in Alaska the whole way down to Ushuaia in Terra del Fuego near Cape Horn in South America. I thought to myself, "this looks absolutely amazing", I took the brochure and plonked it on my office desk to remind me on the bad days, that there was an alternative to what I was doing now.

Road Trip

That Christmas my marriage came to an end and after about eight weeks of wallowing in self-pity, I made a decision to fuck off to Australia for a month on a road trip. I only thought up the idea on the

Tuesday and flew out on the Thursday of the same week; I'm nothing if not impulsive. I packed like a lunatic and headed off to the airport and next thing I knew I was in Australia. I hired a Nissan X-trail and kept driving and driving to try to work the post-marital breakup blues out of my head.

On the journey, I learned a couple of things about myself. Firstly, that I was ok with being by myself for long stretches, and secondly that I really liked long journeys where you didn't really have a place to get to. It was ok to just drive until you got bored and then, pull over, find a place to stay, go out and get some grub, have a pint and at the end of the day, hit the scratcher.

I also started to get a little peeved about having your holiday decided for you. You know how it goes, you tell someone that you're going somewhere and right away they're off telling you that you have to go here, then there and how if you don't go to "this place" well then "you simply haven't been". So I made up my mind that I was only going to go to places that I wanted to go to and not submit to any peer pressure about what I "simply must do" when travelling.

In Australia, I set myself the goal of never driving over the same piece of tarmac twice. This way the road would always change for me and every day would be an adventure because I didn't have to retrace my steps on my way home. I carved a loop out in Australia and knocked out about 14,000km in only a couple of weeks.

Buying a bike

When I came back to Ireland, I made up my mind that I was going to have to buy a bike if I was ever going to consider taking on the Pan-American Highway.

My thinking was that I might start with a small trip; I needed to figure out if motorcycling was something I'd like, if I just upped and went I could end up hating the whole thing. I had my doubts, motorcycling is dangerous, certainly more dangerous than a car.

When you combine that with the fact that you're out in the elements and in Ireland all it ever seems to do is piss rain, I had enough reason to believe that the whole thing could turn out to be pure misery.

I went to see my friend Jason who has always been a keen biker. He had a couple of copies of motorcycle news that had heaps of bikes for sale in the back pages. No sooner had I opened the first classified page and there it was; a bumblebee 1150gs adventurer for sale, the same model bike that Ewan and Charlie had used for the long way round. It came with panniers, crash bars, heated handgrips and some other goodies and the whole lot was on sale for 11,500 euro.

The bike had less than 10,000km on the clock so was practically new. The chap who was selling it was based about four miles from Jason's house so off we went in the car to have a gawk at the beast.

I'd never make a poker player, as soon as I saw the bike I just said, "I'll take it!" and wrote him a cheque for the full amount he was looking for. My penalty for such impulsiveness was I had to listen to Jason for about the next six months giving me the "can't believe you didn't even try to haggle!" routine. I didn't care, I had my bike and I don't think my pulse dropped below a hundred the whole way home.

My first big problem was that I couldn't drive the bike.

I asked Jason to drive it home for me and when we got to my place, I had my first impromptu bike lesson. I was terrified when I jumped up on it, bear in mind that the BMW 1150 weighs over 250kg. If it starts to go to the left or right and gets past about twenty degrees from vertical you'll never be able to hold it up and the whole thing will just crash to the ground. Picking that weight up off the ground would be like shiteing a pineapple.

Every time I tried to move forward on the bike the engine would cut out as I tried to master the clutch. Every jump forward resulted in my shins getting clubbed by the crash bars, a sore bastard I don't mind telling you. I knew that I tended to jump into things, more often than not, it doesn't work out as expected; the niggling feeling that this was going to be another in a long line of bad ideas was starting to grow in my mind.

In keeping with a Hughes family tradition, i.e. full duck or no dinner, I signed up for three full days of intensive rider training with a private motorcycle school. The course was run in March and the weather was absolutely woeful.

At various times it was snowing, pissing rain, sleeting, or howling wind and just to throw some salt and vinegar into the mix; the traffic was mental. There was however a positive aspect; I've always maintained that because I learned to ride in the rain I'm a much better rider in bad weather than most.

Most people start the other way, they learn in the good weather and only tend to go out on their bikes when the weather is good, I never knew any different so having started the hard way I never looked back.

I was struggling to get the hang of the clutch; the instructor had a great analogy to help me get master it.

"Listen horse, you need to think of the clutch as if it's your birds left tit.... would you be grabbing it in and out like that? Eh? Would ya? No... I don't fuckin think so, she wouldn't be long about punching your lights out.... nice and smooth... got it?"

As for the accelerator he said to treat it like a "budgies neck". I think it was the bird's knockers that did it for me; never being one to snatch and grab at a boob, at least not since I was in the cot.

When I told him that I was considering heading off to ride the entire Pan-American Highway on the motorcycle, he simply replied "Me hole".

So now I had the bike and I could drive it; it was time to plan a road trip. I talked to my mate Dave about heading down to the Rock of Gibraltar in Spain; I said I'd chance the run even though I didn't have a full license. So we started planning in earnest.

After a couple of weeks and with the excitement starting to build, Dave phoned me. His opening line was "You'll never guess what", to which I replied, having read the tone in his voice "Sheila's up the duff".

Dave's girlfriend was pregnant. I was delighted for him but knew it meant that the trip to the Rock of Gibraltar was over unless I wanted to go on my own, with so little experience; it was just too risky.

Some months after, when Dave and I were out for a couple of pints, I asked him

"So how come Sheila got pregnant? Did the Jonnie split?"

(A pertinent question, Dave has a hammer on him like an oak tree, sort of thing you would normally expect to see hanging out of an elephants face), Dave replied, "Nah sure I can never get one to fit", which all credit to him, he said with true humility.

Then I asked, "So was Sheila not on the pill?" Dave replied, "Nope". Realising that he'd been bare backing and risking our trip if Sheila got pregnant, I said, "So you were just pulling out! Ya fucker ya! Your some bollix, it's not like the tadpoles would have far to swim, you were practically delivering them to the front door with that baseball bat of a Mickey, You bollix!"

So that was it, there was no other opportunity to go on a medium length trip to see if travelling on a motorcycle for six months was something I would enjoy or even be capable of doing. I was left with the dilemma, if I'm going to go on this trip "Who in the name of fuck was I going to go with".

Going alone?

The summer of 2008 was the time I was targeting to leave, it would allow me to follow the summer south through the America's. There were no organised tours running that year with Globebusters for the Pan American, and none of my friends could go with me. I kept asking myself, was I capable of going by myself, I doubted it.

The sort of things that went through my head centred round that I needed to try to go with someone who's good at fixing stuff. I'm the sort of guy who, if the house was falling down around me, I'd probably buy a tent for the back garden, I'm just not that good with my hands. Now that's not to say that I don't rub a good boob, I do, but with machinery, I may as well be staring up a bull's hole.

So onto the web I went in search of kindred spirits, I was convinced there must be a couple of heads out there with the same sort of thing in mind, I still had a year to plan it so it was plenty of time to meet some guys who might be into same the thing. I got a serious amount of ribbing from the lads about the gay connotations of searching for bikers on the web.

John Mundy

I found a website called Horizons unlimited and just pumped in the words, "Pan-American July 2008, anyone interested?" A lad living near Felixstowe in England replied and said that he was up for it. We talked on the phone and seemed to have quite a bit in common.

We both said that if we were serious about this we'd have to meet and talk, to hammer out what we both wanted to get out of the trip. A couple of weekends later, I flew to England and John picked me up at the airport.

On the phone John sounded a bit of a cockney but was gentle spoken, however when I met him, I nearly fainted. He was about 5 foot 5, a serious looking skinhead with tattoos the whole way down his arms. "Oh my fuck" I thought to myself.

As it turned out he was an ex British soldier who served in Northern Ireland.

Again, I thought to myself "Oh my fuck! Either this guy has gone online to reel in some "ass" or he's logged onto the equivalent of "dial a sucker to murder and leave in your fridge for six months while you take out his torso to have sex with while watching coronation street reruns.com".

We got to his house and headed off down the pub for some pints and grub. On the way we walked down a pitch black lane, for a good while I was certain he was going to knife me. As it turned out I needn't have worried, John was a sound skin and we got on like a house on fire. He worked on the docks and drove the exact same type of bike as me and was interested in doing the trip, if he could get his house sold on time as well as get leave of absence from his job.

While all this was going on Ewan and Charlie decided to do the Long way down, which was a motorcycle trip from John of Groat's in northern Scotland to the Cape of Good Hope in South Africa.

All of this just helped to intensify my feelings of needing to go on the trip. I decided that whatever route I was going to take it had to add up to more miles than the long way round, and the long way down combined. Why? Just, that's the why! Not a good enough answer? Well it's a guy thing, if you did ten press-ups I'd have to try to do eleven.

The Plan

We talked a lot about the route. Flying a bike into the states since 9-11 was a nightmare so we decided to fly into Toronto, Canada. This also happened to be where my brother lived, so would be a lot easier to get lifts out to the airport to collect the bike. From there the plan was to head west to Nova Scotia to Cape Breton, and then track back west the whole way across Canada to Anchorage in Alaska.

Once in Anchorage we would ride north to Prudhoe Bay, the most northerly town in Alaska and then south for many months, the whole way to Ushuaia in Argentina and finally back up to Buenos Aires, a trip I "back of the enveloped" at over 30,000miles. The route had some big advantages, namely you didn't need a carnet de passage in any of the countries, and you would only need two languages, English and Spanish.

The if's and the buts were driving me crazy so I made up my mind that I was going to leave on the 12th of July 2008, and in order to remove one of the variables I went ahead and booked my flight. I also made up my mind that if John wasn't able to come along and I couldn't get someone to go with me, I would go alone. Although I desperately hoped that I would find a riding partner.

John had two kids who were in their twenties and unbelievably, no sooner had he decided to go on the trip than they popped round to his house to tell him that they were getting married that year.

John was torn and he said he was going to come over to Dublin to talk about some things. I knew he was coming over to tell me that he wasn't going to be able to go, and he was too nice a guy to tell me over the phone. He knew it was our dream and wanted to tell me face to face that he was letting me down.

A Welsh guy popped up on the horizons website around this time by the name of Geoff and said he was up for it also, I told him John was on his way over so why not plan to come over the same weekend. Geoff was in his mid to late fifties and his wife had passed away less than a year previous. It was obvious that he was on the run from his grief but he was a nice guy and very friendly; if he wanted to come along "why not?" I said.

As expected, John pulled out, and I hadn't heard anything from Geoff for over two months so I resigned myself to going alone. The piece I was unbelievably nervous about was Central America, "How in the name of Jesus am I going to get through those borders on my own!", the icing on the cake being that I had about as much Spanish as is used in the average Speedy Gonzalez cartoon.

About a month before I was due to leave, I got a phone call from Geoff saying he was going. I was actually a bit disappointed because I had rather gotten used to the idea that I would be a solo traveller. However, when I thought about things like the Dalton highway in Alaska and all the dangerous countries that I'd be going through, it would be better to not have to do it alone.

As the day approached, the comments from people in work all revolved around "It'll be a life changing experience" or "You must be fucking crazy!"

My nerves were at fever pitch. The date was set, and the only thing left to do was ship the bike to Toronto. This part, while expensive was easy. I dropped the bike off at my local BMW dealer and they arranged with James Cargo the shipper, to pick it up about ten days before I was due to fly out. I dropped the bike off with the panniers stuffed with camping gear and every manner of gadget that I could fit into the limited storage you have on a motorcycle.

I had the rough timelines for the trip worked out, mainly dictated by insurance limitations and I wrote in my diary:

"Plan is to take fifty nine days to complete the USA and Canada... Fourteen days through Mexico, another fourteen through Central America and the rest in South America finishing hopefully in time for Christmas!"

I structured the journey this way because in my head I reckoned I could do North America again when I was fifty-five if I wanted to; its easy going relatively speaking. The real challenge would be Central and South America so it's better to allocate the majority of time there.

I nicknamed the bike "Molly", which I later changed to Sam Gamgee, I was Frodo.

What happened to Luke Skywalker? What happened to Han Solo? Well, I decided that I was going to be a mixture of Frodo, Conan, Luke Skywalker, Han Solo, Jason Bourne, James Bond and finally Frodo, and no I don't think that's too many heroes to combine into one persona.

The week before I left, I completed the last mandatory task before undertaking any adventure; I went out on the rip. After about fifteen pints and lots of "You're gonna get raped by FARC rebels....You know that don't ya!" type statements the last task before travelling was complete.

Ready to go

With my flight merely hours away I sat on the couch in my sitting room looking out the window. I asked myself "Am I ready?"

I kept replaying a quote I'd read in my head, "The only way you'll ever be 100% prepared for a trip like this is to have done it before".

I had completed less than four thousand miles on the bike since I'd bought it and I had zero off-road training. With the Dalton highway in Alaska a five hundred and fifteen mile gravel fest ahead of me, I told myself that I would have nearly ten thousand miles done by that stage so I'd be a lot more experienced and it would be ok.

I'd almost no Spanish, but reckoned that I could either hook up with some dudes who did when I would have to cross the borders or I'd get some Spanish lessons loaded up onto my I-pod, again I figured I'd be grand. I was ok for money and had heaps of travel equipment, space on the bike was the only concern and picking the bike up would be a massive problem if it ever fell over.

I had only met Geoff once and that was a worry, what if we did not get on? I couldn't fix a thing on the bike if it broke down; I never even had to fix a puncture so if it happened I'd just have to deal with it at the time. I spent hours and hours worrying, and all I had to console myself with was the fact that there was no going back now.

My brother and his girlfriend dropped me and my cuddly toy rabbit Mr. Fluffykins to the airport in Dublin and as I boarded the plane, I couldn't help notice the lack of fanfare. When Ewan and Charlie had headed off on their adventure there were support crews, a cake and big bunch of well-wishers and it felt a bit weird for just my bag and me to be heading off.

Chapter 2

I flew out on Saturday the 12th of July exactly as planned nearly nine months previous, despite the best attempts of an air traffic controllers strike to halt my progress. As we taxied down the runway I just couldn't believe it was about to start.

The flight to Toronto was wedged with people and I got stuck in a middle seat spending the next seven hours battling for elbow room with two fairly substantial lassies, although I doubt they talked in glowing terms about the hefty dude stuck in between them on the flight either.

Toronto

About ninety minutes after arriving and post a surprisingly gentle rubber glove routine from Gail in Canadian customs, I was out in the arrivals hall being picked up by my brother Ernan and his father-in-law, Jack.

The first question out of their mouths was nothing to do with the trip but was "What's the story with Ireland and the European Union and the whole Lisbon treaty thing?" Ireland had just rejected the Lisbon treaty and it was getting massive airplay, so much for being treated like a superstar biker setting out on a terrifying expedition.

I was starting to notice a trend, as much as I would like to think that what I was doing was the equivalent of Luke Skywalker attacking the death star, I had to be content with the fact, that I was the only one who thought so.

On the way back to the house the three of us stopped for some nosebag and after a pound of wings and three frosty bottles of Coors light it was time to go and meet up with the rest of my extended family. After a lovely evening catching up it was time to unpack and hit the scratcher.

The plan was to collect the bike from customs on Monday morning, which would be the point at which the journey would really start. I'd arranged to collect Geoff on the way to the airport cargo hanger; the plan was that hopefully we'd collect the bikes and be on our way by Monday evening.

I kept thinking about the scene in Die Hard 3, where Samuel L Jackson tells Jeremy Irons to "stick your well laid plans up your well laid ass", and wondered whether or not we were just being wildly optimistic to think that we would clear customs in an afternoon.

Monday came and it was time to meet Geoff. We collected him at the hotel and Shannon asked me do you know where this place is? I said "don't worry, I have a GPS!" Off we went out to the Cargo warehouse or at least to its address, whereupon I discovered the first of many limitations of the average GPS unit.

Always remember when in North America to enter the address in East or West terms, you will find that 2500 XYZ street West is a completely different place to 2500 XYZ street East! After being lost for about forty five minutes, we copped onto the problem and made our way to the correct location where we stood in line to clear the bikes.

When we went up with our paperwork, it was obvious that the gents behind the counter had never done anything like temporary importing of motorcycles before. After a lot of head scratching they told us to come back tomorrow as they needed to take some soil samples from the bike to make sure we weren't bringing in any fungi in the mud on the tires. A complete load of cobblers but there was nothing to do but turn away and come back the next day.

They gave us a number to ring to check to see if the bikes were ready, and told us not to come back out unless we'd checked with the number first. They gave us the impression that it might take a couple of days, which really put a downer on things.

In our eagerness to get going we'd gone out to the airport in enduro motorcycle gear hoping to just jump on the bikes and drive off into the wild blue yonder. With the heat and the fact that the cargo terminal was a solid walk away from the customs area and having to walk back and forward between the buildings, we were cooking in our own juices. Geoff and I got a taxi to a hotel together, and shared a double room.

This was the first of many weird moments on the trip for me. There I was in a hotel room in Toronto with a guy maybe twenty years older than me, who I barely knew waiting to go and collect our bikes to start a trip where, who knows what would be ahead of us. It was surreal.

Sharing a hotel room with a friend is easy; it's a little harder when you barely know the person. As we were nodding off to sleep, Geoff started to snore like a whore's bastard. I lay there staring at the ceiling wondering just what the fuck I had gotten myself into.

Finally on the road

Early the next morning we rang the number customs gave us and we got the news that the bikes were good to go, so off we set to uncrate the bikes and go through the customs formalities, it wasn't long before we were shooting east in the direction of Nova Scotia.

Leaving Toronto gradually five lane highways became four then three and finally two as you get further and further away from the urban sprawl. Gradually we made our way through the traffic towards the town of Cornwall on the St Laurence River.

The stifling heat combined with wearing too much gear and the slow moving traffic made the early going almost unbearable. I was sitting on the bike driving along thinking to myself "Is this it? Is this how I'm supposed to feel? This is the trip of lifetime right?"

It probably sounds unbelievably selfish to say it but I was having a horrible time, after a year of planning I was driving along roasting hot and miserable; when you stopped moving it was easy to imagine what it must be like to be a rotisserie chicken.

It's only when you start travelling in Canada that the sheer scale of the country starts to dawn on you. We drove two hundred and seventy seven miles in the first day, or rather afternoon but if you were to look at a map of Canada on an A4 sheet, you would barely be able to perceive the distance at all.

In Canada you have to stop saying things like its "two hundred miles away" or "its 400 kilometres away" and revert back to saying things like such and such a place is "a three day ride" or such and such a place is "18 hours away". Talking in terms of kilometres or miles would drive you crazy.

To put some numbers on it; Canada is over one hundred times the size of Ireland, and more than thirty six times the size of the United Kingdom, so there!

In Ireland and the UK it's pretty common for motorcyclists to filter between traffic, that means making a second or third lane where there's none marked, it drives the rest of the driving fraternity crazy but makes us bikers feel like kings.

It turns out Canadian driver's don't like you filtering on your bike, in fact, seems like they hate it enough to physically roar out the window "hey a-hole... get in fucking line". By the end of the first day I'd already had a couple of these greetings. Thankfully, due to the lack of availability of handguns in Canada I felt I was able to return the greeting with an extended index finger, not the sort of reply I would consider giving in Texas!

The Canadian highways are full of bikers; mostly driving big Honda Goldwing's made to cover the sort of distances one encounters in Canada. Every time we stopped for Gas or a cup of coffee, which was about every hour, we met loads of people.

My first impressions were that the Canadians were a friendly, if a little guarded, bunch. Based on the first couple of conversations we had with the people we met along the road, most didn't have a bull's notion where Argentina was geographically, although most had heard of it.

After a shower that evening, I headed out to try to find a computer to send an email to my family to say that I'd survived the first day. I looked up Cornwall in my Canada rough guide, it didn't mention it. Hmmm, let me try Google I thought to myself, where I found out that its biggest claim to fame is that its home to one of the biggest distribution centres in Canada, Yawn!

It was the first time that the realisation dawned on me that while there are lots of really great places in the world; in between them are a lot of really average or just altogether boring places. I guess there wouldn't be such a thing as great places if it weren't for towns like Cornwall, so I saluted its boring mediocrity while draining a beer.

I lay in the bed that night staring at the ceiling wondering "Is this how I'm supposed to feel? Shouldn't I be feeling better? Shouldn't I be happier? Why am I still thinking about work? I'm on the trip of a lifetime, why doesn't it feel like it, and how the fuck does Geoff snore that loud without waking himself up?"

Heading for Nova Scotia

The next day we got up early, jumped on the bikes and were off to a town called Riviere du Loup in the state of Quebec. It was my first experience of French Canadians. Much like the "Real" French in that, although they may speak a bit of English, they do not speak it to you. I did my best to remember my secondary school French and managed to get by.

I have to admit to the French mob giving me a pain in the arse. I was a tourist in a place spending money; you would think they'd do their level best to communicate with you. Don't get me wrong I'm all for learning the culture before you go somewhere and having to adapt, but when you know the guy behind the counter can speak English and he's just trying to teach you a lesson it all feels a bit shit.

Although I was only two days into the trip one of my bubbles was about to be burst. Before I started the trip, I had images in my head of driving along the road with women in corvettes or Ferraris pulling up beside me and inviting me back to their hotel room for a shagathon, but over the first two days, I'd yet to see a single looker.

A routine was starting to develop; as I was driving along I tended to be just a bit faster than the average traffic flow. So as I passed a car I could peek into the car to see whose driving, desperately hoping it might be a nude centrefold with loose morals. So far, it had just been Canadian men with big hairy hands and some of the plainest women I'd seen since I studied engineering in college.

I told myself, don't worry when you get to "small town Canada" they'll never have seen anything like me and I'll be kidnapped to become the sex slave of an all women cult.

Geoff and I went out into the town and had dinner in a lovely restaurant and had a good chat. He told me all about how his wife had died; he was completely lost without her.

They had been together since they were very young and you could see that when she died it left a hole in him that he was desperately trying to fill. After dinner we went out for a couple of beers and talked some more. We stood looking out over a balcony, with the St Laurence River in the distance. The whole horizon kept flaring with lightning as a stiff summer breeze blew into our faces. It was the first time I felt like I was having a good time.

The next day we set off for Moncton in New Brunswick, three hundred and eighty miles from where we were, we'd be about ten hours total on the road, including stopping for grub and taking pictures. I was starting to feel just a little hard core as I rested up on the bike at one of the gas breaks when up rode a guy on a bicycle. His name was Alex and he'd cycled the whole way from Vancouver to here, over six thousand kilometres. It just goes to show that no matter how crazy you think what you're doing is, there's always someone doing something crazier, buns of steel doesn't even come close to describing this guy.

Moncton was supposed to be a nice place with lots to do and see according to some folks we met along the way, so we were quietly looking forward to it. On the way into town we noticed a lot of strip bars and tattoo parlours, while not necessarily a bad thing, it's never a sign that you're rolling into a Beverly Hills'-esque type area. I pumped "find nearest lodging" into the GPS and it took us to an Econolodge. It looked a bit rough but my ass was so sore from riding (the bike) that I would have slept under a bull for the night.

As we pulled into the car park three baddies pulled up in a car, got out and checked into a motel room just opposite ours. They left the door open in their room and were all drinking away at a couple of cans of beer sitting on the bed. All four had their tops off; I was beginning to think these lads were on a gay cruise. As I was stripping the bike and bringing the gear into the room, I was worried these guys were going to be doing their shopping out of our stuff if we left the room.

Time Zones

Parking our nervous feelings about leaving our stuff in the Motel, we had to wash some clothes or we'd smell so bad we risked getting hosed down by state officials the next time we stopped. We asked the guy in the motel where the nearest launderette was and off we went.

We got to the place and said, "Hi there, what time do you close?" The girl said 9pm; we said grand and started to load up our stuff into the machines. She said "Eh dufus its 8:50pm, you won't get a run through, we looked at each other and said "no it isn't... its only 7:50" at which point we both realised we'd crossed a time zone, another new thing to have to deal with when riding across very large countries!

After some grub, Geoff was knackered but I still fancied a couple of pints so asked the cab driver on the way back to take me to a good bar. This cab guy starts raving about this place called "Rockin Rodeo" where there were 4:1 ratios of women to men and that he'd gone there the last few weeks and never failed to score, making it clear it was wall to wall women.

Now the cab driver didn't look to me like he'd score in a brothel with a pocket full of twenties so I thought the odds must be good, I said, "take me there Andre!"

He dropped me off, I paid a $4 dollar cover to get in, and yep you guess it, I was the only one in the whole bar, and the bar was about the size of a football field. I nailed a Coors light (watching my figure) so fast that it gave me brain freeze. I said fuck this and left and as I walked out the same taxi driver was still there driving off with another fare. I let out a roar at him, something traditionally Irish, "ya lyin bastard ya".

Feeling a little dejected, I got a cab back to the motel. The next cab driver raved about this "other bar". I think these guys were on retainers from the bars to bring dopey hairy arsed tourists in, but seeing as I was on holidays I tried the "must visit Irish bar", called the auld triangle. The bar turned out to be about as Irish as Margaret Thatcher's underpants, so I had one more Coors and headed back to the Motel.

I finally got back to the motel room where Geoff was up to "high doh", he realised that when he went out for a smoke, he'd left the door open and there were now thousands of mosquitoes and black fly in the motel room. After two hours and more fatalities than in the battle of the Somme, all the wee beasties were dead but I still went to sleep itchy as hell. Moncton left a lot to be desired!

Sydney

We left in a hurry the next day after a restless night worrying about a mixture of mosquitoes and baddies robbing our motorcycles, and drove just shy of three hundred miles to Sydney in Nova Scotia. We had intended to go to Halifax but there was a Harley Davidson convention in Sydney with open air gigs and ride outs. It would be much more our style and it would be great to meet a bunch more bikers. These conventions draw bikers from all over and the closer we got to Sydney the more bikers we met on the road; both our moods were soaring. Every time we'd stop at a garage, we'd end up spending about twenty minutes talking to everyone about where we were from, and where we were going.

Nova Scotia translates to New Scotland and as you travel to it and pass out of the state of New Brunswick, you get an instant reminder of where it gets its name from.

I'm not kidding, the temperature dropped around twelve degrees and it was freezing not to mention pissing rain. I'm certain that two hundred years ago when the pioneers were heading that way, a bunch of hairy arsed Scots hit this spot and said "fuck me jimmy, it's just like Scotland", and the rest is history. Having said that, I would move to Nova Scotia in the morning, it was full of wonderful friendly people.

The first night in Sydney was great, the Harley convention had five open-air bands playing and all these guys could play. All the bands were heavy rock and there was about two thousand Harley heads around the place creating a cracking atmosphere.

The next morning the plan was to do the Cabot trail, which for the great unwashed is one of the top ten road routes in the world; a two hundred and seventy kilometre long ring around Cape Breton. We talked to people who had been up on one of the hills that day looking down into the ocean and they could see whole pods of whales feeding at one of the inlets.

We set out at around 8am and then the heavens opened like Noah was due to take the Arc for another spin. Within twenty minutes and despite wearing some of the best enduro gear on the market I was soaked right through to the butt crack. In the end, we only did forty miles and rode to a place called Baddeck to spend the night. That night we met a father and son pair doing a motorcycle expedition of their own from New York State to Cape Breton. Their names I can't remember but we went out for grub and beers with them and had a cool time.

This part of the world is full of hunters and one stopped by for a chat. I have to say I don't get the whole "hunter thing", this guy was boasting about having killed twelve moose in his hunting career. Geoff started taking this piss out him saying, "Isn't that just like shooting a big cow?" I was asking what he did with the meat. He said that he ate it, at which point we all roared laughing. Apparently there's nearly seven hundred pounds of meat in a Moose, so even if this guy was having moose steak three times a day for his entire life he still wouldn't have eaten that much.

I said to him that as part of preparing for the trip, I had kept reading to be wary of Moose; if you hit one on the bike you're finished. In fourteen hundred miles so far I hadn't even had so much as a sniff of one; I made a joke that it was his fault. The night ended in a sombre mood, Geoff had started to talk about his wife again and I guess by talking about it, he was working the pain out of his system. We spent the rest of the evening out on the motel veranda drinking whiskey and killing mosquitoes.

The Cabot Trail

The next morning it was time to give the Cabot trail another go, the weather looked like it was going to be great and the omens were good, it was simply sensational. Although at this point I hadn't actually logged that many miles up on a motorbike, the Cabot trail was the best road I'd been on. There were sweeping bends, hairpin turns, mountains, cliffs all accompanied by brilliant blue skies and warm sunshine. I was driving the bike right at the extremes of my capabilities and a couple of times I had the hammer down far too hard and nearly flew off a cliff.

On the way round as part of letting the sphincter sort itself out after a couple of near misses we pulled up to a whale tour and went out and saw a heap of Minkey and bottle nose whales. They all looked the same to me despite the protestations of the tour guide. After an hour or so of watching the whales it was back onto the Cabot trail and I was doing as good an impression of Valentino Rossi as a fat bastard from Clondalkin is able to, on an overloaded 1150GS Adventurer.

The Cabot trail is so good you can get caught in two minds very easily. Do I just ride it? The road twists and bends through the countryside like it's a motorcyclist's wet dream. On the other hand the views of the landscape and ocean are so good you want to keep getting off the bike every five minutes to take pictures. My advice is to do the Cabot trail twice, and each time, ride it counter clockwise. That way you'll keep the ocean on your right side. Do it once for pictures, and then do it again just to appreciate the ebb and flow of the road as it makes its way through Canada at its most pristine.

With the sights saw it was time to leave Nova Scotia and blaze a trail for New Glasgow starting the long journey west, the next time I'd see the ocean would be in Anchorage, Alaska.

Chapter 3
*Trans*Canada Highway to the Alaskan border

Having knocked out the Cabot trail, Geoff and I decided it was time to start the long road west to Alaska. Even taking the most direct route it was over 5000 miles away, a lot further when you factor in detours for sightseeing.

We decided that New Glasgow would be a good place to stop for the night, it was about three hours west of where we were. No sooner had we started when the weather quickly turned miserable and we were stopping every forty minutes or so for coffee in the ubiquitous Tim Horton's coffee chain, anything to get out of the rain.

We got to New Glasgow without too much fuss in the end. Much like Cornwall and Moncton, there wasn't a whole pile going on. As we were parking up outside a motel another biker called Ed pulled up driving a 1200GS adventurer. We went over, introduced ourselves, and invited him along for dinner. We headed for a round of wings and beers, chatted for a good few hours about bikes, and shared stories from the road.

As the night wore on Geoff started to talk about his wife again. I guess because the grief was still so near for him, it occupied a massive part of his consciousness; he struggled to talk about much else really. It was at that moment that I decided I was going to break off and go my own way in a day or two. It wasn't that Geoff wasn't a nice guy but this journey represented the adventure of a lifetime for me, I didn't want to spend it helping him through his depression. Maybe if we'd been best buddies before the trip, it was something I would have gladly done but when you barely know someone, it was too much, for me at least.

Obviously, Ed when he listened to the story was very sympathetic but being my fifth or sixth time through it, I guess I looked bored. When Geoff went to the bog I said something I regret, along the lines of "you can't get that guy to stop talking about that stuff, it's really head wrecking". No doubt Ed just thought I was an insensitive plonker.

I knew that I'd cut my losses in the next town and plunge out into Canada by myself. The next day, the three of us, as part of back peddling across Canada decided to strike back for Riviere du Loup, we'd had a great night there first time round, so it made sense to just stay there again.

We covered a lot of ground, over five hundred miles in total arriving and staying in the same guest house we had the first time round. We'd travelled 2200 miles in only a couple of days and I was fucked tired.

Along the way I noticed Geoff and Ed were burning me off the back, which is where the lead bikes keep up a very hefty pace, maybe one just above where you're comfortable to ride at. I was at the back wondering "since when did I become the un-cool guy? When did I become the guy who gets burned off the back?" Ed had obviously thought that I was a dickhead having talked behind Geoff's back.

I found myself thousands of miles from home, rallying down a Canadian highway absolutely miserable, wondering just how the fuck all this bullshit had happened.

The roads in Canada are unbelievably straight, so straight they would drive you to drink. You end up counting every mile and end up just sitting there bored out of your fucking mind. Every now and then you might slip into a trance where you don't notice the miles passing, but it doesn't last long and then you're back in the helmet; just you and your thoughts and your very sore arse. At times I'd have conversations with myself along the lines of "Hmmm, what do I usually think about when I'm trying to pass the time? I can't think of anything!"

The next morning I met Geoff for breakfast and said to him that I was going to go a different route around the great lakes and was he ok with that. I think he knew it was coming and I think he was happier that way anyway. Once we cleared the air it was amazing, we were back getting along like a house on fire. Ed by this stage had already left so we agreed that we would go as far as Montreal together at which point he was going to burn south towards the USA. His plan was to circle the great lakes from the south; mine was to continue to cross Canada. We made a remark about meeting up on the other side of the lakes, but never did.

When it came time to part ways it was very sad, we had stopped for lunch and talked some more about his missus and I really did understand how he felt and felt very sorry for him. As we drove up towards Montreal we got to the turn off, Geoff blazed to the left and I went to the right. I held my finger on the horn and then held my left fist high in the air as we both went our separate ways. I was on my own now and I couldn't stop from welling up, and having a good old cry.

Arnprior

I just kept riding to try and work things out in my head and ended up doing just short of four hundred and fifty miles as I pulled into the town or Arnprior in Ontario Canada, just west of Ottawa. The town sits on a river and is very easy on the eye. I walked down to the riverfront and sat on a bench to try and soak up the summers evening. Tens of people were casting their fishing rods into the river as the sun was setting just behind the town on the far bank of the river.

I was feeling a bit lonely and thought to myself "you're gonna need to come out of your shell more or your gonna have a shit time, you need to start meeting people".

If you've ever travelled by yourself I'm sure you'll agree that at times things can be weird. If you're a guy and you just go up and start talking to a guy, the guy will think "this dude must be gay". If you go up talking to a girl "this loser just wants a shag".

People in the western world can tend to think that there must be a reason why this "fucker" is talking to me. The last thing we would ever admit to ourselves is that people might be just looking for company.

Everyone I talked to said that once you got west of Toronto and passed the great lakes there was nothing but flat farm land for thousands of miles. In a way I was quite looking forward to it, in my mind's eye I reckoned that I might be able to get "in touch with myself" and really work some stuff over in my head, realistically I'd no clue what was ahead.

My next port of call was Sault Ste Marie, a town on the border between Canada and the USA. The town was formed as a result of connecting two parts of the great lakes and its locks are busier that the Suez and the Panama Canal combined. I don't remember much about the road there, it wasn't very scenic, that's not to say that the countryside wasn't nice, it just wasn't very memorable. The land was largely flat with crop forests of ever green pines running right up to the road intermingled with the odd farm.

I went down to the locks to take a look, and went to see the movie Hancock. I'd developed a little routine when I pulled into a town. In the evening I'd take off the enduro gear, head in for a shower and then go for a spin on the bike with just a leather jacket, jeans and a pair of sun glasses on. I'd ride around the respective town looking for something to do, but mainly just to look cool. I reckoned that none of these red neck Canadian women would be able to resist it. So plenty of just me on my own then!

Prairies

The further west you go in Canada, the less and less populated the country becomes so I had to contend with being on my own a lot, I hadn't met anyone at all in two days. I guess crossing Canada on a motorcycle isn't something that too many people do.

I was driving over four hundred miles a day, its sounds a lot, and it is, but there's so little to do in this part of the world, its best to just push on. I would love to be able to say that there were some fun spots to pull over and have a good time but the only thing to keep you amused was the clouds in the sky. I crossed the 3,000 mile mark which meant I had completed about 10% of the total journey eleven days after leaving Ireland, at this rate I'd be finished sixty days ahead of schedule. I consoled myself by saying "Dude, spend your time in the happening places."

The next day I was on the road again looping north around Lake Superior on my way to Thunder Bay. This was the first time since Nova Scotia that there was a decent bit of scenery. The lake itself is huge, bigger than Ireland by over ten thousand square kilometres so for the whole day I had a lake on my left side and forest on my right. It's hard to believe the lake is fresh water; it looks just like the sea with waves lapping up onto gravel beaches.

I stopped every hour or so pulling over and walking by the lake having a chat with anyone who looked in the least bit friendly. Yakking away to the locals in any given area you tend to pick up lots of little titbits of information, for example; believe it or not, they get waves of up to thirty feet on Lake Superior during storms and it's fed by over two hundred rivers. Some of the great lakes are officially dead with all the pollution, Lake Superior is still hanging in there though.

When I was about an hour from Thunder Bay I pulled over to the side of the road to take a few pictures. The sun was low in the sky on the right with the lake stretching out in front of me flickering in the evening sun shine. On my left, still a few miles distant a thunderstorm was starting to go into high gear. I don't know if it's how the town got its name but I can tell you the whole time I was there it was thundering away like crazy. The whole reason for the town to exist is to transport grain from the prairies out onto the great lakes where it's ferried off to various ports.

I got up the next morning absolutely knackered and couldn't bear the thought of riding, but the town was so dull that I said to myself "c'mon push on to the next town and stop there." I was a bit down in the dumps and was feeling pretty lonely.

I'd lost my phone and I was wondering whether or not to replace it. I was starting to get pissed off that I wasn't getting any text messages from home; it was like the whole world had forgotten about me and was getting on with their lives. The phone in a way became a reminder of "people not getting in contact with me", so I made a decision to do the rest of the trip without one.

When I look back on it, it was a stupid idea, if anything bad happened I would have been rightly fucked, but my thinking on it was; what would phoning someone do anyway, it would only get them worried. I was really on my own now.

Dryden

I pulled in at a town called Dryden, which was built around a large paper mill. I hadn't been able to get near the internet for a couple of days so once I booked into a motel I headed out to look for the local library. Internet cafes are noticeably absent in most towns in Canada and the US. I guess there's an assumption that everyone has a computer so why would you bother.

As I went looking for the library a guy pulled up on a bike beside me and said "hey how are you doing? What are you doing here?" I told him and next thing I knew I was back at his place swinging out of a couple of beers. He was a keen biker and I got a lot of "off road" tips from him, which would come in handy in Alaska which was getting closer every day. The suspicious person in everyone always thinks that someone just walking up to you must have an agenda, and I have to admit to thinking "maybe this guy is a serial killer or gay and he's gonna take me back to his place and stab me up the arse."

As usual, I needn't have worried, he was a sound skin. Over a couple of beers I told him all about the trip so far, and that I thought it would have been better, that I thought I'd meet more people and that it wasn't really working out as a dream trip, and to top it all not a whole pile of interesting things had happened so far. He really understood and told me not to worry; there'll be lots of bikers once you get to the Pan American highway. I headed back to the motel after about eight bottles of various types of beer; it was just the tonic I needed to get my spirits up.

Relatively rested after a short run the day before, I headed for Brandon a town west of Winnipeg. On the way I passed through the geographical centre of Canada; I was officially half way across. Half way seemed hard to believe when I thought about the distance I'd covered, some 4300miles completed, almost the distance from Dublin Ireland, to Mumbai in India.

My ass was officially turning into a different life form, every time I sat on the saddle it felt like I was sitting down bare arse in a field of thistles. With the heat my motorbike boots smelt so bad I reckoned they might force an early migration of the Caribou herd.

Mossies and black fly had by this point taken a penchant for my extremities and on average I had about twenty bite marks on the go at any one time. I even had a couple on my bum, that mossie was taking his life in his hands I don't mind telling you.

I had hit prairie land, namely Saskatchewan, the Canadian equivalent of Montana in the United States; big sky country. The whole "flat land and big sky" thing is an amazing thing to drive through. You can see right to the horizon in all directions.

The roads are completely and utterly straight with no bends for hundreds of kilometres and once the novelty of the landscape starts to wear off you, the tedium of the road starts to grow.

You just sit there. The road is straight, your speed is constant, the horizon is perfectly flat and the blue sky extends the whole way to the horizon. The fields by the side of the road are sown with same crop so nothing changes. The only things on the road are trucks and the occasional car. Everything seems constant. You become aware of every mile you're riding, and every minute you're driving. There is nothing you can do to take your mind off the vast unchanging landscape. It takes days to cross.

It is like driving through purgatory, the only thing to keep you company is a really noisy wind. The farmers in the area all joke that because the land is so flat, if your dog ran away, he could run for three days and you'd still be able to see him in the distance.

On the way to Brandon I had my first "nearly killed" moment. There were two big eighteen wheelers blocking the highway doing about 50mph, they were talking to each other as they were driving up the road and no one could get by.

This went on and on for about 40 miles or more and yours truly not being known for his patience, especially while getting the shit kicked out of him by both the wind and the turbulence from the juggernauts was quickly losing the rag. I decided to bomb up a very skinny hard shoulder to the right at close to 100 mph and lashed by the lads in the trucks, giving it a bit of "yee hawwwwwwwww!" in the process.

It was only later, that a couple who saw me passing the trucks on the road, came up to me at a filling station and said that the trucker swerved for me as I was passing on the inside.

They had called the police so I spent an hour or so talking to the cops who had arrived before I knew it. Most of the time was just spent talking to them about where I was off to I didn't really want to bring up the fact that I used the hard shoulder as my own private race track. We chatted for a good while and to be honest I was glad of the company. Seemed to me that these guys were glad of the company too, I doubt too much goes on to keep the police busy in these parts.

I got into Brandon that night too late to get any grub and there was absolutely nothing to do, not surprising as the town is an agricultural hub. I hit the hay starving and my stomach started talking to me as it often does, "Aren't you forgetting something fat boy? Where's the fucking nose bag!" Too hungry to even have a hand shandy, I just headed off to sleep.

The next day I was back on the road in a familiar routine; rise, ride for about an hour and then stop for breakfast, then ride for another hour and then stop for gas and so it would continue stopping every hour or so in an attempt to break up the monotony of the flat unchanging land.

The further into the state of Saskatchewan I went the more encounters with storms I had. A prairie storm is a thing to be feared, and can get violent enough to send you running for your mammy.

In the distance you can see black clouds and as you approach the storm day becomes night. As you get into the middle of it you start to notice some "off" yellow colours in the clouds, an almost sulphur colour; round about then you know you're in deep shit. The temperature drops about ten degrees and you turn from roasting to freezing in just a couple of minutes.

The rain starts to come down in sheets and the rain drops are so large that your visibility drops to about fifteen feet. Fork lightning fires all round you and the thunder is so loud it drowns out the sound of the engine on the bike. You start to remember all the stories about how a car is the safest place to be during lightning and then start to think "hmmmm...don't recall hearing anything about motorbikes". On these vast planes there are very few places to shelter so there's nothing you can do but put the hammer down and try and run like a blue bastard straight through it. Every second you're in a storm on a motorcycle is spent shitting bricks, feeling like a nervous dog at Halloween when the fireworks are going off.

Often when I would stop for gas, the locals seemed to take relish in filling me full of fear with phrases like "there's a Tornado warning about son". I was driving along saying to myself "just my luck...the day the hairy arse dub shows up, a twister the size of Galway bay will drop straight on me."

Living in Ireland or the UK, realistically we never see a real storm, at least not like they have them in North America, and you ain't seen nothing till you've seen a prairie storm. The mad thing is that once you drive out the other side of it; it's like it never happened. You're back clear skies and roasting temperatures and uttering some choice phrases like "What the fuck just happened?"

The influence of the Native American communities who originally inhabited these lands starts to jump to the fore as you continue west, towns called Moose Jaw, Medicine Hat and Swift Current all conjured up images for me of what this country must have been like before the wagons started to roll west. The towns may have had cool sounding names but as with a lot of towns in North America, they were all grid towns with no centre square and for the most part impossible to tell apart.

The colours of the crops either side of the road thankfully started to break up the monotony. It was still July so most were in bloom and there was a sea of yellow rape seed and flax planted as far as the eye could see. One farmer who I met in a garage told me that there was now an area the size of Germany planted with flax in Canada that used to be planted with wheat and corn.

With Oil prices shooting up and food prices dropping the farmers were turning to non-food crops. I wondered what would the implications of it be, surely you can't take that much food out of circulation without causing a famine somewhere.

Riding through this sort of terrain you go through the full range of emotions. The day always starts well; you knock out the first two hundred clicks in two or three hours and stop for a coffee. Then the second leg is always tougher; your brain starts to go crazy looking at a road which never bends and just keeps going straight for an eternity. On top of that, as the miles pass your boxer shorts start to ride higher and higher till they're literally sawing you in two by the end of the fourth hour. With another four to five hours in the saddle, you start to feel like your arse needs to be put in a sling.

The wind never seems to let up, ripping your head one way and then the other. When you're passed by a huge truck, the turbulence punches you so hard you almost take it personal. Train tracks run in parallel to large sections of the highway and often you encounter massive trains which snake for miles through the vast flat countryside. They all stop at massive grain silo's which stand like sentries along the train track visible for miles.

The people you meet along the way are normally farmers. Most are friendly up to a point but keep their distance, not surprising really when you consider they're talking to a bearded loony from Ireland "So you've over here doing what?"

The prairies were very tough, not in the dangerous or physical sense but mentally challenging, maybe akin to the doldrums for sailors. Straight roads for thousands of kilometres, long distances, storms, howling winds, maniacal truckers and boring one horse towns, I was bored to tears. But every now and then the wind stopped blowing, everything was calm and there were no trucks or cars on the road. I was riding along surrounded by a sea of yellow and light blue flowers under a cloudless blue sky, with the fragrance of the field coming in through the helmet. For a fleeting moment I imagined this must be what heaven is like.

Canmore

I made myself a promise on the trip that I would where possible, avoid big cities unless I was getting the bike serviced and in keeping with that promise I burned straight through Calgary and headed for Canmore, a town in the Rockies.

I can't tell you how good it felt to see mountains again; after nearly two weeks of flat unchanging landscape to have the horizon dominated by massive snow-capped peaks had me smiling like a Cheshire cat.

I headed out that night for one of the biggest pizza's I've ever had and washed it down with a couple of celebratory beers. I was sure that now I was in the great north west of North America that I'd meet a lot more people on motorbikes or at least lots of tourists who might be kindred spirits.

The road turned north for the first time in nearly two weeks as I drove the road between Canmore and Banff and then on up to Jasper and from there on up to Hinton.

The route took me through the Ice field parkway, one of the most famous roads in Canada, no matter who you talked to this was a "must see" area and it didn't disappoint. For almost three hundred kilometers this road ambled its way through the feet of giant snow-capped mountains. The mountains, three times the size of Ireland's largest mountain were so impressive I doubted if anything would ever top the sites that lay before me, I rode completely silent and just lapped it all up, it was unbelievable.

Glaciers feed the rivers and lakes in the area making all the water turquoise; as if the scenery didn't stand out enough already. Every time I'd see a mountain or a scenic view and say "yep that's it ... nothing will ever top that", just around the bend would be something even more spectacular. The Rockies chain stretches down the whole way to the Andes in South America, I liked the idea that this mountain range would be like an old friend by the time I was done.

The day ended in Hinton, a small town based around lumber. The bucket in your head where you store images of nice scenery was completely full for me, and after what I'd seen I had a strange feeling, namely that nothing could ever top it. This area is renowned as one of the most beautiful areas in the world; would it be downhill all the way from here?

At moments like these I told myself "it's an adventure ya big bollix", it's about driving from Prudhoe Bay to Ushuaia and going coast to coast at the widest point in the Americas so stop your whingeing and fill the tank up with petrol, it's time to get going again.

I decided the following day would only be a short run of about five hours or so taking me from Hinton to a town called Grande Prairie. The day started out pretty crap as it was pissing down and for the first time on the trip it was really cold. Hard to believe looking at the calendar, that in July, things would be this cool but the chill rolls off the Rockies and joins cascades of wind and rain.

I was absolutely freezing on the bike and after about only thirty minutes I had to pull in and put on my arctic gear. That involved stripping to almost naked by the side of the road and putting on an inner body skin, and an outer layer which is both water proof and wind proof and over that that the enduro suit. I also put on a balaclava to turn off the chill factor on my face which was quickly turning into something approaching the colour of a beetroot.

I'd expected to encounter this weather on the Dalton highway in Alaska or down towards the south of Argentina, not in Alberta Canada. The problem with a bike is that once your cold it's almost impossible to get warm, like I said before it's not like there's a heater you can turn on and after about forty minutes rain, wind and cold I was thoroughly miserable. I pulled into the smallest town I'd ever seen off highway 40, called Muskeg.

Frenchy

I sat down in a diner dripping wet and shivering with the cold and ordered two of the biggest mugs of steaming hot coffee in the world with some hot sandwiches to try and heat up. The lady behind the counter obviously took pity on me and was quick to refill the rapidly emptying mugs of coffee.

Just then the whole room darkened when the biggest man I've ever seen walked into the room, comfortably six feet eight inches and built like a brick shit house. He nodded to the woman behind the counter who said to him "were pretty busy Frenchy, you can sit down with that guy over there (that's me) if he doesn't mind", not at all I replied.

I was sitting in a booth where you'd normally sit 4 people me with my motorbike gear on one side and Frenchy sat down opposite me taking pretty much the entire booth opposite; he barely had room just for himself. He stretched out his legs and I quickly moved mine out of the way apologising as you do.

(Especially when a white version of Shaquille o' Neil sits down opposite)

The dimensions of Frenchy were something to behold, his shoulders were gigantic and had a set of hands which were like a bunch of bananas. His rib cage was like a barrel and he looked like the incredible hulk (except not green obviously) sitting opposite me. Anyway you get the picture, he was a massive dude, and I reckoned he had about fifty five years on the clock but that would be a guess.

"Usual Frenchy?" said the lady behind the counter to which he just nodded twice. With that I put my hand out to shake his and said "Hi I'm Oisin", he shook my hand, mine looked like a little girls in his, and his skin had the texture of tree bark. One shake had me wanting to grab a tube of moisturiser! He didn't say anything, I guess he'd figured out I already knew his name.

Somewhat awestruck I said to him "dude if you don't mind me saying so, you are the biggest bastard I've ever seen", to which he didn't say anything. Thinking the bastard remark might have offended him I quickly back peddled, saying "no offence on the bastard thing, it's just a turn of phrase.... in Ireland... that's where I'm from", I was dying on the vine.

He still didn't say anything but at least he didn't look offended. Just then Doris showed up with the coffee saying "How are you today Frenchy?", to which he just replied; "Doing good Doris" to which she smiled and walked off leaving me with the behemoth.

I started to try and make conversation with him and I'm not bad at this sort of thing normally, shy and retiring are not attributes which feature anywhere on my resume but this guy was a piece of work. I was also anxious that Doris bring him his breakfast just in case he started to butter me and eat me.

The rest of the conversation went on:

Oisin: "So I'm over doing this big motorbike trip...y'know shipped the bike in from Ireland to Toronto...went to Nova Scotia..and then over to here..heading for Alaska"

Frenchy: uh huh

Oisin: "yep and from there I'm going to Argentina...will be 30000 miles total...."

Frenchy: nothing

Oisin: "Cold out today huh?"

Frenchy: "Guess so"

(Think what he really meant was... you wouldn't know cold from a cabbage ya big Irish dumb ass... as it gets to -40 here in the winter)

Oisin: "So are you from here?"..."like Canada? I mean ".."or...."(was desperate that he'd latch onto that "or")

Frenchy: "I'm from here"

Oisin: "So Alberta..? or this town...or "

(Was pushing my luck with the "or's")

Frenchy: "here"

(Jaysus this was tough going...talkative oul bollix aren't ya I wanted to say to him if I wasn't in absolute fear of my life that he'd either eat me or punch me in the head for yakking so much)

Doris arrived thankfully with the grub for Frenchy which was really a trough of food poured onto a serving plate where one might expect to find the carcass of a roasted pig at a banquet.

Oisin:"Holy fuck!!...that's some amount of nose bag!!!"(It was a nervous knee jerk answer)

Frenchy:"nose bag?"

Oisin: "yeah like a horse's nose bag... know what I mean?" and then made a motion like a horse emptying nose bag into itself and through in a neeaahhhh for good measure, Frenchy smiled and said..."you're a bit crazy y'know that!"

Seeing my opening and not that I needed any invitation, I just kept blabbing on and Frenchy sat their listening at least I think he was listening. He asked me why I was doing the trip, I told him, to which he just said "hmmmm ok"

I asked him did he ever do any travelling, to which he just replied no.

Now that we were getting along just dandy, although it wasn't so much a conversation as a monologue I did a Hughes classic and looking at the size of his hands I just blurted out: "dude with fingers like that who needs a dick!", "although you'd want to get the oul Oil of Olay on the go before any birds would let ya near them." Frenchy roared laughing; one of those laughs that was so deep, almost like he'd been holding onto it for years.

After he'd finished laughing he took up his cup of coffee which looked like a play cup in his hand and said "Irish man.... you're ok in my book"

Oisin: "glad to hear it... I thought you were gonna fuckin eat me there for a while"(more laughing)

Frenchy sat there eating the rest of his breakfast shovelling fist sized pieces of scrambled eggs and ham into his mouth seldom looking up from the plate, although his eye level was still above the top of my head; like I said the dude was massive!!!

Frenchy: "so looks like you got pretty wet huh?

Oisin: "right through to the crack" after a delay of about 3 seconds Frenchy roared laughing again; no way was anyone going to tell him to quieten down.

We got talking then about all sorts of stuff, me desperate for a reason not to go back on the road because of the rain and cold, and him, well because I was yakking his ear off. We got talking about willow herb, a plant which dominates the side of the roads here; I told him we have it in Ireland too. It was left there by the last ice age, probably didn't need to add the last part

I asked him was he married, he wasn't wearing a wedding ring but that wouldn't have mattered, it would have required a kilo of gold to round one of his fingers so unless he was really a masquerading Saudi prince there's no way he would have been able to afford it.

When I did finish the question he just looked forlornly out the window into the vast expanse of forest; "nope" he replied after a time, I didn't pry any further.

He went on to tell me he'd worked in the woods all his life as a lumber jack and that he loved the mountains and could never leave them. I remarked that he didn't need a saw for the trees all he'd need to do was lean against them, to which he smiled.

We walked out together to the car park and I showed him the bike. I asked him to jump aboard and try it out; he did and made the bike (one of the biggest motorbikes anywhere) look like a scooter. I told him about the blog and that if he was ever online to check it out; he replied that "don't have much call for computers... wouldn't have a clue about the internet, too old to learn now"

We shook hands and said goodbye. I watched him get into his truck really testing the suspension as he sat in and started her up, "watch out for bears" he said as he smiled and drove off. I stood there for a while thinking, oh my god I forgot about the fuckin bears!!!

Frenchy in my memory was the biggest dude in the whole world but also one of the most gentle. One of the downsides of the trip is that you only ever meet people once and then you move on most likely never to see them again. In some peoples case that's great, but Frenchy I still think about. I reminded myself of one of things I'd read, that it's not the places you visit, it's the people you meet

Chapter 4

When you travel alone you have no one to give you a second opinion. Once in the Rockies I cut further north from Grande Prairie which as the name suggested brought me straight back out onto the prairies. When I realised what I'd done I didn't have the heart to double back on myself so I just pulled into a motel, had a bath and headed out to watch a movie.

I invested in a small portable laptop which was great for keeping in touch with people, but if I'm honest was great for looking at porn mostly. So after only three hours in the saddle which you'd expect to knock out in Canada with one swing of your John Thomas I was off to sleep with the prospect of a better day to come tomorrow.

The next two towns I'd planned to stop in conjured up for me what life must have been like in Canada in the early part of the 20th century, namely Fort St John, and Fort Nelson. I could imagine wooden forts and lads with beaver skin hats all trading furs and whiskey, and Daniel day Lewis telling "yer one", "I will find you. I will find you!"

The next day I'd hit the wall after only two hours so I pulled over not having the heart to continue. I was lonely and apart from Frenchy I hadn't had a meaningful conversation with anyone in ages. My arse was officially on strike, so instead of passing through Fort St John, I just stayed the night there. The further I headed north the longer the days became, by the time I'd get to the Arctic circle there would be no "night", just 24 hours of light.

The next morning I got up in bad form again and just jumped on the bike and left. I was starting to doubt the reasons why I'd come on the trip. I realised that the attraction of the long way round TV series for me wasn't actually the bikes or the trip, what I really liked was the camaraderie that the guys on the trip had.

It had taken me 9000 miles to figure it out, but there was no turning back now.

That day I was driving along and I passed a lay-by where two bikers who were both driving BMW's were parked up. I drove over to say hello, in a weird sort of way you almost expect people to greet you with open arms "Yay! you're a biker too!, and you drive a BMW, and you're on a big adventure... let's be buddies!"

These two chaps were about as friendly as a bull with a sore hole so after a few minutes I was back heading north again. I also hadn't seen a moose or a bear or any form of wild life really so I was really struggling to keep my sense of "this is the trip of lifetime" about the journey.

Manitoba

That night I couldn't sleep. At 4:17am I was still awake and wrote the following into my journal:

I'm in a town called Fort Nelson right now in British Colombia and am going to make a break for Whitehorse, which is over 1000km away. The reason for the long burst is because the only town between here and there is Watson lake...and staying there is the moral equivalent of having to stay the night in a nursing home.

Fort Nelson is not a place you would ever visit, it's a town you drive through to get somewhere else and its sole existence is based around lumber. The whole town is stained by debris from the forests, a by-product of pulling trees out of the woods. Fort Nelson is supposed to be way better than Watson Lake so I'm making the trek for Whitehorse sooner than stay in another crappy town for the night. I guess that's what you should expect of what was essentially a frontier town but when you've ridden such a long way to get somewhere a part of you just expects it to be better.

I was watching the news tonight and about the tenth story into it; the tenth story!!! was about this guy you kills another guy on a greyhound bus in Manitoba in Canada, unfortunate you'd say but can happen. Well, wait till you hear the details the guy killed him with a Rambo knife and then cut off his head.

The eyewitness was interviewed at the scene by the news guys and said the dude beside him was just asleep and the dude with the knife had just got on the bus. Can you believe *it! One minute you're asleep and the next some dude is walking down the bus isle carrying your head!! The eye witness said that the killer blamed the truck driver for making him drop the guy's head and had then proceeded to follow them with the knife.*

Anyway so now you know why I'm awake, but as if the thing wasn't bad enough it's that the news guys had the story about 10th in the order and they weren't shocked enough. The story was followed by some kitten that got its head caught in the fuckin drain!

So as if there wasn't enough to be worrying about with bears, moose on the road, maniacal truckers, getting a puncture, dubs winning the Leinster football final, now you've got getting your head hacked off by some lunatic and to add insult to injury having it dropped on a greyhound bus floor which let's face it, is dirtier than a coal miners arse.

The goal was to get to Whitehorse before nightfall, a journey of over six hundred miles most of which would be done on the famous Alcan Highway. It also represented the end of the Trans-Canada portion of my trip, as it was less than a half days ride till I got to Alaska. Starting at about 5:45am I set off on what turned out to be an assault on the senses.

After about an hour's riding I had seen bears, wild dear and wild goats so was well chuffed. I stopped for a coffee in a campsite which also sold gasoline. I had a wonderful chat with the owner and this older

American couple who were up driving the Alcan Highway to celebrate their retirement. This is a good point to mention that with soaring gas prices, all of North America was in crisis. Families who would have normally taken RV's up to this region were staying at home and it was regular enough to drive for an hour at a time and hardly meet a truck or a car on the road. It added to the dreamy feel of the whole thing, that you were alone and all this incredible scenery was just for you.

I passed through a place called Charlie Lake, one of the places where Ewan and Charlie had stopped and filmed a scene for the long way round. They had remarked that they had only fifteen days left to go in the program and I loved the look of the place. I hadn't planned to pass it; I just saw the sign and pulled off the road. It felt magic to be in one of the places that had inspired me to do the trip. The sun was shining and at the end of a small wooden pier there was a boat parked up. The lake was a mill pond of beautiful blue water and the gentlest of breezes was blowing into my face as I soaked up the moment. For the first time since Nova Scotia I really felt great.

Further along the road I met three guys who were motorcycling up to Fairbanks from Washington State and we rode together for a good few hours. I'm not a skilled enough writer to describe how awe-inspiring the scenery was we drove through. Whether it was a mixture of having some company, the great weather and some of the most beautiful countryside anywhere in the world, I'm not sure but I was having the time of my life.

Isaac, Roger and Bruce and myself had some great chats about what all bikers tend to chat about. For example what was the best pound for pound motorcycle in the world, given I knew nothing about motorcycles bar how to drive one and that the BMW 1150 was my favourite only because it was the only one I'd ever owned I offered little to the debate.

I also love the way people who are familiar with stuff shorten everything down to the shortest possible sentence. For example when we had stopped for lunch a bunch of motorcyclists passed us on the road. Bruce said "Dude did you see the bunch of Twelve hundreds that just passed us, man they were some machines", as if to say that all and sundry would automatically know what a 1200 was.

Later on we ran into a herd of buffalo which is probably ok when you're in a car but when you're on a motorbike it's definitely not ok, these animals are massive. The buffalo are not owned by anyone and certainly aren't tame, and much as they've always done, they are allowed to roam free.

All I could think of was the movie dances with wolves, I definitely had some "Tatanka" ahead and was really worried one of the bulls would charge me on the bike, thankfully they didn't and I lived to fight another day. I had been terrified by stories which I'd heard about loose buffalo "hooking" you, a process whereby a buffalo takes one of its horns and drives it straight into you.

It was like someone turned on the wildlife switch, at various points I saw three black bears all out near the road, a dose of caribou, chipmunks, mountain goats, deer, I loved every minute of it.

I kind of developed a theory on travelling that your mood pretty much maps the way it does at home except your peaks and troughs are higher and deeper.

So for example if you're a moody bollix at home it's likely that you'll be the same when you travel, except that if you're in a good mood it'll be better. Conversely if you're in a bad mood it'll be worse because you don't have any of the support structures you have at home that might get you out of it.

It could also be very tough on you physically. Motorbike 101 for those of you that don't drive them, the contact area of a motorbike tyre, unlike a car, isn't flat; it's semi-circular. It's by leaning the bike right and left on the highways that you turn it, i.e. moving the contact area of the tyre on the road to the shorter circumference areas cause the bike to turn; yawn, I can hear you but I'm going somewhere I promise.

So this is where the fun starts. Imagine you're driving down a 1 lane highway with oncoming traffic in the other lane. On your side of the road is a hard shoulder but it's made of gravel, great if you're in a car with four wheels, really dodgy if you're on a motorbike with only two wheels contacting the surface. If you hit gravel straight on its no problem on a bike, however if you hit it while your turning there's a really good chance the bike will just slip straight off the road. So the key point is that you really don't want the bike going onto the gravel on a bend where you've a much smaller amount of tire contacting the road and the bike is leaning to one side.

Ok, so next up as you're driving straight ahead there's a forty mile an hour wind coming from the left side, i.e. which is doing its best to push you off the road or at least closer to the pesky aforementioned gravel. Now throw in that it's gusting up to about sixty five miles an hour and things are starting to get a bit awkward.

So how you cope with it is that you lean your body into the wind and keep the bike straight, i.e. compensating for the wind. If you didn't it would push you straight off the road. With the gusts you can find yourself sweeping up to three to five feet across the road, so you adopt a position on the road close to the divide at the centre to allow you to drift a little if an unexpectedly large gust comes up.

Now the pot is beginning to simmer, throw in the rain and truck drivers coming at you from the same direction as the wind is coming from. In pissing rain an eighteen wheeler can throw up more than ten gallons of water per second and when they pass they shower you with a waterfall of turbulence bad enough to make your kidneys wobble. Finally, watch out for moose, deer, bears, pot holes and every other manner of obstruction that you're likely to find out in the cuds and do it all through a visor on a helmet speckled with rain droplets and grime.

Driving through the above is a little something like this, in my mind anyway. Imagine doing this as you're riding along for the whole day:

> Ok Ois ya big ride ya... keep her steady... keep her steady.... oh jaysus big bastardin gust....adjust ya big bollix or ya'll be in the ditch....adjust ...done it...nice one...like i said ois....your a big ride.....jaysus the feckin rain is brutal....cant see a feckin thing....find a gap between the drips on the visor...right ...nice one have it..can see a bit... oh jaysus another big gust... hold er... hold er....jaysus ..big bend and gust...slow her down ya big bollix...slow her down.... holy lantern devine theres gravel in the middle of the road...avoid it... thank jaysus .. only just...more wind...ah me neck is feckin killing me ....oh fuck...heres one of these trucker bollixes coming straight for me... can barely see him with rain...ah jaysus gonna get soaked... holy fuck..can't see a thing... wipe the visor.... gust of wind...only one hand holding the handle bars...nearly over into the gravel.... hold her ya big bollix...hold her....nice one horse... nice one.....jaysus i'd murder a cup of tea.... and a shag.... fuck more wind....5 ft drift...keep your mind on the

road ya big bollix... or a moose will be shagging ya in the ditch this afternoon!

Like I said earlier, I was having the time of my life.

Whitehorse

I arrived in Whitehorse that evening checking the cheeks of my arse with my hand to make sure that they were still there, I felt like I was sitting bare arse on a bed of nails for the last couple of hours of the ride.

I booked into a motel and went out for a bite to eat. My initial experience of the town wasn't great, lots of drunken angry Native Americans. I knew I'd be stopping here on the way back so this was just a place to get a door between me and the night. I lay in bed that night thinking that everything I'd done up to this point was just bullshit, what if every day was like today, how good a life would that be!

I'd now travelled without a break every day for twenty one days and was getting a bit worn out but I knew I was close to Anchorage where I'd get the bike serviced and have a bit of down time. I drove off for Tok, Alaska and coming across from Whitehorse the impact the oil prices were having on the tourist industry up in the Yukon and Alaska was becoming increasingly apparent. The roads were empty; I drove through one section albeit in the morning time for two hours without seeing even a single car.

The knock on of the above was that over 50% of the gas stations I saw on the road were closed down due to no business, the usual supply of massive RV's from Canada and the USA had dried up due to the massive costs incurred from running the beasts, most averaging less than eight miles to the gallon.

It was like driving around in a dream, the scenery was breath taking and I was driving completely alone on the road. If you pull over to take pictures, no cars pass, there was literally no one around, the only sound you can hear is the sound of high flying birds or the breeze blowing but nothing else; eerie doesn't come close to describing it.

It's weird seeing some of the most naturally beautiful sights in the world and being completely alone doing it, it's like getting a ticket to see the biggest band in the world and you're the only guy there. In a whole days travelling where I stopped many times I met a total of five people, a Dutch couple, a German couple and another German guy, there were seemingly no North Americans on the road. By Midday I was at the border and ready to cross into Alaska. I'd successfully crossed the second biggest country in the world, I treated myself to a diet coke and a snickers.

Chapter 5

North to the Top of the World

I got to Tok Alaska having crossed the border into the United States from Canada. The town is really just a bunch of services centred on the crossroads of the Alcan and Glenn highways.

I stayed the night in the Golden bear motel, a family owned place. After a shower I went for dinner in the restaurant, and in true Alaskan tradition there was one choice, you either wanted it or didn't. I loved it.

The owner walked in and sat at one of the other tables and after a while he swung over and we chatted for about two hours about all sorts of things. I asked him what the weather was like in the winter, to which he dryly answered "Cold!"

Apparently it has dropped on occasion to sixty degrees below freezing. He described what it's like and how everything has a blue appearance, even the air. The family made me feel very welcome and I headed off to the scratcher that night feeling wonderful.

I arrived in Anchorage the next day and started to find out about getting to a place called the motorcycle shop where I'd planned to get the bike serviced. At this point I was still in a work frame of mind, i.e. "let's go, c'mon man got to make up the miles" so was looking for a pit stop to get the bike prepared for the Dalton highway rather than a place to hang out for a couple of days.

It takes time to learn how to relax I think.

About a week into the trip I started to get less worried about the time and after two weeks I'd pretty much completely forgotten about it, at any one point in time only being able to tell you was it morning, afternoon or night. As the third week had progressed I started to forget about what day it was but I think a month had passed before I stopped thinking about schedules or distances and really started to just enjoy the ride and forget about the destination.

I didn't care for Anchorage, it's a nice place but it's not why people go to Alaska. It's a town just like every other town in the states so after spending three days there getting the bike fixed up I was more than ready to get going again.

There was one highlight that sticks in the memory that happened on a bus tour of the town. A girl tour guide told us that there were twice as many men living in Alaska as women, and she said "While the odds are good for us women, unfortunately the goods are odd!"

I had run into lots of people who were after getting me very worried about taking on the Dalton highway without any off road experience. I kept telling myself to only take on board information from folks who had actually driven the road personally; the rest was probably just hype.

Some of the stories I'd heard included advice to make sure my throat was covered because the eighteen wheelers will throw up huge amounts of gravel, "a guy got a lump right into the throat last year and it killed him" one guy had told me, I was starting to become shit scared.

The Alaskan highways with the on-going oil price problems continued to be like ghost highways, and I was starting to fall in love with the fact that the roads were so empty. I had driven so many miles on empty roads that it was uncomfortable being back in a city in some respects…in my journal I'd called it "solitude available on tap!"

Over 60% of Alaska's population live in anchorage. The state which is almost 3 times the size of France has less than 500,000 people, which gives you an idea of how empty the whole place is.

It doesn't get dark in Alaska in the summer, at least not as we know it in Ireland. The sun was setting around 11pm but it was still bright out and stayed that dusk colour for the whole night. In the peak day of summer in Anchorage they get twenty two hours of daylight, that's with the sun up but the other two hours it's still bright, it's just that the sun isn't in the sky.

It was there I learned why the Arctic Circle got its name; it's the line of latitude where you get complete darkness and complete brightness for a whole day on the various solstices.

With the bike serviced and sporting a set of brand new knobbly tires I made the three hundred and seventy mile trek from Anchorage to Fairbanks, a trail which takes you through the Denali national park. There were lots of mountains with snow-capped peaks, lovely rivers and nice bendy road, it was heaven.

The further you head north the colder it gets and the icy wind chills you right to the marrow.

Fairbanks

I had about twenty kilos of clothes on me at one point. Here's the list; a helmet, a balaclava, a buff (yoke that goes round your neck for keeping your neck warm and making you look cool), an enduro jacket, and enduro set of pants, motorbike boots, motorbike gloves, wind/water proof under layer jacket, wind/water proof under layer pants, two t-shirts, two pairs of socks, a thong (just kidding) a pair of football shorts, ear plugs, glasses and breathable under layers which act as a second skin.

Even with all that I was brass monkeys. I guess the bottom line is that once you get wet and throw in the wind from riding through the countryside at 60mph not to mention the fact that you're only a stone's throw from the Arctic Circle you're bound to have a chilly willy not to mention a face redder than a baboons arse.

The next part of the trip was the first major challenge I'd encounter. For me it was the mental part, going to

Prudhoe Bay without having the skills on a motorbike to take on the road.

I surveyed the route in my motel in Fairbanks and sat with my mouth wide open.

Wait till you here the three towns you have to pass to get there; I was sure there was an omen in there somewhere. Livengood, Coldfoot and finally the peach, Deadhorse! I'm not kidding.

"Fuck me" I thought to myself, if that isn't a bad omen, the horse may finally meet his waterloo; I'd bitten off way more than I could chew.

I sat working out how I was going to approach the trip. It was about a hundred miles to Livengood, a town about the size of a toenail. You can get petrol there however it'll have an octane rating lower than whale shit.

Then it's up to Coldfoot which was about a hundred and eighty miles further up the road testing the two hundred mile limit of the BMW fuel tank especially as I'd be riding mostly in third gear and wouldn't have great fuel economy. There is a place to stay there but it costs about $285 dollars a night and from reports it's the equivalent of staying in an orang-utans arm pit, "warm but don't expect anything else" was how I'd heard it described.

Now the hard part would kick in, from there it's about two hundred and seventy miles to dead horse, seventy miles beyond the capability of the bike so I would need to get a jerry can and carry spare petrol on the back of the already overloaded bike.

I thought to myself "If I slide of the bike and catch some sparks of the gravel… the bears are in for some char grilled Oisin steaks", although if the octane of the gas was any lower it may not even light, at least I wouldn't be crispy!

Once you get to Deadhorse which by the way is over two hundred miles north of the Arctic Circle you can't get to the sea. The oil companies own the land and you have to pay $30 for a bus tour where you can get out and go for a swim in water that's about 2deg C, not very romantic at all.

If that wasn't bad enough a hotel room equivalent to the size of a priests confessional can cost up to $200 without any of the fringe benefits!

Now the nice part, it was to rain all day and despite me trying to find someone who was heading this direction on various motorcycling websites I was doing it all on my Sweeny Todd.

When I'd done the trip planning based on what people were saying on the various websites there were going to be so many people going up this way on bikes around this time of the year that it would be a veritable traffic jam. The truth however as with many things in life is that when it comes to game time, nuff said.

As I sat in the motel with the map in front of me and thought about the journey I was completely shitting bricks about the whole thing, I hadn't been this scared or nervous since I asked Lorna Donoghue for a dance at the rock disco when I was fourteen; she said no!

As I lay in the bed trying to get my mind into the right frame to take on this task I said to myself; "So Lorna baby.... this one's for you..... And just for your information... I'm a great break dancer."

The day had finally come, today was the day I was taking on the Dalton highway, over five hundred miles of some of the worst driving conditions between here and the planet Pluto. I had burned so much nervous energy thinking about this part of the trip that I was a nervous wreck that morning. I left my motel at 6am with more layers on me than a Spanish onion and rode out of the town of Fairbanks in the pouring rain.

Prudhoe Bay

The road as far as Livengood was fine apart from the freezing cold and pissing rain, the first ninety miles were over and everything was going fine. For a moment I allowed myself to think maybe this isn't going to be as bad as everyone was making out. Two kilometres up the road I came to a sign saying the Dalton highway, it may as well have read "Abandon hope all Yee who enter here" and fifty yards up from the sign the tarmac finished and the road became gravel, I couldn't believe it.

The early part of the road was easy enough going, just kept the speed at about fifty miles an hour and stayed on the most used track through the road, and all of a sudden I'd knocked out nearly a hundred miles.

Things were going well although my hands were so cold that they'd gone beyond numb and now were just stinging.

The road then deteriorated from gravel to pure "muck and shit".

I was looking up a really steep hill in the pissing rain with the makings of a decent size river cascading down towards me when as I started to go up the hill the back wheel just spun around and struggled to get any traction. At the same time the front wheel of the bike was sweeping everywhere, moving around like a hard boiled sweet in the mouth of a granny with no teeth.

As I started to go up the hill the bike kept on inching further and further left until I was fully on the opposite side of the road, in the middle of where the other lane would be, if it were a road and not just a dirt track.

With that a truck started to come over the crest of the hill; seeing me and knowing there's no way he could stop before he hit me he started giving it lackery on the air horn.

Meanwhile at the bottom of the hill I was revving the fuck out of the bike to try and get it moving in the direction I wanted. I was stuck on the upward slope of a hill with very little control, I was panicking. A thought came into my head "just give her the hammer….if in doubt accelerate"; sure enough the bike started to bite and I was out of danger, at least from the impact of a truck, my heart was beating so fast I thought I was going to keel over any second.

When driving a bike in the muck and shit there's some golden rules; the most important is that the engine is always biting i.e. keep the rev's high and the traction high.

If your idling or cruising with the clutch engaged the bike has no traction and when you try and brake you'll probably just come off. The other one to avoid is gurgling, i.e. when you're going too slowly for the gear you're in ….keep the bike hauling ass with high rev's and you have a chance of getting through it.

The other thing that's counter intuitive is that your only way out of trouble is with high revs, in other words more throttle. If you get into trouble your instinct says "FUCKING BRAKE!!!!!!!!!!!!!" but you have to do the opposite.

If you brake you'll just slide straight off in the gravel and muck so you have to kick down a gear and always keep the bike at about 4000rpm, breaking only with the engine and never the brakes.

Another thing is that the faster your moving the more chance you give the bike to cut through the gunge on the road with just sheer momentum, its only if you go slowly that you struggle. Can you imagine telling someone back home how you crashed your bike and ended up in hospital "yeah, I was going too slowly!"

I made it to the first milestone of the Dalton, a place called Yukon River. This was the first sign of life that I'd seen since I left Livengood, Alaska really was living up to its billing as the last wild frontier on earth. It was still before 9am so I fancied my chances of making it the whole way to Deadhorse in one day.

As I was at breakfast, rattling like a set of maracas with the cold, I said to myself "why am i going up here in the first place, maybe I'll stop at the Arctic Circle and turn back.... hmmmm." I ordered a roasting hot breakfast and heaps of coffee and talked with the waitress.

This was probably the tenth restaurant or Cafe that I'd gone to in Alaska. The women who work in these places are about three stone heavier than the equivalent waitress in the lower forty eight states. I reckoned that a women here has to display different qualities, namely "Stick with me sugar, there's great heat in me in the bed for those long winter nights"

I mentioned to the waitress that I was wavering on whether to go to Deadhorse or not and she said "look you've made it this far... it doesn't get any worse...

and from here to Coldfoot (which was about 190 miles) there's lots of paved sections so you'll be fine."

My resolve stiffened and with a full tank of fuel and a full pot of hot coffee in the system I headed off for Coldfoot. I just kept on going at 4000rpm and bar a good few scares on corners where I had come in too hot and ended overrunning completely onto the other side of the road, things were going fine.

A thing to note is that on the Dalton you just pick the best line on the road, it doesn't matter if it's on the wrong side of the road.

I got to Coldfoot in one piece and was starting to feel like a bit of a hero, "Dalton slayer is what they'll call me" I thought to myself. I filled up with gas and also filled up both jerry cans so I'd make the next gas station. Keeping things simple by just keeping the rev's high and the speed at around 50mph things were going great the only problem was I was so cold and wet, I was hallucinating; signs on the road from a distance off started to look like bears and moose, I was going a bit mental.

I got into the Brooks Mountain Range; it was like being on a different planet. They still had snow on them and they looked very harsh, like the way you'd expect mountains to look near the Arctic Circle. Parking up to take some pictures with no one around for hundreds of miles in some of the most severe terrain anywhere in the world I was starting to feel like how the first explorers of this land must have felt, minus the huskies obviously.

The only thing you bump into along the way is oncoming trucks covering you with a shower of mud, shite, gravel and water, this road is one of the routes featured on the TV series, Ice Road Truckers.

Things were going ok, at least from a "miles on the clock" perspective. I passed the Arctic Circle, stopping to take some pictures. I continued on and passed the point where no more trees grow and hit the Arctic tundra. Every twenty minutes I had to stop to heat my hands on the piston heads of the bike, beyond the Arctic Circle I was introduced to a whole new meaning of the word cold.

I was just seventy miles from Prudhoe Bay when the road turned into Swiss cheese. Gravel three inches thick abbreviated with millions of potholes, massive trucks spraying you with muddy water and gravel hitting of your visor and body like someone firing bullets at you was making the journey impossible.

I was on the road for over twelve hours at this point and my teeth were chattering uncontrollably, I couldn't feel a thing with my hands and the cold had even got to my John Thomas. When I would try to drive forward the front wheel was either washing out completely, or the potholes were so bad or numerous it was like driving over the rhythm section of a band.

I pulled over to the side of the road completely and utterly fucked. I couldn't go back; I didn't have enough juice to make it, nor the stamina. I couldn't go forward at that moment because I just couldn't control the bike.

I stood there in the pissing rain completely covered in head to toe with mud, myself and the bike almost unrecognisable. I had to get off and take a leak. When I went it felt like I was pissing barbed wire, the end of the John Thomas was like something someone had glued on.

In the arctic tundra there is no shelter, no trees, nothing to stop in under out of the rain; it really makes you appreciate how hardy an animal a caribou is out here grazing the whole time.

In my mind's eye I just said "dude you're Luke Skywalker"... "No you're his older better looking brother.... the one with the beard"... "c'mon its only seventy miles you can do this... when you get into Prudhoe there'll be a parade for you...you'll be washed down by fifty five naked women who'll all refer to you as the "Dalton highway slayer"....Britney spears will get on the phone and she'll say dude on your way down why not pop over to see me, you can give me a lick of the cango".

I filled my mind with hundreds of motivational thoughts to pump me up and for the next ninety minutes I battled through the worst conditions I've ever come across making it to Deadhorse fifteen hours after I started in Fairbanks.

When I got there they were booked out so I had to stay in place called "camp 1", it's where they house oil workers. For $179 dollars I got a room in a prefab which had three other beds and had no toilet or hot water.

The toilets and wash rooms were communal and there was no restaurant. When I went in to the wash area I was faced with two naked dudes in the shower, one of whom had the hairiest arse I'd ever seen, it really was just like a pair of fur shorts. Desperate not so see the front section I went over to the sinks to brush my teeth where I looked in the mirror and smiled to myself "I did it, I rule the world."

I went to the camp cook guy and asked him could I have something to eat, he said "dude were done" to which I replied "dude just give me a plate of hot food, anything I don't care, just once it's hot." He returned with a plate of pasta and two pieces of ham which looked like they were just pulled straight off a boar's hind quarters and I sat in the corner eating like I was about to go into hibernation.

There was no parade, no welcoming committee, no fifteen chicks in the shower, no alcohol (banned in that area). I just went to bed at 9:20pm with a smile from ear to ear. I had to do it all again in reverse tomorrow.

Turning South

The road back down to Fairbanks the next day was much easier and dryer and with the experience gained from the previous day it took only ten hours to get back, fully five hours quicker. Having talked to lots of folks who completed the Dalton highway it's a coin toss, if you get good weather its very doable, if you don't it's gonna hurt.

The Dalton highway did extract a heavy toll though, my back pannier hopped off somewhere on the road no doubt jarred off by potholes, I didn't even notice and I certainly wasn't going back five hundred miles to get it.

It was laden with much needed stuff but I knew I'd be able to replace the stuff in Fairbanks so I wasn't overly upset. By the time I got to Fairbanks after over a thousand miles of dirt roads through some of the toughest terrain in the world in just two days, I was too tired to care about what I'd lost.

The motel I stayed in while in Fairbanks had two guys from Alabama working behind the counter. They saw me coming in off the road destroyed with mud, and asked "Where the hell you bin boy?" I told them and also told them where I'd been so far on the trip and where I was going, to which they replied "Mayannnn that is baaad Ayass, ya'll must be one hardcore son of a bitch!"

I went to my room beaming; make no mistake there is no greater compliment for a biker than to be called hardcore. I headed off to sleep with the guts of 1100 miles on brutal terrain under my belt and slept like a hedgehog in the winter.

Before I started to head south I decided to take three days in Valdez, Alaska, famous for many things but mostly for the Exxon Valdez oil spill. I met a Scandinavian guy who was over there training the military on survival tactics and he told me that Valdez was the most incredible place that he'd ever been, never one to doubt a Scandinavian, I decided to go.

It was a detour of over three hundred miles but nothing is close in this part of the world so I just puckered up and set off. After the previous two days on the Dalton highway my ass felt like I'd been on the wrong end of some prison love in Sam Quentin so there wasn't a lot of joy in the helmet, I needed a bit of time off the road.

When I was about a hundred miles from Valdez the road steadily started to climb until you reach a place called the Thompson pass, which is a route through the mountains to Valdez. While the pass peaks at about 12000 feet, the mountains still stretch even higher all around you and you can see snow beneath you on the mountains, that's right beneath!

The cloud formations were a wonderful spectacle, every now and then they would part to let the sunshine through and reveal a massive snow-capped peak and just as quickly it would vanish only to be replaced by another on a different section of the road.

Valdez

Valdez is a small fishing village on the coast and is completely surrounded by mountains. It doesn't matter which window you look out of, you are looking directly at mountains with white wispy clouds floating just above your head. I went for a walk around the town stopping to eat in a Thai restaurant, owned by a lady who came here on holidays ten years earlier and never left.

The next day I took the whale watching cruise with a whole heap of European tourists, and at various times we saw Killer whales, Minkey whales and seals all on a waterway surrounded by gigantic snow-capped peaks.

At breakfast one morning I introduced myself to a guy who was also driving a BMW around Alaska, Helmar from Los Angeles. We went on a tour of the surrounding area on our bikes even took the time to take the bike off road onto a rock precipice and take some pictures.

I was standing there taking some pictures with my small Canon point and shoot camera, and over my left should Helmar appears carrying a camera you'd expect to see in a fashion shoot, while it wasn't quite penis envy I did feel a bit girly standing there with my palm sized camera.

Helmar was an American of German extraction and ran his own business. It was a software company which allowed him to spend a lot of time on the road, sounded like the ideal life to me. We went out for a heap of beers in a local Irish bar, hard to believe that even in Valdez Alaska you can find an Irish bar! Helmar was the sort of guy who would just love to camp out by a river for a couple of days by himself and do a bit of fishing. At this moment in the trip I was saying to him "For three fuckin days, what the fuck would you be doing for three days beside a river by yourself?"

We said goodbye and I left Valdez. The biker community on the road is quite small so people run into each other quite often and Helmar mentioned that he'd met a guy from Venezuela and a guy from Switzerland and some other Europeans, especially this bird from Switzerland and that I should look out for them.

At the time I said to myself, man Alaska is a big place, no chance of bumping into them. I made a note in my diary that night "Heaven is a place called Valdez", it's that simple

Tok

That night I made it to Tok and the place was jammed with travellers, it seemed like a different place than just a week earlier.

I met lots of people who were all on different stages of their journeys, two of them Rafael and John from Venezuela and Switzerland who I had just talked about with Helmar the night before had just finished the Pan American trip going south to North. We talked about Central America, Colombia, the Ruta 40 in Argentina all of the places which at their mere mention sent shivers of fear down my back.

Rafael only had one piece of advice for me, "Open your mind, but more importantly open your heart and you'll have the time of your life." I was awestruck that the guys talked so nonchalantly about locations that I was scared shitless about. We talked for about an hour in the rain and they allayed all my fears for the trip, I was beaming when I left them. These guys had completed what I was about to undertake, they were so chilled out it was untrue, any more laid back and they'd fall back!

Chapter 6

The next day I swung north to traverse the top of the world highway on the way to Dawson city in the Yukon. A point well worth mentioning is that the Yukon Territory is bigger than France but has a population of less than 30,000 people, with over half of those living in Whitehorse.

My first stop was in a tiny gold mining village called Chicken, Alaska. I sat down in a small cafe and had an amazing slice of apple pie. Lots of people had told me about Dawson City and said that it was a great night out and not to be missed, so being Irish and never needing more than a tenuous link to having a good night somewhere with drink involved, I headed off all guns firing for the town.

On the Taylor highway aka the top of the world highway I crossed the 10,000 mile mark of the trip, I'd about a third of the distance completed for the trip and I still hadn't got out of Canada. I'd talked to a lot of people about this road and they said that seeing as I'd survived the Dalton highway this one would be a cinch. It started to rain which made for a couple of hairy moments but bar a couple of minor scares it was no hassle.

Dawson city is only accessible via a ferry, seeing as I think it must be one of the only inland towns in North America where this is the case, I was surprised that no one had mentioned it. The ferry is small with room for about eight cars and it struggles to manoeuvre on what is a very large and fast flowing river. I imagined I was crossing into the planet of the apes.

Most of the people I'd met who were incidentally all North American said "no doubt about it Dawson City is an absolute must see" and after visiting the place and spending quite a few hours walking around I have to be honest; I don't get it. It was an overpriced cheesy place if you ask me. It's kept the older type building facades, and the roads don't have tarmac so its feels fairly earthy but at $179 for a cheap hotel I was expecting a bit more.

I went to the casino which was mediocre; the centrepiece was a stage and a bunch of slot machines with a large wooden bar. I think the reason the North Americans like it is because it represents their recent history, as close to a frontier town as you can still get. Not my cup of tea, but everyone to their own as my old gaffer used to say.

As I was walking around I met this German guy who had just spent the last sixteen days kayaking in the Yukon, pulling off the rivers at night to sleep in the woods. He didn't even have a tent, man this guy was hardcore!

He told me that he does this every year, coming over from Germany and he heads out into the Canadian woods for seven weeks, alone. He had me oohing and aahing at some great stories about bears and moose. He was like talking to Michael Schumacher. The Germans would put you to shame coming from Ireland; most can knock out about three languages and don't get me started about the pesky Dutch!...more languages than fingers!

Over a couple of tall frosty beers in Dawson city watching some particularly lame entertainment laid on for visiting tourists I started to reflect on the fact that I'd 20,000 miles to go, and 10,000 under my belt.

It was 33 days since I left Ireland and only 30 since I left on the bike from Toronto. I knew that while in North America you could knock out two to three hundred miles in a morning with the roads being so good, once I got to Mexico all the distances that you'd be capable of completing in any one day would be far less aggressive.

I left Dawson city the next morning feeling a little blue. I missed the conditions of the Dalton highway in a perverse sort of way; I loved the excitement of it; so I decided I was going to set the GPS to take me to Moose creek using off-road tracks.

I got about fifty miles of dirt and then was back on the highway. I was now circling south via a different loop back to Whitehorse along the Klondike highway. It's straight as a ruler for hundreds of miles and after the off-road escapades early in the morning this was a cruel torment.

Jolly Green Jim

On the road I met a cool gent from Washington State called Jim Green and we rode a couple of hundred clicks together. We were both headed the same general direction so we decided to hook up for a couple of days.

Jim had also completed the Dalton highway and said it was very emotional for him as it was something that he'd dreamed about since he was a boy. He was driving a BMW 1200, a newer model than mine and he was like Inspector gadget with all the bits and pieces he had round the bike. He was also armed with a big "fuck off" SLR camera. I was beginning to think that they gave them away free with BMW's in the states.

Jim was one of the easiest going characters I've ever come across. While we were parked up having a soda I looked at the back of our bikes, my wheels had gnarly knobblies and he had a worn out looking street tire. I said to him "Jim did you ride the Dalton on that fucking tire?"... To which he replied... "Yep... there's still plenty of rubber left on that bad boy too". I couldn't believe it. I wouldn't have dreamt about doing it without the best of tires and there's Jimbo cruising along on a slick without a care in the world.

We got to Whitehorse, for me it was the second time round; I couldn't believe the amount Native Americans who were absolutely wasted drunk. Apparently the Native Americans lack an enzyme to break down alcohol so get drunk quicker and stay locked longer, that could really take on in colleges in Ireland. However the sad thing was, none of them looked happy they all just looked really angry.

On my first run through Whitehorse a guy offered to suck my John Thomas for $20 as I passed him by on the street, he looked out of his mind on drugs and was in a wheel chair. I tried haggling him down to $15 but he was having none of it (only kidding about the haggling), I gave him the $20 and declined the BJ.

The motel I stayed in became night of the living dead at around 2am with nothing but druggies and Alco's all wandering around the car park and streets outside, if there's a sadder place on earth I've yet to see it.

The night was topped off when I went to a bar beside the motel for one Coors light to celebrate a long day on the bike and knocking out some massive miles, when a woman who was obviously a close relative of Jabba the Hutt asked me if I was "looking for company sugar?" I downed the Coors light in one go and walking out the bar door couldn't help wonder what sort of dudes would take up that offer; I guess in a town when you get BJ's on wheels anything's up for grabs.

I'm sure there's a good side to Whitehorse but in two visits I hadn't managed to see it; but hey, at least it's lively!

It was my second time through this part of the world so I was pushing things fairly hard, averaging four hundred miles a day; my thinking was that this would allow me to drop to a hundred miles a day in South America for a good period of time. I was having a ball with Jim who was ex-army, ex law enforcement and was just a world of stories and fun. When two people are travelling on the road I think you tend to meet more people, I think people tend to shy away from people who travel on their own "He's travelling on his own, that fuckers weird!"

Every time we stopped on the road we would get talking to bikers or fellow travellers who all seemed really interested in who we were and where we were off to; we were having a ball.

Coal River

We stayed for a night in Coal River in a motel come campsite and about half a mile from the back of the motel there's a river. We strolled down to the riverbank harassed the whole way by giant mosquitoes. When we got there we were greeted by a river flowing east as the sun set in the west. The dusk air was cold but the sun was warm on our faces as we stood watching the river slowly pass us by. The moment ended quickly when Jim spotted bear tracks close to where we were standing so we both hauled ass back to the motel.

We had great weather for days at a time now and met great people on the road everywhere we went. Everyone you meet is travelling. You stop at a rest stop and people come up to you and say "so where you headed to?" You share twenty minutes of stories from the road and you're off again.

There were plenty of obstacles on the road, more buffalo, gravel, and bridges with a grated bridge deck which almost pushes you off the bridge as it catches the knobbly tires, certainly gets the heart racing! We stopped at the sign forest in Watson Lake and I left my mark, as people from all over the world just pop along and leave a sign on one of the masts. There must be easily 20000 signs and when we stopped for some water at a lay-by we saw a crow the size of small donkey. I gave it some fruit and nut mix before it tried to fly off with my motorbike.

Both Jim and I just loved to ride the motorcycles and in just three days had knocked out over a thousand miles. The days tended to start foggy and burn off as the sun rose. The sun turns the scenery on if you know what I mean, when I passed this way ten days earlier it was lashing rain and I didn't think too much of it. Well today the sun was out and it was mesmerizing.

I'm also pretty sure the company made it feel a lot better too, every time you stop you have someone to share the experience with. The roads continued sweeping left and right as they meandered through mountain passes all the time flanked by jade green rivers and forests. The roads continued to be almost completely deserted so we had the run of the highways; I was living the dream.

After Fort Nelson the sun started beaming and the temperature soared, for the first time in over two weeks it was time to put away the fleece lining and water proof layers so I was down to just a t-shift and the enduro suit with all the vents open, long live the heat!

As the evenings drew on with clear skies the bike would cast long shadows and as the roads circumnavigate large hills your shadow dances to the left, front and right of you as you're making your way through the passes. The roads sweep unendingly left and right, as you carve a path through the countryside. At the time I wrote in my journal that "I've never felt as good as I do today."

The only real downside of this part of the world is mosquitoes and black fly. Canada and Alaska are overrun with these gurriers. They actually stalk you, if you're walking home they actually follow you and wait till you leave some bare skin open and then dive straight on it. In these parts of the world they have real mossies, not the caffeine free diet mossie that has made its way into Ireland, for one thing they are about three times the size of the Irish variety.

If that wasn't enough there's black fly which is basically a flying set of teeth which tries to bite you a new bum hole when it lands on you. And the final piece of the jigsaw is completed by a little cur called a noseem, no-see-em get it? It's the North American equivalent of a midge.

So, as soon as you hang a bit of bare skin out the door one of these three amigos is going to try and feast on you. The only way to minimize it is to spray two litres of deet on you or use countless other home remedies like bathing in yak piss; never a yak around when you need one eh!

As you're driving along on the motorbike in the summer your visor gets hit with a variety of insects; about one every five minutes, normally right at the centre of the visor so you can see it with both eyes. This part is quite a bit worse than a car because at least you're three feet from the windscreen in a car, with a helmet you're about two inches away so you get to inspect the lower intestines of anything exploding on the visor.

A June bug hit my visor and it was like someone threw a bottle of Colman's mustard at the helmet...ewwwww! I was straight off the bike gollying onto the visor and wiping him off. If you don't get off and clean the visor the only way to get rid of them is to try and turn your head to the right or the left and see if the carcass will blow off the visor in the wind.

We met a lot of hunters, all card carrying members of the NRA. Like I said earlier I don't get the hunting thing, but again everyone to their own. They would come up and ask you "Hey did you see any caribou?" Yeah like I'm gonna tell you so you can go up and shoot it! It's mad you've 99% of folks looking out of the windows like oul ones waiting for the postman for any sign of a wild animal and then these boys are out shooting them! There's a huge debate in the states about hunting and its relative merits, so no point in taking it any further here.

Pablo Escobar

As Jim and I were pulled over on the Ice field parkway a bike pulled up and Rafael from Venezuela jumped off and said hello. It was great because today was the day when Jim's road and my own would diverge and I wasn't looking forward to it. It was like fate was paying me back for all the lonely riding in Canada, "Don't worry Ois, here's another biker buddy for ya".

We spent the day mucking around on Glaciers, looking at bears and mountain goats and generally having a great laugh. The three of us were pulled over at a glacier and given there was an Irish, USA and Venezuelan registration plates we were attracting a lot of attention. Lots of folks asked if they could take a picture of us, it was one of the first times that I really felt other people thought, what we were doing was cool.

It came time to say goodbye to Jim, we had rode from Dawson city the whole way down to Lake Louise where he cut off to Washington State. We'd a great four days covering almost 1600 miles together and I knew I was going to miss him. Rafael was a completely different sort of character. He was a tall Latin dude with long black hair who was too cool for school. We immediately hit it off and were straight away having a great time. He was headed for Houston in Texas so our roads would likely be the same for over a thousand miles which suited the two of us down to the ground.

I was constantly badgering him with questions about Mexico and Central America, he gave me one piece of advice, "Never look at the news in these countries, if you do you'll be afraid to leave your room!" The first question I asked Rafael was what did he do for a living to which he replied "I'm a drug dealer."

Black Diamond

After 12,500 miles it was my last day in Canada. Pablo Escobar, aka Rafael and I pulled into a town near the USA border with Montana called Black diamond. The town was as dead as a door nail but was a nice place. We went out for a couple of beers in the local hotel and while I was getting petrol I bumped into the ugliest women I'd ever seen. She was dressed like a nurse, and if this is what nurses looked like in this part of the world, I reckon people didn't stay long in the hospital; she had a face like a bull dog licking piss off a nettle.

We had spent most of the day getting some new tires on the bikes, and I had a full service, the bike had been through a bit of an ordeal by this stage. We didn't go to a BMW dealer to get the work done, and the only thing I can say is that this was a mistake, and I'll leave it at that. While we were waiting on the bikes we went over to a place called Blackfoot BMW to see if they had any bits of kit worth picking up. We met a guy there from Chile while we were hanging around and it turned out he was a veteran over lander who had done the Pan American highway a bunch of times.

He was the spitting image of a friend of my brothers called Foxy in every way except he spoke with a Spanish accent. This guy was fifty eight years old and was married to a thirty year old polish girl who was really hot and about a foot taller than him. I asked him what's his secret and he said, exactly like Speedy Gonzales would have said it "eets coz I'm sexy no?!" In his wallet he had a picture of him in the Atacama Desert but the stories he told me made me more nervous than ever about crossing into Mexico.

We rode out of Calgary into a thunder storm as the sun was setting on the Rockies in the distance while being completely black overhead. We spent that night in a hostel, first time in a while for me it has to be said and because we arrived late I got one of the top bunks in a room holding six people with three bunk beds. There was a Japanese lad beneath me who if I did end up falling through the top bunk on top of him, was going to end up rightly fucked.

The top bunk was about two foot from the ceiling and had a wooden surround. I hadn't been in a bunk bed since I was about five years old, which was about the last time I was able to fit in one and things hadn't changed. I was too tall for the bed and too wide and with the really low ceiling it really was like looking out of an open casket coffin. I hit the scratcher late to be more tired than normal so I'd sleep but looks like everyone does this so I ended up being first in the scratcher.

For about two hours, on the half hour the rest of the guys in the room would come in, turn on the light, go in and brush their teeth etc, then go to bed, turn off the light. The whole time all I was thinking about especially after the guy got his head hacked off on the greyhound bus in Manitoba "ok this fucker is a serial killer...he's gonna take out a bowie knife and do me in the goolies with it."

I guess I'm just not comfortable sleeping in a room with five strangers. Also the people who go to hostels here aren't the same as in Europe. They aren't inter-railer's, or students. A lot of them are hunters, and other types of cabbages most not the sort of folks you'd be striking up a conversation with.

I talked with one of them earlier in the night and he was on sick leave for some reason and here was the only place they had a doctor, he didn't elaborate. In my spinning mind this translated to "ok this guy is a nutter, no way they have a doctor here in Canmore and not in Calgary." The fact that he had a moustache and a real dodgy comb over didn't do anything to allay my worries. I thought to myself, if I'm gonna get slaughtered in the middle of the night; I don't want it to be by a dude with a tache and a comb over!

I could see myself in the serial killer year book. On the left page a full page picture of the serial killer, and on the right a montage of all the people he'd killed, and on the top row, two in from the left was me.

Chapter 7

South to the border with Mexico

The trip had been getting better and better and hit a new peak as we crossed into Montana in the USA. It was early in the day and we were headed for the Many Glacier International Park to drive the Logan pass.

It was a straight forward border crossing and I threw in a joke that I was a Jedi, "you don't need to see my ID, and these aren't the droids you're looking for", the border guard laughed charitably, I think he'd heard it a few times before.

For large parts of the day it absolutely bucketed down but it did nothing to dampen the scenery. The route through the Logan pass takes you higher than most clouds and the sensation of travelling up through, and above rain clouds is sensational. The road hairpins right and left above massive chasms cut by glaciers and the whole way through you have massive mountains on one side which were intermittently coming into view through the rain clouds.

We finished the night off in Hungry horse. If I'm honest my only motivation to stay there was because of the long way round. It was one of the small villages Ewan and Charlie stayed in, and by chance we stayed in the same motel. Rafael thought I was a spacer but the two lads were my inspiration for going and I was feeling magic.

This was the point at which the guys turned east to head for New York and I would be turning south to go to Ushuaia. For me it was the point at which the whole journey became my own adventure. Everything from this point on was just me. If you think it all sounds a bit sad, you're right.

We then popped over to a great cafe where the folks were really friendly and had a great bit of grub and a good laugh with the waitresses. Rafael was winding the girls up that we were gay saying things like "two deserts but only one spoon" which the girls were lapping up. It was a perfect end to a great day, certainly the best day of the trip so far, and for me the best since Liverpool beat AC Milan on penalties in the European cup.

Montana

We met a biker when we were stopped for coffee that had just come up from a massive Harley rally. He was from Australia and he was now turning south to do Route 66. He was average height with a beard that would have gotten him a job with ZZ top in a heartbeat. He was a man's man, he told us that he left the missus back home to go on the trip, he didn't tell her where he was going or how long he'd be gone for; just that he was heading off and he'd be back when he was ready.

Rafael was teaching me some Spanish for Central and South America. Just some key phrases like hello, good bye, please don't kidnap me, no I prefer sex with women, please don't spit in my dinner, the usual stuff they teach you in first year Spanish class in Dublin.

Since I'd the bike serviced in "wankerworks" there was a rattle whenever I'd get towards 4000rpm. Given that on a trip like this your completely and utterly dependant on the bike, I had to bite the bullet and drive to a BMW dealer in Helena Montana, a day's ride of a detour all told.

I'd been separated from Rafael that day, he had been in a bad mood as a result of some bad news from home about his business and I'm not sure that he didn't just want to be on his own anyway, one way or another I was back on my own and feeling a bit blue.

I got to Helena and a guy called John, armed with a stethoscope came out and started using it to listen to the engine. Within about three minutes he'd found the source of the problem and five minutes later had it fixed. It's great to see guys who really know their game in action. It's amazing how your mood goes with the bikes condition; if the bikes in great shape you feel great, if there's anything wrong with it at all, you turn into a freak show.

He gave me a route from Helena to Yellowstone Park, about four hundred miles long of which I'd completed three quarters when I stopped in a town called Ennis the following night. I thought it was good karma as I passed my bike test in Ennis Co. Clare in Ireland.

As long as you have a map you'll never be lonely in the USA. If you happen to find yourself alone and want some male company in any restaurant or bar anywhere in the fifty states just pull out a map and spread it across the table you're sitting at. Draw yourself up a pensive looking face and men of all ages will flock to you. Men are attracted to maps like wasps to jam. When a man is driving a car obviously he doesn't need a map, nor instructions or directions for that matter. Like the swallows finding their way to Capistrano every year, a real man will find his way.

However, a map in the hands of another party, well that's another matter.

The first thing they'll say to you is "You need some help buddy?" and that's it they are sitting at the table pouring out the best routes, towns, scenic areas and places where they spent "quite a bit of time". It's a wonderful trait; if you don't believe me give it a go.

For the last couple of days the weather had been perfect for riding and the landscape had turned a golden wheat colour which stretched off as far as the eye could see. Montana has a reputation for being flat but it also has huge mountains with great roads that sweep and weave their way through the Montana Rockies.

Surround by such natural beauty it's impossible to stay in a bad mood and I cured my melancholy by having a fantastic time on the bike, there is nothing like having the bike leaned over as far as you can take it cornering bends to get your mood back firing on all cylinders.

I got stopped by the Rozzers, I was doing 45mph in a 30mph zone. They were a bit pissed off and made me strip down the bike to get the vehicle registration and do a concealed fire arms check, but in the end let me go with a verbal warning. The day finished on top of a hill looking at the sun setting, not for the first time over the foot hills of the Rockies.

The variety in every day sends you to sleep in a daze, it's like there's only so much you can take in and every day you completely fill your mind with memories. Even on bad days you cover so much ground and see so many things it's really hard to remember what day certain things happened.

The next day I knocked out another four hundred miles and ended up in Red Lodge after completing the Bear tooth highway, renowned as one of the best motorcycle routes in the world. My poor bum had gone through some savage treatment on the motorbike and I'd a huge blister on it which burst when I jumped on the saddle too quickly.

When it happened first there was the relief as the awkwardness and uncomfortable feeling went "ahhh...oooh.." The original pain was gone but was replaced now with a new pain like someone was washing the area with lemon juice and a brillo pad ...ARRGGHH!!

I saw a mammy bear and her two cubs crossing the road about twenty yards ahead of me on the road that day which is about as close as I ever want to be to a bear. I'd seen one crossing the road at full clip a few days earlier with Jim and it was only then I realised why people say you'll never outrun a bear.

Since I got to Canada I'd been having a recurring nightmare with bears in it. I drive around a bend in a dark forest and there's a bear standing on the road. I break and stop about ten feet away. The bear stands up on its two hind paws and lets one of those noises that Ben from Grizzly Adams used to make.

I try to turn the bike quickly to haul ass out of there, too quickly and end up falling over and dropping the bike. I quickly jump to my feet and try to lift the overloaded bike worried that any moment I'll feel the heat of the bear's breath on the back of my neck. I throw the bike back up, jump on, start it up, lash it into first and rally out of the bears reach.

When I'm about a hundred yards from the bear I look back and it's standing there, with a leash on it and a woman is standing beside it. I turn the bike around and drive back to her and sure enough, exactly as you'd expect, its Brittney Spears wearing the red leather outfit from oops I did it again, absolutely appropriate as it's a recurring nightmare after all.

I drive back up, take off my helmet and say to her..."what's the story with the bear?" She says to me "do ya fancy a cup of tea sweetie?" I reply that depends... do you have any Jacobs Mikado or coconut creams? She then says... Nope I only have Kimberly and some fig rolls. Yuck!! And that's the end of the nightmare....I wake up in a cold sweat..... Imagine.... going for tea in Brittney's place and not a decent biscuit to be had!

Yellowstone is massive at over 3,000 square miles and is an excellent place to visit. The park consists of lakes, canyons, mountain ranges and the largest super volcano on the North American Continent. I had been given a ticket in the park for stepping on a thermal feature. The park wardens didn't try to coach you and tell you why it's a bad thing they just issued the ticket. A bigger pair of condescending pricks I've never met.

There are some great sayings over here for being tired. Jim told me one after a long days riding, he was very tired and he described it as "I'm beat.. Like a red headed step child!" and the best one after a really hard day, "I feel like I was rode hard and put away wet" which is used all over Canada and the US, there are a lot of places I could go with that saying, but I'm going to take the high road.

I've left Wyoming and Montana both behind, and went like a fart through a G string through Idaho. Why the rush? Well after Yellowstone and the bear tooth highway you start to cut into Idaho, and to be honest there wasn't really much of anything that grabbed my fancy in Idaho, just lots of agriculture, so on days like this I tended to eat up the miles.

Bonneville

I took a right turn at Salt Lake City made my way to the Bonneville Salt Flats in Utah. To get here you have to ride right into the Utah desert, and with the temperature at 48deg C I thought I was going to explode. With no mountains and very little in the desert that you would need to build a road around, the road stretches straight as far as the eye can see.

Gradually the desert becomes whiter and whiter (that's the salt n'est pas!) until if feels like you're on the moon. As I was driving along I started to wonder hmmm.... so is this it? (i.e. the salt flats) or will there be a sign up here somewhere as pretty much one salt flat looks like the next I guess.

So after about twenty minutes of deliberating as I was driving along I said "fuck it I'm pulling off the highway onto the flats". Now a couple of things were going through my noggin at that point and there's nowhere to escape from these thoughts inside a motorcycle helmet.

1) Its 48deg, the oil in the bike is 20/50 which means it's rated for -20 to +50; if it got any hotter I'd be in trouble. 2) Would the bike sink? It's a heavy machine; if I went too far out would I be able to get it back onto the road? 3) What if I came off the bike? Out on the flats no one would ever find you, after half a mile out you just vanish into the heat shimmer. 4) Is this the actual salt flats or is there another area which is not so soft? 5) This place is like being in a dream and finally 6) I need a shag.

So off I set and drove out about two miles just far enough so that I couldn't see anything in all four directions but white salt, the blue sky and the brown of the distant mountains.

When you do this sort of stuff you get all uppity and Marco polo within yourself. I struck up an inner narrative "A lone Jedi treks off into the nothingness, with only his ...blah blah blah" I'll let you fill in the rest. A couple of things to note, there's no sound, nothing, just you, the bike, some distant mountains and blinding whiteness all around. As they say back in Clondalkin... "Deadly buzz".

After only a short period of time, either because of the heat or the unchanging surroundings I was starting to get disorientated. At times like that I was thankful that I'm a fat bastard and I just followed the hefty track me and the bike had made through the salt to find my way back to the road.

I was also glad I didn't have a sensible travel mate, to warn me off doing stuff like this, all that "be careful" "you'll regret it" "it wasn't me father, I pulled out" type stuff.

I suppose I was testing myself every day in terms of "gowan ya big scardy cat, ya big girl's blouse, ya mohair cardigan". If I found myself saying "don't do it" because I was a little afraid I constantly said to myself "Fuck it...I'm just doing it..You only live once".

I kept trying to get in the moment; I was obsessed with it actually.

Everyone had told me before I left to make sure that I "Stayed in the moment". I have to be honest I didn't really understand the concept, having worked so long for a corporate giant you tend to spend all your time either forward planning for performing post mortems on things that went wrong in the past, never leaving much time for "the moment".

I thought back to some Billy Connolly DVD's I'd seen, every time he went somewhere cool he'd strip off into his nude and do a dance, so not to be undone I said I'd give it a go. I did, and it felt great. No sooner had I completed the jig when I noticed in the distance a biker making his way in my direction out on the flats.

I noticed him starting to slow down no doubt thinking "Is that fucker naked?" Then he slowly arced to the right and burned off into the distance. I was rolling around laughing. For my troubles I got absolutely burnt alive, with the intense heat and glare I was glowing like a gas heater.

I stayed out there until it got dark, and because I was in a place where the world is flat and very dark, I could see stars right down to the horizon in all directions.

When I got back from the salt flats that evening, I was gassing up for the following day when a chap driving an old BMW pulled up. He was a school teacher named Barry in the town of Wendover, which is where I was staying. We got talking and he took me to one of only two places in the world, other than at sea where you can see the curvature of the earth.

You drive to the top of this hill and you look out onto the salt flats, because it's so flat the lights from the cars driving from Salt Lake City and back create a light Arc around the curvature of the earth, too cool.

Barry was also a pilot and we went down to where the Enola gay was stored and where they store the plane prop from the movie Con Air. Now we were there well after hours around 10pm or so, and I found it amazing how your natural suspicion is that people don't just come up and talk to you. They must be serial killers or worse, maybe republicans.

On a trip like this you just have to go with your instinct, if someone comes across as genuine, you have to go with it. But I will say one thing, when we down at these airplane hangars in the pitch dark, at one point the air conditioning went off in one of the buildings and I nearly jumped twenty feet!

The following day I was supposed to push on towards Lake Tahoe but I stayed another day, the salt flats are too incredible a place to just pass through so I wanted to have another day out there acting the maggot.

I went for dinner in a casino in the town, and got talking to Lieutenant colonel Vader, fate or what. We went for dinner and had a great chat about his time in Korea, Vietnam and Desert storm. After dinner the magnet that is the salt flats pulled me back out for more fun.

In Utah you don't have to wear a motorcycle helmet and driving around with just a pair of sunglasses and no armour in the heat of the desert gives you a tremendous feeling of freedom; it really is how motorcycles should be ridden. Out on the flats I got talking to guys who were doing motorcycle speed trials, it was a pure "guys" moment, standing around looking at things going very fast.

Nevada

Leaving Bonneville I drove towards a place called Wheeler national park in Nevada. It's a pass that takes you up to about 10,000 feet above sea level with a seemingly endless view of the desert below. The roads up there were in great shape but above 9000 feet were hard top with a very fine layer of gravel which had built up on top of the surface. The back wheel washed out from under me twice and if I didn't have the Dalton highway experience under my belt I'd have come off for certain. When the back wheel starts to wash out now the instinct kicks in and says "MORE GAS FAT BOY!!!!!" which let's face it is a pretty imprecise instruction!!! If you don't give enough you're off the bike, and too much and you'll bronco off the bike as it corrects itself.

I was now firmly in the Nevada desert and took B roads for large portions of the day so I could check out two ghost towns, not a single car passed me for the entire time I was on one B-road, a full eighty eight miles.

I pulled up to the ghost town and to be honest I was shitting myself. The combination of not having seen anyone on the road for so long, and a town full of ghosts was giving me the heebie jeebies. (Yeah yeah I know that's not what a ghost town is!)

I had a twenty second wander around and I burned out of there like a scalded cat. There wasn't much to see really. I thought it would be like a western town or something like that, but looked more like a knackers' yard.

The temperature continued to rise eventually peaking at 49degC. How hot is that? Well it had me running to the internet to see how far off a world record it was. Pesky Ethiopia had a day of 134degC, about 56degC. Still it's so hot you've a headache for most of the day, and your goolies feel like you've a burning lump of coal in your nether regions.

It was a good few days since I'd talked to anyone and I woke up the following morning feeling home sick; not sure why that day of all days. I think it might have been because I was getting closer to Mexico, and it was looking increasingly unlikely that I'd meet up with a riding partner to go through the tougher parts of the trip. I didn't speak the language and I was starting to fret.

Then, to add insult to injury the girl who ran the motel (who it turns out was from Mississippi) asked me where I was from; "Where ya'll from". I said Ireland and then she said in her southern redneck shit-kicker drawl; "Reckon I shoulda known u havin red hair n'all". She came an inch from me breaking my foot off in her ass, calling me ginger, cheek of her! That's strawberry blond I'll have you know, bitch!

So in a fairly low mood I headed off to Bryce canyon.

I decided to get my spirits up I was going to do as much unpaved roads as possible, as it's pretty hard to feel homesick when your front and back wheels are struggling for traction. The roads I picked were mental. In reality I've nothing like the amount of experience on a motorbike needed to be taking on this sort of terrain, but that day if there was a trail, I went up it, even if it only looked like a donkey once might have went up there for a piss, I went up there on the bike.

At one time I went up trails which had about three inches of fesh fesh (really fine sand) on them, I didn't come off and really felt that I could handle any type of trail on a motorbike, which no doubt would be tested in South America. By that evening my mood was a lot better, in two conversations with other bikers today, at separate times they both referred to me as hard-core, I felt like I'd won the lotto!

The next day the temperature hit 51deg C, my only reaction was to take a picture of the thermometer, "no one will ever believe this!" I thought to myself. It's a curious thing when you see 51deg on the readout; all you want to do is see it go to 52.

Zion

While stuck in a traffic jam in a town called Hurricane, with 51deg and a glacial flow of traffic on the way to Zion Canyon, I genuinely thought I was going to spontaneously combust. To cure it I just pulled off the road into a garage, went in and pulled a bottle of water out of the fridge, drank about half it, and split the remainder pouring it straight down my back, and the other half down into my boxer shorts; mannnn!, did it feel good.

Zion canyon was breathtaking, every now and then you'd find yourself saying a spontaneous "Jesus Mary and Joseph!!", or its close relation "holy fuck", it was that good. Having lived in Phoenix for a while, I was amazed I'd never heard of it, from memory I thought the place was better than the Grand Canyon, mainly because with Zion the road travels right into the depths of the canyon.

As you drive in the canyon, your head fills with the theme sounds of westerns, the magnificent seven, Bonanza, The high Chaparral, you get the gist.

Every now and then a silly song would jump in "Oh the milkman is your friend in the neighbourhood, in the neighbourhood." When I start singing the theme sound from Sesame Street I know it's time to get off the bike.

I was inching my way to the Grand Canyon, North rim. I plumbed the destination into the GPS and selected "shortest distance". I started out from a place called Kanab and ten minutes into the journey I was back on the heavy gravel. I don't mind it but not ten minutes after a lad is finished with his ham and eggs.

In total the unpaved portion was about forty miles long, and in the middle of it a mega storm opened up and the road turned to shite. The main worry I had was that I was passing through woods which were supposed to be full of bears and ill-tempered squirrels; the North American grey squirrel is known to have a penchant for goolies.

I parked up the bike and went under a shelter to dry off a bit. I was talking to a guy when a lad overheard my accent and said "Where are ya from?" I said "Ireland", pretty standard so far... "What part?"... Dublin I replied and this is where you know you've just met a paddy... "What part?"... Clondalkin!!

There were three lads all from County Cork and were on a road trip from Vancouver in Canada to México and back, and all needed to be back in Ireland for college on the 6th of September. We'd a good natter and took some pictures around the canyon. The lads are travelling back in a jeep Cherokee which they bought in Vancouver for $800; they were having a great time.

From there I headed off for the south rim of the canyon, and even though its only ten miles away as the crow flies, it's over two hundred miles to drive. For the entire ride on one side there was pink desert and on the other side large red cliffs so the ride was awesome.

Once done with the canyon I bolted for Flagstaff where I would stay that night. Along the way I was chased by storms and I wrote in my diary that night that it was "thundering and lightning like crazy outside so I got here just in time".

I was well ahead of schedule so I decided to knock out about four hundred miles on Route 66, which runs through Flagstaff. It was just like the movie "Cars" with all these old towns now kept alive only by tourists coming in to buy 66 memorabilia. The diners sell some of the best pie anywhere; I'd say the average person who completes the whole of Route 66 must end up putting on about twenty pounds with all the good eating en route.

In a petrol station I picked up a brass token which said "good for 2 screws in dolly's", not bad for $3.69. The whole place was full of European tourists, as one biker remarked to me, "neva saw so many eye-ties!"

There had been an unseasonal amount of rain in Arizona, and large chunks of the road were lined with beautiful yellow flowers which encroached onto the road. The reason for all the mileage apart from doing the whole "it's cool to ride on route 66" thing was because I woke up like a boar with a sore hole.

I hardly got a winks sleep because the motel I stayed at in Flagstaff was right beside the train station. The trains ran pretty much all night and the drivers kept blowing their horns on the way past, I was picturing the driver in the engine room, "c'mere Cletus I'm gonna toot da horn an wake up all dem der fellers"

On top of that they must have been serving oysters in the diner because the couple in the next room were going at it hammer and tongs for about two hours, yep that's right two hours.

It started out gently enough but pretty soon it was all "oh yeah.... oh yeah.... right there honey... right there.... yeah...that's it...right there...", followed by some course correction, "no honey, like I showed you, yep..that's it... right there.....oh yeah baby...right there", and this was just the woman talking. I resisted the temptation to roar in "Ride her sideways!"

To drown them out I turned on the TV and what was on? Basic instinct, more sex, nothing but reminders everywhere and the last time I had a shag you could buy a snickers for 25cents. I was contemplating "y'know I'd take an ice pick in the head to shag Sharon Stone, easily worth it."

The only cure for when I'm grumpy is to get on the road; I knocked out the first two hundred miles without even stopping. I pulled in and filled up and did another hundred, then stopped for some scrumptious apple pie and knocked out the final hundred staying in a town called Williams for the night.

Phoenix

I had kept in touch with an Intel colleague who had moved to Phoenix and he invited me to stay with him to get the bike fixed up before heading south of the border. I met Andy about two hours north of Phoenix and we burned down for his place. I planned to give the bike to the BMW dealer and tell him, "Change anything that may or could go wrong between here and Quito in Ecuador, I can't afford to break down in Central America".

Phoenix is always roasting, it was the 1st of September and each day was over a 100degF. I spent a great three days with Andy and his family and Andy who's also a keen biker, ferried me around all the motorcycle stores so I could restock any of the gear I was missing or that was damaged.

After having had a great rest it was time to get going again. The only wrinkle was that the guys in "WankerWorks" in Calgary had broken a part of the rear shock where it connects onto the transmission, so it would be a $1200 dollar repair. Had I gone to the BMW dealer they would have covered the damages, but there it was, blue locktite, the BMW garages only used green so I had to fork over the cash.

Before I went further south it was time to go shopping for new underwear. Gone were the cotton boxers. While they looked nice they were sawing me a mangina as a result of the many atomic wedgies one gets when riding around on a motorbike all day. I replaced them with black Lycra jocks, lovely stuff!

In Mexico you don't have as many launderettes, so all you do at the end of the day is take these bad boys into the shower with you, do a disco on them while your showering, squeeze em and hang em up, and the next morning they're dry as a pistachio. The only downside is that they're ultra snug, so you've a male camel toe going on while you're wearing them, y'know, the "division sign" rotated ninety degrees.

Based on conversations I'd been having with people along the way, the paranoia about driving into México was intense. Nearly everyone I talked to thought I was just plain crazy. I was beginning to doubt myself as these people lived just next door to Mexico, what made me think I knew more coming from Ireland?

Most people who go to México go to a resort or on package holidays so don't ever get to see the underbelly. Apparently the border towns with the US are very violent, frequent robberies, murders, muggings etc. Needless to say I wasn't looking forward to it.

As I got closer and closer and was stopping in gas stations the tales of woe increased. One chap in particular really put the willies up me, he said "Man they'll fuckin shoot you, they'll see you coming through and radio ahead and they'll be fuckin waiting, they'll take you into the desert and kill you, rob your fucking bike and probably rape your ass!"

When I consulted the Irish department of foreign affairs they didn't fill me with hope either; on their website the following warning was posted:

There have been a high number of drug related assassinations in 2008 so far, particularly in the northern border and Pacific states. Seven people were killed and 130 injured when grenades were let off at Independence Day celebrations in Morelia, Michoacán on 15 September, most likely by members of a drugs gang. Foreign visitors and residents have been among the victims in the border region, including the cities of Nuevo Laredo, Tijuana, Ciudad Juárez, Nogales, Reynosa and Maramoros.

I didn't want to go to Mexico, and I certainly didn't want to go to Central America, these were areas on the trip that I had to get through to get to Ushuaia. I was petrified and was a bit pissed off that with so many folks all online saying that they were doing these trips yet there was no one who was actually near me. I started to think that maybe these websites are full of bull-shitters who make up that they are out in the world travelling. I left Phoenix and headed for Tucson, it was my last night in the USA and I'd no idea what tomorrow would bring.

I took some advice on what area to cross, and to avoid the bandits I decided to cross in a quieter town called Douglas, just to the east of Nogales. I had no idea what to expect.

Realistically, travelling in Canada and the USA is a holiday. Sure you can have days where you have a hard ride but you know that at the end of the day you'll always be able to find a place to stay, and find somewhere to get something to eat. There's a lot of certainty when you're travelling there. Once I crossed that border my certainty was gone.

I left Andy Flanagan's place and burst out for Tucson the plan being to get close enough to the Mexican border so I could get to a town called Guaymos about two hundred miles south of the US border in the same day. W

hen I left Tucson I headed south east and I wasn't long into the journey when I realised that I'd completely underestimated how far Douglas was from Tucson, and despite leaving the motel at about 8am, I arrived at the border at midday.

This was "it" I told myself, this is where the shit hits the fan, where the fun stops and the adventure begins. The amount of times I told myself, "don't worry you'll meet up with people before you have to go through the borders", and sure enough there I was going through on my own.

Chapter 8

Mexico

I was absolutely shitting myself as I crossed the border. The downside of arriving at midday was that I was hiking between customs and passport control in an Enduro suit and motorbike boots in 100-degree heat; I was sweating like a whore in confession.

I parked up the bike and of course there was no one to watch it, and with a lot of my gear simply bungee corded to the top of the bike I was certain some of it was going to get swiped. In fact, if half of the stuff that I'd heard in the USA was true any moment now I'd be robbed of my every possession. I went in for processing and the Mexican border guards were great, they didn't get too many Irish passports coming through; the guards took a real interest in the journey and had me out of customs after about forty minutes.

It was the first moment that I knew I was rightly fucked though; I had no business being south of the border without any Spanish.

Most people who go to Mexico go to resorts like Cancun or Acapulco where the locals are used to foreign visitors and most of the folks working in the tourist industry have some English. In the border towns I was surprised to find out that no one spoke any English, and certainly couldn't comprehend what a big hairy arsed Irishman was saying.

The difference between the USA and Mexico when you cross the border is night and day. I thought it might get poorer as you go south, but once you get across that border, that's it; people don't have a pot to piss in, at least that was the case in Douglas and a couple of the towns I drove by that first day.

The route I chose was supposed to be quiet; inadvertently I'd picked one of the most scenic areas to drive through in northern Mexico, the Ruta Sierra. The scenery was top notch, but all I wanted to do was to get as far away from the border as possible, so if I'm honest I was a bit too nervous to enjoy it.

The advice on Mexico I'd been given was that as long as you "get the hell out of the border areas" you should be fine.

The speed limit on the roads was 80kmph, a speed most three legged donkeys could do so I ended up just ignoring the limit and tipping along at about a 100kph.

In the first day, I was stopped three times by customs, the army and finally the police and none of them were for speeding. The customs dude was checking for the motorcycle permit, the army was checking for drugs and had these two North American girls stuff all over the road, and finally the police were just stopping me to say hello and wondered what football team I supported. He'd noticed the Irish Registration plate and wanted to know was it "Liverpool" or "Manchester United".

Out on the road, I passed at least five people openly selling weed, think they call it Juanita (wan-ita) down here I think, not sure and I was afraid to ask in case I was taken up the wrong way.

The Mexicans appeared to be a devout crowd, all over the roads there were little houses for praying in and shrines where people were killed on the road. On cliff faces, I saw at least half a dozen murals, mainly of the Madonna. My first impressions of Mexico were that the people were very friendly and God fearing and I thought that I was going to like it. I spent that night with a copy of Spanish for Dummies; not being able to speak the "lingidy" left me feeling dumber than pig dribble all day.

Hermosillo

I got as far as a city called Hermosillo, better known as the Sun City, the largest town in the state of Sonora. I lay in bed that night and I had to keep pinching myself; "Dude! You've just ridden your motorbike to Mexico!!" The trip odometer was up over 16,000 miles and my head was all over the place. Hermosillo was a nice town and the first thing I had to get used to was the food; Taco's Tortillas, rice, beans would become staples for the next couple of weeks.

That night the heat was brutal. Gone was the air conditioning ubiquitous in the US, replaced with a fan that just rotated hot humid air around the motel room. I only had to comb my hair to break into a sweat. Walking out into the air was like walking into a warm wet sponge, and this wasn't even supposed to be a humid area.

I kept on thinking to myself what is it that this temperature does to the human body that the reaction it fires physiologically is "All the water in the body....get out now!!!!!" With all the sweating my motorbike boots smelt like an old used gym bag that you'd left in the boot of the car for a year.

The next day I headed for the coastal town of Guaymos taking the Ruta 15 to the pacific coast. The last time I'd seen the ocean was in Valdez Alaska and it seemed such a long time ago.

That day I did quite a bit of wandering on the bike touring around the mountains, one in particular called the Sierra Libre really caught my attention with its name. The scenery was good without being spectacular, but I couldn't help thinking that I'd made a mistake by going to Alaska and the Rockies so early in the trip, would anything be able to compare to it?

I spun over to San Carlos which is the tourist zone of Guaymos and spent a day mucking around by the beach. The hotels owned huge sections of the beach, and you couldn't just walk out onto it, large areas were reserved just for guests.

The pier in the town is full of American owned boats and yachts that are sailed down from the US. I'd seen a lot of very poor people so far that day and something just felt wrong to be looking out at the sun setting with all these expensive boats in the foreground.

I had put the bike up onto the centre stand and was sitting relaxing with the lovely view when a red pickup full of drunken Mexican youths pulled up and walked over. I got the distinct impression that if I'd been from the USA I would have got a lot of hassle but I just played the dumb Irishman card and it all passed off without a hitch.

Alcohol is sold everywhere along the road. You can stop in a shack by the side of the road and have a Corona or a Pacifico and it seems that drink driving is no big deal.

The driver of the red pickup was completely wasted. When he was done drinking cans by the pier with the rest of his buddies they hopped straight into the truck and drove away. It's tough to listen to drunken people at the best of times, but when they're Mexican and only know two lines of English, which was one more line than I knew in Spanish, it was tough going.

Navajoa

I continued on the Ruta 15 for the third day to a town called Navajoa. I was only doing very low mileage, an average of less than a hundred and fifty miles a day for the previous two days; it was just too warm and humid. The people at this early stage were brilliant, genuinely friendly although I didn't have a clue what they were saying; I just kept smiling and nodding.

It was strange for a guy like me, I've always used humour (or at least tried to!) as a way of getting to know people and communicating with them, but no one there had the slightest clue what I was on about.

In Navajoa I stopped in a motel which had a pool, it was scorching all day so the thought of cooling off in a pool was more than I could resist. That night I lay floating in the water looking up into a sky full of stars with the most gorgeous soft warm breeze blowing against my toes and face, "Man... this is the fucking life!"

On the down side, I'd two cockroaches in my bathroom the size of a fox, like I said Mexico is a country of extremes. Navajoa was completely off the English-speaking tourist trail as were most of the cities that far north in Mexico so I just kept moving on. I set off early the next morning, the trees in the car park of the motel were full of birds that made a fantastic racket as I was pulling out and on my way they covered my bike with shit.

The poverty in the small towns was humbling and the gap between rich and poor seemed vast, it seemed like there was nothing in the middle, you are either very rich or very poor. I made a point of only going to places to eat and drink which looked clean and poor if you know what I mean, I wanted to give the peso's to people who were struggling, obviously I was keen not to risk blowing out an O-ring in the process.

People get to work by whatever means they can in Mexico, it was common to see six or seven people all piled into the back of an open truck. It seems so farcical that in the western world we have laws that say you must fasten your seat belts in the back of a car and here everyone bundles in wherever they can find room.

Mexico has two types of roads, the Ruta Cuota, which are toll roads, and the Ruta Libre, which are obviously free. On the Cuota roads, it seemed that about every sixty miles or so you hit a toll road, and these weren't cheap, you would have to pay about five dollars to get through. The fallout of this is that given so many people are poor in Mexico, the Ruta Cuota's are completely empty and the Ruta Libre's are tremendously congested.

Military check points are very common and combined with police checkpoints it would make you wonder "what's the undercurrent in the society that makes this necessary?" I surmised that it was probably drugs; I didn't think I'd ever get used to seeing half a dozen young men with guns, but in fairness to them, they were always very courteous and polite.

Anytime I hit a check point I'd go through the same routine, passport out first "No Norte Americano Senor, Soy Irlanda Irlandes!, Irlandes si?" and smile like I just won the lotto, they would look at the picture and look at the head on me and I make a face which was supposed to say "Eets the sun Senor!"

Being in Mexico made me feel very far away from home, on top of that I was getting lost about twice a day (GPS doesn't work down here). The maps I was carrying and the road and street signs gelled about as well as oil and water. Getting directions unfortunately was the next chapter in Spanish for dummies. Why not read that one first I hear you ask? I was still trying to get through ordering grub, eat first travel later my friend.

I passed into the state of Sinaloa, which I thought sounded like something from the High Chaparral or the Magnificent Seven and stopped in the city of Culiacan for a bite of grub. In these places wearing a big enduro suit and being about a foot taller than the average Mexican made me stand out like a purple cow. There were only about ten customers but there was a twenty-piece brass band beating out samba like music, the din was unreal, but it was magic.

You can get a savage feed for about five dollars in Mexico, not surprising then that it's the world second most obese country the first is a couple of hundred miles north.

Mazatlan

The next town on my itinerary, which by the way I was making up as I went along, Mazatlan, was a tourist destination and so was a bit more built up than I normally like. The motel I stayed in obviously doubled as a knocking shop because in the room was a pole sitting up on a table surrounded by chairs and by the bed there was a dispenser for tissues.

It was only when I turned on the TV that it fully dawned on me, it was wall-to-wall porn! I should have tweaked it when the hotel charged by the hour. I bought twelve hours for $18 dollars, not bad eh! The chap on the way to the room kept asking me something in Spanish which I didn't understand, looking back, it was did I want any women.

As it turns out Mexico has a big population with lots of small houses, so if you have a girlfriend it's very unlikely you'll get a free house to have a shag. So the youth, people having affairs, not to mention people who pick up prostitutes all converge on motels to take care of the Dick Dastardly deed. I found this out later on and it explained all the funny looks I had received up until that point, when I asked people were there any motels nearby.

That night I went out to a seafood restaurant and had a massive plate full of freshly caught shrimp washed down with plenty of drink; suffice to say I left the table late. While I was chowing down, a really loud storm hit, it was the monsoon season so the rain was torrential. The whole area was being battered due to several systems in the Gulf of Mexico sending their storm tails that direction.

On the way back to the motel I had to drive through about eight inches of rain lying on the road, standing up on the pegs of the bike going through this sort of stuff is great fun. Further on the road, as I came over a hill with a beautiful tropical wind blowing into my face and out in the distance lightning was flaring in a completely black sky, the view was magical. I went off to the hotel for a good night's sleep and just a bit of porn to help drown out the noise from all the amorous couples busy shagging all round me.

As I checked the route for the next day's ride I realised I had also just crossed the Tropic of Cancer, which gave me a tremendous sense of achievement.

Most evenings there were storms filled with lightning and many flash floods. Far from being a hazard I genuinely thought this was one of the peak experiences of the trips for me, the stuff that was happening was just so completely unlike anything that happens in Europe or North America.

The next day I set off for Manzanillo on the Ruta 200, a Ruta Libre. I took the free roads because the tolls were brutal, in one day I handed over almost $70 dollars so I said "Fuck this for a game of soldiers", when in Rome and all that good stuff.

The Ruta Libre takes you through every small town on the pacific coast and the poverty is overwhelming. The roads disintegrate and at times are no more than just gravel and mud tracks. It was time to pay the piper for having such a good day, the day previously. When I was coming around a bend in the pissing rain, doing about 30mph the bike skidded out from under me.

The bike and I slid along the ground for about twenty yards or so with my left leg trapped underneath the bike. Three of four Mexican lads jumped out of a truck and picked the bike off me and helped me to my feet, my left ankle felt like I'd broke it. The only thing that saved my life apart from the fact that I wasn't going too fast was that in Mexico you drive on the right side of the road, so as I slid I just went off the road and not into oncoming traffic.

About ten minutes later the police arrived and started yakking in Spanish, well why wouldn't they it was Mexico after all, but I didn't have a clue what they were saying.

One of them spoke a bit of English and told me there was a lot of diesel on the road at the bend. Within about fifteen minutes we were off to the hospital in a town called Tepic in a police car. The bike was driven behind the police car by one of the police officers who appeared to be having a rare oul time. The bike had come off remarkably unscathed, one mirror was fucked, the wind shield scratched to fuck, the panniers were scratched, my tank bag was scratched up a bit, and the ABS no longer worked but other than that it was tip top, the BMW is a bullet proof machine.

I got to the hospital in Tepic under police siren at about 10am and the police brought me to the emergency area. It was absolute chaos. I guess because I was a gringo I was seen quickly.

The doctor aided by two nurses told me to strip off in Espanol by doing the motions. I cringed, remembering that I was wearing the trusty Lycra long johns so when I dropped the enduro trousers the nurses started bursting their shite laughing.

I was hobbling so they got me a wheel chair and wheeled me down to the x-ray area. It turned out there was no break just a lot of swelling; thank you my lovely motorbike boots! Armed with painkillers and anti-inflammatory tablets I was sent on my way, the only trouble I had driving was changing gears which hurt like hell. As I'm sitting here, writing six months later my left leg still hurts which should give you an idea of how sore it was at the time.

At about 2pm I set off for Puerto Vallarta, in the state of Jalisco. It's a resort town on the pacific coast, it was a good ways off but I needed to get some miles up on the bike to get my confidence back. I kept imagining problems with the bike, "was that a wobble"; "steering feels funny" "the weight distribution is a mile off".

In spite of my paranoia, I got there about 4pm but it really was just like an American town in Mexico. I decided I'd drive through it and stay in one of the towns just south of it. This turned out to be a huge mistake as town after town that I went through were complete and utter shit holes with no hotels or places to stay anywhere to be seen.

Don't take me the wrong way, the Mexican people are the best in the world, the food is amazing but the conditions in some of these towns were just horrific. Mexico's modern cities rival anything in Europe or America, but some of the country towns and villages are in appalling condition.

For the next three hours riding on the Ruta 200, it wasn't so much a drive as an obstacle course. Pot holes, horses and cows on the road, lunatic driving, torrential rain, dogs trying to take a lump out of your boot as you're driving and in places heaps of sand on the road. In case you don't know, putting sand on the road from a biker's perspective is like putting a couple of gallons of KY Jelly down, you can't get traction and slide all over the place.

At about 7pm I was stopped by the federal police at a checkpoint. At this point I was so tired, fucked off and sore that I couldn't be arsed with my big smiling paddy routine. I reaped having to unpack all my stuff from the pike so these hombres could check through it. I tried to explain why I was having difficulty getting off the bike but it got lost in translation. When they were done I had ninety minutes of driving still to go to get to Manzanillo all of which would be on the Ruta 200 in the pitch dark.

In those hundred miles, I hit rock bottom. The road was full of massive potholes that nearly throw you over the handlebars and with the fading light, it was almost impossible to see them. On top of that, there were many hidden speed ramps, not the sort of thing you want to be hitting in the dark. In places the roads were covered with sand I nearly skidded off about four times (ABS not working as a result of the crash), I was nearly driven off the road twice by oncoming trucks, soaked to the skin by torrential rain and to top it all off I had to contend with a couple of mudslides covering the road.

With the visor down you are blinded by oncoming traffic as the light reflects through the rain on the visor, conversely if you keep the visor up the light from the bike attracts millions of insects so your eyes and face get milled out of it. In the end you reach a compromise position, which is the visor half up and your viewing angle just above the wind shield with a view area about three square inches in size.

It took me until 10pm to get a place to stay, after one of the worst days ever. I got into a hotel, completely fucked, didn't even bother showering and just hit the scratcher.

I kept trying to tell myself as my mood descended into the abyss, "it's not everyone who gets away so light after coming off a bike." I lay in the bed that night and said what every man over the age of thirty says when confronted with a crisis; "I want my mammy!"

The next morning I only had time for a cup of coffee and a bite standing. I had to head off to the BMW dealer in Guadalajara and while I left the bike there to be checked out and fixed up, I headed off to the hospital to get my side x-rayed. Even though it was 24 hours later, I woke up that morning feeling as if someone had helped themselves to one of my kidneys.

Everything checked out ok on both fronts, in the hospital I must have come across as a total Benny, trying to explain what happened with just a phrase book and a poor mime display. A doctor came along who spoke English and he laughed like a hyena when I told him the tale from the previous days.

I left Guadalajara and rode to a town called Morelia, a nice colonial town with the centre completely preserved in the colonial tradition. The only downside of the town is that it has throngs of beggars, mostly Indians, it was pretty clear that in the pecking order of society in Mexico as was the case in Canada and the US; the Indians were at the bottom.

The roads that day were great. I treated myself by mostly riding the toll roads and they cut a beautiful path through rolling hills and farmlands, the countryside was full of bushes in flower, it was like riding through a painting. It turned out that the following weekend was Mexican Independence Day and most of the towns I rode through were gearing up for the festivities. Judging by the preparation that was going on, this is a serious party.

I stopped by a roadside cafe, which was just a place with an impromptu cooker fired by flames from sticks, with four tables and chairs, where you could either sit or stand. I pulled over and asked for quesadillas, it had been almost a week since I talked to anyone bar the Doctor in Guadalajara so I decided I was going to just talk to this oul one whether she understood me or not. It went something like this...

Me: Buenos tardez Senorita (Good evening)

Oul one: Buenos tardez Senor

Me: Me no hablez espanol senorita…. (forlorn hope that she might speak English, yeah right..It's common for poor people who operate roadside restaurants to be bilingual! not!!!)… "you have quesadillas por favor?" At this point I was getting disowned by the publishers of Spanish for Dummies.

Oul one: Si!… something in Spanish followed which I think meant how many would you like?

Me: cinqo por favour (Giz five missus)

She then started to cook away at the grub

Me: Feckin rain is brutal eh?… making motions with my hands like it was raining

Oul one: Si…. blah blah blah blah blah blah rafeal benitez blah blah blah

Me: Jaysus I'd love a skin full of Carlsberg in the laurels (local pub)… or even a couple of pints of Guinness… although you´d probably need to go to steering wheel (alternate local with decent Guinness) for them, down stairs bar… (Gratuitous hand gestures by the big fella)

Oul one: (english translation) I´ve no fuckin clue what you're saying you gringo bollix, and if you don't stop annoying me I'm going to put the juice of a camel into your food

Me: You know the only problem with the laurels is there's no birds in it... only a pack of fart arse oul fellas all letting sly farts , really need to go to Quinlan's (pub of last resort, with nice birds) for the oul hula hoop

Oul one: (english translation) My husband has a gun you know... ya dirty lookin edjit´

Me: So do you have a coca cola light por favor

Oul one: Que?

Me: Coca cola (smiling hopefully)

Oul one: Si Coca cola (grabbing one from a cooler beside her which had no ice, but mucho tepid water)

Me: No senorita... coca light? rubbing the belly

She looked at me like she'd just caught me pissing in her roses...

Me: "ok ok... coca cola... Gracias senorita"

She gave me the grub and the coke and I went to sit down and eat it....she said something in Spanish to me which I'm pretty sure meant "hurry up and eat that, you think I've feck all to be doing besides listening to a gringo pox bottle like you!""

Me: Gracias senorita

Oul one: De nada

One of the biggest challenges of Mexico lay ahead of me the following day, namely to get to the other side of Mexico city, a teeming urban sprawl with over twenty million inhabitants. I made my way from Morelia to the city outskirts and after coughing up nearly $80 in tolls, I hit instant logjam. The traffic was insane, I don't think anywhere in the world except maybe India compares to it (I've never been to India but it looks bad on the TV). The traffic just stopped and made no sign of moving. There was a flood of people, no different than any big city there, the difference being that so many of these people are walking on the road.

When the traffic stops, an armada of people walk into the traffic selling every manner of goods. Rafts of window cleaner's descend on the cars and beggars bring their most pitiable face to the fore to scab money from the car and truck drivers who are just stuck there hour after hour.

The smog is horrendous, and the fumes coming from trucks and buses that should long ago have been used for spare parts was awful, no such thing as emissions tests in Mexico I fear.

The only way to deal with it is to just turn into a happy nutcase, beep the horn at everyone, copious use of the finger, break red lights and weave in and out of stalled traffic. If you lined up all the traffic offences I made trying to move around Mexico City it would be enough to put me in Sam Quentin for ten years, but it was good fun in a perverted sort of way. I'd hate to have to live through that every day but to do it once was an experience.

After about two hours battling through it and making only ten miles I gave up and headed south to break free of it, which took another ninety minutes. I made my mind up that this would be the last big city I would go to on this trip except for Santiago in Chile and Buenos Aires in Argentina.

Once you head south out of Mexico City the scenery is excellent, lots of mountains and rolling hills with whole acres covered in beautiful pink flowers, on top of winding roads with great surfaces. I did my usual grub at the roadside cafe, this time without the fireside chat; the nosebag in this part of the world is delicious.

When it comes to enjoying the scenery in Mexico, the only gripe I would have is that the Mexican tourist board have not bothered to put any lay-bys or scenic sign areas on the side of the road. You might have a great looking mountain, river or lake but there's nowhere to pull in and take a picture of it. I guess if you are the government of Mexico your first priority would be better roads I suppose, and then work on the lay-bys.

Taxco

When I arrived into the town of Taxco in Mexico, the trip odometer just clocked over 18,000 miles and per the original plan I'd about 60% of the journey complete. In the process, I had crossed different time zones no less than ten times, and driven well south of the tropic of cancer.

The reality is that I'd done about 3000 miles more than I expected at this point with all the diversions and detours you end up taking every day, so the final trip distance was likely to be somewhere between thirty and thirty five thousand miles. It was also the 12th of September so it was exactly two months since I arrived in Toronto, fair to say the bike had a good workout since then.

I decided that I was going to stay in Taxco for five days all told mainly to rest up after the crash; my body still felt like a wet week so I wanted to get myself right as rain before taking on Central America.

The town is the silver capital of Mexico and they have some really unusual jewellery, inevitably I ended up buying a good bit of stuff and had to stop myself before I ended up looking like Mr T.

This was the first time I'd really stopped on the trip and I was keen to soak it up. It was such a culture shock but it's the culture that makes the place what it is I guess, and it was definitely starting to grow on me, although it had taken a while. You've got to love mayhem to love Mexico, it's that simple.

Taxco was declared a national monument by the Mexican government. Every old Volkswagen beetle or van ever made seemed to be there, there was thousands of them.

I stayed in a hotel perched on the side of the mountain and the balcony in my room was perched on the Cliffside looking down on a yawning valley below. I spent the first night in the room reading the Lord of the rings and I heard an unbelievable scream from the valley below the hotel. It turned out there was a pig abattoir down there and the screams from the pigs all night was exactly like the ring wraiths from the Lord of the Rings.

Obviously they use traditional methods for slaughtering, the noise would scare the living shit out of you, especially if you're woken from a sleep at 4am by it, but no one seems to mind.

The noise the whole time I was in Mexico, especially in towns is way above what one would come to expect even in the busiest of European cities. If you're out in the square having a coffee, at any one time you're competing with election cars screaming out their candidate's merits, construction of various stands, mental traffic with more use of the horn than a Kerry Ram and hundreds of street sellers selling every manner of good imaginable. Suffice to say if its peace and quiet you like, Mexico is not for you.

There is no doubt it creates an incredible buzz and atmosphere. I was sitting at the square reading a book when this oul one of about eighty-five sat down beside me. After about ten minutes she cleared her throat and hocked up as big a greener as I've ever seen and gollied it onto the ground beside where we were sitting. I hope there are birds like that around when I'm eighty-five, she was a real find.

The murder rate in Mexico is twice what it is in the USA, and its thirteenth on the list for AID's and HIV, so as I was advised very wisely; if in the highly unlikely event that I was to meet a Senorita, "make sure you double bag"! I just gave it a miss, although it wasn't like I had to turn down any offers.

I met my first English-speaking person since arriving in Mexico in Taxco. She was a tourist and her name was Alex. She was a trainee doctor from Wales volunteering near Mexico City in a hospital for the summer. I took one look at her and said to myself "where were ya in Guadalajara Alex!"

She was only twenty years old, a fine thing and over in Mexico alone, it turned out that travelling alone came easy to her as she did the same thing four years previous hiking in Namibia. There is always someone who will knock you off your hardcore perch.

It was great to have a yak with someone who spoke English and I just blabbed my head off for a couple of hours over a couple of tall frosty beers. She told a great story about hiking for sixteen days without changing clothes while in Namibia and at the end of the hike, the whole group just burned their clothes. I said to her "no wonder the lions didn't come near ya!"

We yakked about Mexico and all the things you see that you don't see in Europe, and stole Leonardo de Caprio's line from the movie Blood Diamonds about Africa; "TIA baby, This is Africa" uttered every time you see something completely fucked up, and changed it to "TIM, This is Mexico"

The next day Alex headed away to Mexico City and she was almost running from me. I knew what had happened, the last time I had talked to anyone was Andy Flanagan in Phoenix and I'd given her a pain in her hole. Talking to me was like trying to drink from a fire hydrant, it wasn't to be the first time that I scared people off with this particular character trait.

When I asked Rafael what are the women like in Mexico over a beer in Black Diamond in Canada, he made a face something like you would make after being asked whether the weather is good in Ireland.

Well, let me take Rafael's comments a bit further. The women here are very nice, but they age like milk, lots of lovely looking young ones but once they hit about thirty, well, the wheels come off the wagon; ill tidings indeed for a thirty seven year old Dublin lad travelling with a stork on him that would knock apples out of a tree!

Independence Day in Mexico was one I won't forget in a hurry.

Jail House

The day started out great, lots of singing and dancing in the square with kids dressed in colonial dress dancing on a stage, the place was packed and the atmosphere was electric. Later in the afternoon, I had the first of the day's dodgy encounters namely English gap-year student travellers.

If you come across them, don't approach them for they are deadly. I met them just outside the church in the square, two girls and a guy, all from in and around the London area. They were all about twenty, a bigger bunch of "know it all's" you have never met. They asked me what I was doing here; I just used one of Rafael's lines and said I was a drug dealer. I said good luck and wished them well.

As the early afternoon wore on everyone went home for a siesta as beer stands and bandstands were set up in the square. I knew how many people were going to be down there later so I went back to the hotel to drop off my valuables, had a bit of a kip and headed back down to the square packing lightly, just cash and the key for the room in the hotel. I was certain there'd be a heap of baddies down there at some stage so best not to carry a wallet or anything valuable like that. Another in a long line of mistakes as it turned out.

The beer stands were selling corona for about $1.50 a bottle, but pouring it into plastic glasses as people bought it. Everyone was in a great mood and as the band cracked open a few tunes there were lots of

"Viva Mexico" to be heard all round the square. By about 10pm the mood was getting a little bit more aggressive and there were plenty of dodgy looking hombres knocking around so I said to myself, ok, after this one call it a night, note I'd only four bottles total, so not even the slightest bit drunk.

I was standing off to the left of the square where two cobble lanes met at right angles, one to go downhill to the circulation road, and one to go up to someplace else. All of a sudden, an Indian girl who was selling cakes was beset upon by two other Indian girls and one other guy. My guess was that they have turfs where they allow certain groups to sell stuff, or maybe something else, I'm just guessing.

The guy landed a hefty smack on the girl's face, up until this point it was really just hand bags at six paces and nothing serious. The girl started crying so I went over to her aid, pushed the guy against the wall and stood between the two girls and the girl they were attacking.

I turned to her and said "Vamoose... pronto", while at the same time I motioned to a guy who was standing beside me to come over and help "Senor...por favor!.." it wasn't difficult to guess what I meant, but he just turned and walked away into the crowd. I roared after him "Hey Rat features... come back here... give me a fuckin hand ya prick".

Before I knew it, a sea of people had descended on us. There was cake, drink, nachos and god knows what else flying around not to mention pushing and shoving coming from every angle. I was in the middle, comfortably a foot taller than everyone else saying to myself "nice one Ois...nice one."

Next thing I knew whistles started going like crazy and what felt like about twenty police officers showed up; thank god I said to myself, except that they started loading me and about forty other people into the vans. I was saying to the officer "Hablez Ingles, I was only trying to help, where the fuck are we going?!"

The door slammed shut on the van and a moment of complete and utter silence followed.

I was sitting on a small bench looking around at about twelve or thirteen other people who once we got going started roaring and shouting. I sat there feeling a right fucking idiot and in keeping with every other day I'd spent in Mexico, I didn't have a clue what people were saying. I wasn't overly worried as the police officers weren't too aggressive as they were loading us in; it wasn't a riot if you know what I mean.

After only about five hundred yards, we arrived at what turned out to be a police station and we were marched into an area with rows of seats like a church in front of a desk where I guessed we were going to be processed. I sat there thinking to myself "If one of these lads can't speak English I'm fucked!"

Sure enough, as people were getting led up to the desk it was the turn of one of the girls who did the initial attacking and she started pointing to me and shouting angrily, while talking to the police officer. Then, another who I guessed was her sister jumped up and started shouting and making similar gesticulations. "Ah here!" I said to myself and I walked up the counter thinking I'm going to say my piece and I couldn't give a rats ass if no one understands me.

"Hablez ingles?" I said to the officer to which he replied "No". I looked to the ceiling and said "fuuuuuuuuuuuuck it anyway!" Undeterred I went into a monologue in English.

"Right Senor..." says I, "I was standing there just having a beer when Pocahontas here.." (about five police officers started roaring laughing) "and Pocahontas dos(2), and Hiawatha over there started attacking this senorita".

"All I did was block them, that's it." Seeing that the officers were laughing the sisters went ballistic, all of them were about four foot max and it was like getting roared at by a bunch of Lilliputians.

"Calm the fuck down!" I roared as the noise in the place descended into anarchy. The police came out from behind the counter with hands on batons and told everyone to sit down and be quiet, or at least that's what I think they said. Everyone else was sitting saying nothing in about five seconds flat, I was the only one left standing in the room. Seeing as I was standing they started to take my details, first looking for ID.

"Booooolllllllllliiiiiiixxxxxxx" I thought to myself, all my ID and wallet was in the hotel where I'd intentionally left it in case I got pick pocketed.

It seemed like not having ID was a big deal, so I started to play the paddy card, "Irlandes Senor!", to which he looked at me as if to say; "So what?"

With that, none other than the guy who walked away from the disturbance in the square walked in and started talking to the police men, pointing at me.

Right about then I was really sorry that I'd called him rat features but he walked over to me with the police officer who said "Amigo...You are free to go" to which I replied "Nice one....nice one... Gracias amigo..Gracias".

They asked me what hotel I was staying in and the gent (rat features) gave me a lift home. He had broken English so we didn't have much of a conversation. My hotel was less than a mile from the police station, but I picked up enough from the chap who was giving me a lift that all of the folks would be let go in stages over the next hour or so, they were just getting them off the streets.

I thanked him and was lying on the bed sipping a bottle of water by 11:30pm thinking to myself "All that in ninety minutes...? Zorro me bollix!, he doesn't have a patch on me!"

Mexico celebrates independence over two days, during the second day I kept a very low profile, but to be honest, the above probably reads worse than it actually was, it never really felt out of control. The stupid side of me wanted to get put in a cell for a while just to say I'd been in one, the non-stupid side gave the stupid side a good kick in the goolies and told him to cop on.

Oaxaca

I left Taxco in the rain and headed for Oaxaca one of the more highly recommended towns in all the travel guides. It was supposed to be a great place, full of old Colonial buildings and a Mecca for back packers in this part of the world. It was about two hundred and fifty miles away and the vast majority of the road was Ruta Libre, which just meant absolutely shite roads with large amounts of mental drivers all over the place.

The journey there was slow going with almost all of the miles running through fog-covered mountains, it took every minute of eight hours to get there. The road surface was appalling with huge tire shredding potholes and hidden speed ramps all over the place.

When I finally got to Oaxaca, I realised that one of my bags was gone. No doubt, it was shaken off due to all the bumps and potholes.

What was in it? All my memory cards holding the pictures of the trip so far, my laptop, my journal where I kept all the trip logs, a copy of all my confidential information, Spanish books, maps and a copy of Lord of the Rings which I'd bought in Phoenix.

I lost the rag completely, I had lost all record of the trip so far apart from what was posted on my blog site and I had no one to blame but myself. It's not like I didn't know the roads were crap here, but because it was raining I rushed packing up my stuff. I lost thousands of pictures of parts of the world that I was unlikely ever to see again, it was a sore blow.

Worse was to come.

I stripped off, changed, and said I better go down to the police station and let them know, maybe someone will hand it in. On the way, I hit heavy traffic and these guys, as is normal when you come to stop in busy traffic came out onto the road cleaning windows. These weren't the normal squad of down and outs as it turned out. I was stopped, boxed in on all sides by buses and cars. Next thing I felt a blow to the right of the head and on my left out of nowhere a guy was pulling my watch off.

I was trying to pull back but in his sponge he had a knife which he waved at me.

Startled, I pulled back, in the process getting another punch in the back of the head. He pulled at my left arm and because my left leg was weak, being the one that slid under the bike when I crashed, I fell to the ground with the bike on top of me as this guy ran off with the watch. Just to complete the misery the GPS hopped off its mount and hit me straight on the coupon (face).

Thankfully, the bike didn't land on my leg so I was able to pick myself up, by which time the bandits were long gone. It was a strange feeling I went through just then, calm just before I boiled. I picked up the bike and put it on its stand. I was surrounded by traffic and starting to boil like a kettle.

At that moment the guy who was stopped behind me beeped his horn, as if to say "Move! You are blocking the road" This was the same dude who saw everything that happened and did nothing to help me.

In a complete fit of rage I pitched the GPS unit straight at his front windscreen smashing it in the process. I walked the bike over to the side of the road out of the traffic, and he pulled in behind me. I saw him on the phone and knew the police would be on the way soon. He never got out of the car; he knew I was in a fit of temper.

I sat there for about ten minutes boiling over till the police arrived. The whole process with the police took about ten minutes and I ended up having to pay about $200 for the guy's windscreen. There was never any chance that they would catch these guys, and the watch I didn't care about. Would you believe after standing there talking to them I forgot to tell them about losing the bag.

I just headed to the motel and boiled the night away. I think the annoying thing about the whole losing the bag, and getting robbed "thing" was that I'd only myself to blame, but that doesn't make you feel any better about it, it's worse if anything.

I spent the night "shoulding"... shoulda done this, shoulda done that" As soon as I realised I'd lost the bag I just wanted to leave Mexico, actually I just wanted to go home.

The only cure I had for a spiralling mood was to get on the road, which I did at 5 am the next morning and drove for over four hundred miles over mountain roads through some of the worst driving conditions you're likely to find anywhere.

Mexico was too much like hard work for me. I decided that I was burning for the border with Guatemala via San Cristobal de la Casas the next day.

San Cristobal is in the Chiapas region of Mexico known to be a revolutionary stronghold. As soon as I crossed into Chiapas, people were waving hello and it seemed to me that it was a particularly friendly place. To get to the town you climb out of a valley and onto a plateau. As I climbed the sun was setting bathing the entire valley below in orange light.

San Cristobal de la Casas turned out to be a magic spot despite the fact that the town is ringed with people living in excruciating poverty.

I stayed in the Hacienda Don Juan, which was run by a very friendly innkeeper; he couldn't do enough to help me. I stayed there two days to get my documentation and my head in order before heading into Guatemala. While I was wandering around the town I went into an English bookshop run by an elderly American lady, I'd only one question to ask, "Do you have the Lord of the Rings?" "Of course I do" was the reply, I was over the moon.

I met two folks in the town who used to work for the same company as I did; Jennifer and Lorraine who were off backpacking, and we headed out for a couple of beers and a bit of nose bag.

Both were on the road about two weeks and it was magic to have a natter with folks from home for a couple of hours. The next day I met two aid workers for Trocaire, Mary and Maureen who worked in Guatemala on various projects and they did a lot to allay any concerns I had about crossing the border.

I had a read of the lonely planet regarding Guatemala and based on what it said you wouldn't go to Guatemala in a million years, a direct quote "In villages lynchings are a near daily occurrence…"

I was coming to the end of my time in Mexico, and I reflected on the variety that was in every day, good roads, bad roads, check points, lovely scenery, people crammed onto the backs of trucks, grossly overloaded vehicles shedding their load, horrendous poverty, but every day the constant was that the people were wonderful.

I passed a poor oul bastard in a wheel chair sitting in the middle of the road collecting coins from passing traffic; he was about ninety years of age. Imagine in your retirement having to look forward to being wheeled out into the middle of the road and beg from passing cars; with the way they drive in Mexico! I tell you a nursing home doesn't look so bad after seeing that! He was smiling his head off, I guess there was nothing on the telly or the missus was giving out "I've had enough, roll me out on the road!"

While I was in an internet cafe, I started to instant message a friend back home.

I was telling him that I was terrified about crossing into Central America, he told me to just go back up to the states, that I'd gone far enough and also that no one would have expected me to make it the whole way anyway. "Well fuck that for a game of soldiers" I told myself, "finish what you've started Oisin."

The form had completely turned; I was back in good spirits. When you see how poor some of the people are in Mexico, and how little possessions they have and yet they are smiling and seem very content you just can't stay in bad form for long.

I talked with a friend on the phone about it and we concluded that the reality is that these people have almost no chance of escaping poverty whereas I was only ever a flight away from home; it helped put things in perspective for me.

I left San Cristobal and headed south for Guatemala. I only knew one thing for certain, it was going to be more difficult than Mexico, more dangerous, worse roads, poorer and it officially marked the start of Central America, the bit of the journey I feared the most.

Chapter 9

Central America

I did some research regarding travel advice for Guatemala before I crossed the border and one paragraph which I copied from the British Travel advisory website summed up how I was feeling about it:

Guatemala has one of the highest violent crime rates in Latin America with around 40 murders a week in Guatemala City alone and a total of 98 per week in the whole country. Although the majority of serious crime involves gangs or narcotics and does not occur in tourist areas, violent attacks on tourists, including carjackings, assault, armed robbery, murder and rape have increased in the past few years and can happen anywhere. Guns are commonly used, and there is a low arrest and conviction rate for perpetrators. You should take your personal security seriously and be aware of your surroundings at all times

If the above doesn't give you a feeling of how bad things could get, another way to put it is that there are more murders in Guatemala in a year than there were in over thirty years of the troubles in Northern Ireland.

Rafael had warned me not to watch the news or I'd be too scared to go out. I'd also been told that a week earlier a chicken bus had driven off a cliff with all fifty-five people killed; the bus driver had been drinking. The two Irish missionaries I'd met in San

Cristobal had also told me that they were afraid for me based on what they had seen on the roads there.

With all this in my mind I got up later than normal, went and had breakfast and for the first time on the trip I caught myself arseing around the place. I was putting off the cross over into Central America, I was absolutely terrified.

Some of the stuff I was doing when I look back on it was surreal; it felt like all that stuff you do before you start studying for a big exam; buy new pens, and jotters, for what I had no idea, anything to put off the inevitable crossing.

The cafe where I had breakfast was blaring out some awful Jazz music, which was enough to spur me to muster up the courage to leave, so off I drove a distance of about a hundred miles from San Cristobal to the border.

As I approached the border the road deteriorated more and more until it was almost impossible to drive on. No one seems to care about this last little section of road because you're leaving Mexico anyway. The border was a sea of people, and near every bank or entrance to an official building there were armed security guards holding pump action shotguns, not the sort of place you would get into an argument with the chap behind the counter.

The problem with crossing these borders on your own is that you have to go through three steps normally in three different buildings.

Firstly you have to stamp out of one country, then stamp into the next. Lastly and more often than not the most difficult part, you have to import the motorcycle into the next country. The whole time you're doing this, there is no one to watch the bike and with all your stuff packed on the top of it with lots of people around, it's impossible not to feel helpless.

The only protection I left on the bike was a set of Rosary beads hanging around the handlebars. The people here are devout and even the worst rapscallion might think twice about robbing from a Catholic Gringo, not that I'm religious but if drinking horse piss would have made it easier to pass through, then that's what I would have done.

I made it through eventually after much gnashing of teeth and copious amounts of tsk tsk's aimed in my direction. I was bluffing the whole way and decided enough was enough, I had to take some Spanish lessons; I couldn't hope to continue to get by playing the lovable "Mick".

I made my way to a town called Quetzaltenango (say that with a couple of pints on you!) and for once what I had heard about the driving conditions i.e. the roads were even more chaotic than Mexico, was absolutely true.

"Yeah yeah" I hear you say. Well, to put some statistics on it; your 16000% more likely to get killed in Mexico and Guatemala on the roads driving a

motorcycle than you are driving a car in Britain or Ireland. Now put that in your pipe and smoke it!

The further I drove, the further the road safety conditions continued to go through the floor. Over taking on bends happened so often that it seemed almost to be mandatory. I saw three near miss collisions, and every couple of miles there were landslides destroying the road surface.

As you drive along there are no lay-bys, no hard shoulders and no places to pull over and take a picture or have a rest. The result is that the journey can get frustrating, on your left you pass something you would dearly love to take a picture of but you can't find a place to stop which is even moderately safe.

Everyone overtakes on bends, obviously that's not a problem for traffic ahead of you going the same way, but a big deal if you're taking a bend and you've some hombre coming around the corner on your side of the road. The ride to Quetzaltenango was a massive eye opener for what lay ahead for the rest of Central America, if you drive expecting other folks to obey the rules of the road you will get killed.

The only way to avoid it is to take every corner hugging the very right side of the road, right over at the right line so if some Benny comes round the corner on the wrong side of the road at least you'll have a small bit of space and be able to get up the inside.

The next big problem is the ramps or as they are called in Guatemala "Reductors!" They are a good idea with all the lunatic drivers on the roads; it's no harm getting them to slow down. The problem for us lily livered westerners is that they are not always signposted and are not always a different colour than the road and can pop up almost anywhere.

So, you can just be driving along at about 60mph, and whack!!!!! Two things happen to you on the bike when you hit a reductor at this speed. First your whole body gets thrown up off the bike as the front wheel hits the ramp leaving you in the air just holding the handle bars, second as you're in the air and the back wheel hits the ramp all 300kg of motorbike jumps up and smacks you in the balls.

For about the next ten minutes you're driving with two lumps in your throat with a forlorn wish that you were five years old again and the jewels were still safely nestled just under you nipples. Suffice to say, I started this trip with a pair of rocks and would no doubt finish with a pair of saucers.

Lots of trucks, vans and even motorcycles were completely overloaded with people, the amount of times I saw three people on a motorcycle or people hanging off the back of trucks, buses and vans, or whole families sitting in the back of trucks was too many to count.

On the flip side Guatemala has wonderful countryside; in fact its forests are so vast they are called the Earth's fifth lung. I got a weird sense of

Irony that a country I only wished to "survive and get through" was so beautiful.

Quetzaltenango

I made it to Quetzaltenango and tried to find somewhere to stay. As I was pulled over getting gas, a guy driving a motorbike from the town came over, his name was Juan Antonio. I told him I was looking for somewhere to stay and asked him did he know where the nearest hotels were? Juan brought me to his friends place to stay, not knowing either of the lads but bowled over by their kindness at the same time, I asked again were there any hotels.

The guys were trying to do their best for me but what I wanted was a hotel with a shower in it, somewhere to safely park the bike and see about getting some Spanish lessons, eventually I got the message across.

I stayed in the second best hotel in the town for about $25 a night. The hotel felt like a hotel in Cuba to me, not having ever been in Cuba I'm not sure how I came to that conclusion but was happy not to question myself any further.

This part of the world on account of the altitude is cold; I slept with my arse hanging out one of the nights and caught a cold for my troubles. There was no hot water in the hotel so taking a shower in cold water when you've a cold had me sneezing like I'd inhaled a barrel of pepper.

The town has a nice centre square with lots of statues and official buildings; every other part of the town was in bad shape. I booked in for Spanish lessons at a local school for five days. The lessons for a full week cost less than a $100.

My first Spanish lesson was done on a serious hangover, if you haven't tried a margarita, may I wholeheartedly recommend it, just make sure you´ve plenty of aspirin in your pocket because the next morning, it's like a cement mixer going off in your head.

There were many interesting people in the town, for the most part, folks from the United States. I'd met eight folks in total from the US, five of whom are missionaries or volunteer workers, two trainee doctors and another person who was off to see the world. All of the folks were top class! You have to hand it to the missionary workers and volunteers; there are a lot easier places to come than Guatemala to donate your time and energy to try to help people.

I had lunch with one of the folks, Katie from New York and she was the type of person who would tell you anything. I asked her what was the maddest thing she ever did as we were getting tanked on Margaritas and she said "I gave a Police officer a Blo-job so as he wouldn't do me for DUI", I just said; "yeah, that beats mine."

She was meeting her boyfriend the next day and they were heading to South America for a couple of months, we wished each other well and went our separate ways.

I talked with one missionary guy who was telling me what the conditions were like out in the countryside and I really admired what he was doing and what he had to put up with in the process. We had a bit of a philosophical discussion around was it ok to feel bad when your football team loses when people who live in abject poverty surround you.

Sure it puts the thing into perspective, Liverpool only drawing with Stoke making you feel bad, and here's people poorer than church mice, but we both walked away believing that it was still ok to feel bad about our football teams losing.

Talking to all these US expats keeps you in mind of how much America is a land of extremes. Here were all these enlightened individuals all down here trying to make a difference, when I compared them to some of the rednecks I'd met near the border with Mexico I just shook my head.

No matter where you go there are lots and lots of guns around the place, anywhere there's money-changing hands there's a guy standing with a pump action shotgun.

It had rained continuously for three days and I'd seen all Quetzaltenango had to off so I was longing for the road again. Despite only completing two days of Spanish lessons, I headed for Antigua.

I was mulling over a couple of things in my mind, first amongst them was whether or not to avoid Guatemala city and the second item I was going over was would it be worth bypassing El Salvador altogether, just go from Guatemala into Honduras.

The choices were to take the southern road thus bypassing Guatemala City however; this meant having to go through El Salvador, or take the north road and get into Honduras and in the process bypassing El Salvador.

The problem with the northerly route was that it wasn't clear whether or not I could make it to a "safe" town in the daylight hours, and getting stranded out in the Honduran countryside at night was not my idea of fun.

These were the thoughts that were dominating my mind as I left Quetzaltenango. Getting out of the town was easier said than done, road signs are about as common as hens teeth so after an hour's driving I ended exactly back right where I started. Yes you're right, I am a real man and we don't ask for directions.

I solved the dilemma by grabbing a taxi, telling him to drive to the exit of the city and that I'd follow and pay when we got there, it worked a treat and it wouldn't be the last time I'd use that way to escape from a big town when I was lost.

The bane of my life in those early days of riding in Guatemala, were the chicken buses. I wondered why they were called "chicken buses" but I'm pretty certain it's because they play chicken with oncoming traffic. I saw two crashes that day, it didn't look like anyone was really hurt but negotiating your way through the countryside was absolute mayhem.

In many places due to deforestation and the rainy season, the hills were collapsing onto the road, leaving a trail of muck and shite all over the place that you have to try to find you way through. The last time I'd seen roads this bad was on the Dalton highway in Alaska, the difference there was that you were the only one on the road, here the roads were jam packed.

Atitlan

I went to Lake Atitlan, which was tipped to be one of the wonders of the world. Well if it does become one, the first thing they'll need to do is signpost it. As far as I could make out there were none, at least as you approach it from Quetzaltenango. It was like a big secret and when I did find it, there was nowhere to pull over and take a few pictures.

As I approached Atitlan, there were three or four pull in spots, where you could get out and take a few snaps from the road. Now remember, this is a prospective wonder of the world we are talking about here. Two of the stop points were being used as police checkpoints and another was a makeshift rubbish dump. I met a guy there who was so keen on the motorbike trip I was doing I was worried that he was going to club me over the back of the head and rape me.

The lake itself is a wonderful place. The view I remember most is of parking the bike out on a ledge and looking out in the distance at two volcanoes whose sides seemed to dip right into the lake. From there it was on to Antigua, which is renowned as the nicest town in Guatemala

I had so many near misses while driving to the town; I felt like a cat counting down from nine and was already at about three. Sometimes something would happen and you'd just pull over and shake your head and say, "That was too fuckin close, fuck this!"

While it was very difficult to find, If I hadn't bumped into two Mormons from Montana I think I would still be looking for it.

The Mormons are a great bunch, no matter how shitty and decrepit a town is, you'll find two Mormons there in a perfect set of pressed blue trousers and white shirt with a matching tie. Whatever your feelings towards Mormon's, I've always felt that they are the most courteous people you could ever hope to meet. We had a good laugh and one of the lads when he noticed on the stickers from Calgary on my pannier rolled out a "Dude!!! You went through Blackfoot! That's my home town!"

Antigua is a beautiful cobblestoned town and is a popular stopping over spot for backpackers who want to "Do" Guatemala, and generally anyone who is making their way south or north through Central America. Antigua is a picture of how Guatemala "could be" if the country could get rid of its corruption and is chock-a-bloc with tourists and people learning Spanish.

Antigua

I got myself a hotel anxious to have my first hot shower since Mexico but not unexpectedly the water was fucking Baltic, the heat of a warm shower would have to wait till another day. I went out for a couple of pints knowing that I had probably the most mental four or five days of my life coming up with El Salvador, Honduras and Nicaragua standing between me and relative normality of Costa Rica. My passport was starting to look like a colouring book with all the stamps I was collecting for me and the bike at the border posts.

The town is full of young Indian girls selling everything from necklaces to head scarves. They're all about eight or nine years old and are so cute that you just keep putting your hand into your arse pocket to buy stuff. They all have a couple of catch phrases; "Business is Business, I no sell much today, you not buy nothing from me mister, how much you pay for this mister" and so it went for the duration of my stay.

I met an Aussie guy called Sam, an Icelandic gent called John and a cockney couple in an Irish bar in Antigua and we all got pissed drunk, although I was back in bed a little before eleven, I knew I had a big day coming up. When the clouds cleared I saw why this place is such a Mecca, standing there right at what seemed like the end of the street, was a huge volcano, I thought to myself, if that thing ever goes boom this place is never even going to get a warning.

The next morning started with a dose of the trots, Central American style. I woke up and had about three seconds to get to the jacks, thankfully I made it in one. For about thirty minutes, I was doing a fantastic impression of an upside down fire hydrant with intermittent machine gun fire. The whole time this was going on, in the hotel courtyard which all the rooms surround, the hotel pet parrot kept saying "Ola!... Ola!" As I sat there flexing my stomach muscles so my heart wouldn't plunge out along with the rest of my alimentary canal, I thought to myself "where's a good oul cat when you need one!"

I packed up and left the room, and as I opened the door I realised the bog faced also out onto the courtyard, there were three or four old ladies all having breakfast, they all gave me a sympathetic look while breathing in sharply through their teeth.

From Antigua to the border was about three hours and I bit the bullet and drove through Guatemala City. It ended up not being too bad and I was only lost for about ninety minutes. I met a bunch of bikers who were from the city who were meeting up for their Sunday afternoon ride, something that happens all over world.

When they saw me coming they really laid out the red carpet and made me feel like I was the king of the world. They gave me some directions as there really aren't any signs at all, and I used the GPS to keep my direction south and got through the city ok.

The whole time I was travelling, I was flexing my arse cheeks together so hard I gave myself a brand new set of wrinkles, thank the lord for Imodium. The road quality had improved once I got to Guatemala City too; I guess the government know that most people come to Guatemala to visit Antigua so they may as well build a decent road. From there it was on to the border town of San Cristobal (Lots of towns with that name in these parts). The El Salvador border took about three hours to get through.

El Salvador

Two lads had become my self-appointed fixers through the border, although I'm pretty sure it took longer because of them, but they were nice fella's so I was happy enough to give them some money, if only for the company. The bureaucracy is incredible when you're trying to get through, if you were going on a bus it would be easy; just flash the passport, but because you're bringing a motorbike in, it's much tougher. The humidity while waiting around at the border was enough to drown you, I felt like my boots were filling up with puddles of sweat.

I made it out in the end without too much of a fuss and I drove down the road chuffed that I'd made it through my second Central American border unscathed. I drove under a gathering thunder storm to a town nearby town called Santa Ana which wasn't a bad spot. I arrived soaked and stinking of a mixture of sweat and lord knows what else and tried to find a hotel.

The town was intimidating in places and I got the feeling that if I rode down the wrong street here things could get nasty. All of sudden a passing private security truck told me to follow them and they escorted me to a hotel. Never in my life have I had an experience which compared to being escorted by five armed guards to a hotel room. They took me under their wing, no doubt because I looked lost at the traffic lights.

There were no tourists there and I couldn't help but feel that people kept staring at me, I kept checking to see if I had my underpants on over my jeans. I didn't plan to spend any time in the country, it being only about a quarter the size of Ireland I planned for just one night. There are those who might say that how can you say you've been to a country when you passed through it like a dose of Epsom salts, my answer would be that most of the Central American countries were just obstacles in my mind, something that had to be overcome to get to the good stuff.

I was cooked up in my room from about 6pm that night and couldn't believe how quickly it got dark. It was the 25th of September and it felt like it went from day to night in only a couple of minutes.

I left Santa Ana and headed for the Honduran border. Even though El Salvador was a tiny country, the roads twisted and bent through the mountains so it took me nearly five hours all told to get there.

Along the way, I pulled over for a swig of water. A guy walked out of a field with an eight-finger forehead, his shirt unbuttoned to the waist and in his right hand he was wielding a machete.

He was just a farmer and just said "Hola!" I was ready to hand him the keys of the bike and hope he didn't cleave me in two. Machetes are as common in Central America as mobile phones are in Ireland. No matter where you drive you can see people by the side of the road carrying them, its normal for here, but as I kept telling myself, "here ain't normal."

Murder remains one of the El Salvador leading crime problems with an average of ten murders every day. It has one of the highest per capita murder rates in the world; 59 per 100,000, by comparison the murder rate in New York City is just seven.

For the heck of it I went through San Salvador the capital, traffic wasn't too bad and from there pushed on to the border with Honduras. Every day you survive you tend to test yourself more and more, I was amazed how unafraid I was driving into one of the most violent cities in the world.

Just before I got to the border I stopped for gas, and was immediately beset upon on all sides by six guys all vying to be the one to take me through the border. The roaring and shouting they were doing was deafening. I followed one of them on a motorbike up to the border when another ten or twelve guys all jumped out of nowhere all roaring and shouting, obviously all in Spanish.

The competition to take the gringos across the border is violently intense. They were unbelievably aggressive and a fight even broke out between two of them.

The day was quickly descending into a nightmare, I told them "Fuck off the whole lot of you!" and I drove down the road to see if I could find a less dodgy looking fixer.

Eventually I picked what I thought was the least dodgy looking one and we darted ahead of about three miles of trucks all queuing to get through the border. It was quickly becoming apparent, to me at any rate that the corruption in a country was directly proportional to the bureaucracy you encounter at its borders and when I got to the border, I had the shock of my life waiting for me.

Now it wasn't like that having passed through Mexico and Guatemala and into El Salvador that I was expecting the Ritz but what I came upon was easily the worst place I've ever been, by a country mile.

There were literally thousands of people all pressing on each other, hours of Q´s, the whole place stunk of piss, emaciated dogs roaming around barking and people throwing rubbish and pouring all sorts of stuff right out onto the street.

Everyone there was on the con; the whole thing is a setup to get as much money from people making their way through as possible. From the moment you get there you are harassed, chased, lied to, robbed, bullied and manipulated right to the moment you leave.

I had six or seven guys around me telling me that it would cost me $70 to get my bike through fumigation, which I knew I didn't need. All these guys kept roaring and shouting at me and I was standing there just telling them "no way". At this point my passport, bike registration, and licence were off being processed by one of the "ass wipes" in the office and he was just letting me rot outside with this melee of people around me.

Being at one of these borders is enough for you to lose all faith in people. Everyone was in on the conning and exploitation of people who were moving through. The police were taking bribes, the customs officials, even bank officials and all doing it openly. The guys who were doing the vehicle importing in the office were just wearing jeans, no shirts or anything, just a bunch of thugs with a title.

The bank officials only take Honduran currency, no credit cards, or Dollars and then send you out to a moneychanger who charges you ridiculous rates, no doubt the moneychanger is the "bastard" in the banks "man on the outside". I completely lost the rag with the place, and thought to myself that I would love one of those guns that Jesse Ventura had in the movie Predator; I could have done a lot of good with it!

After about four hours I was making no progress and was almost despairing when three lights in the darkness showed up in the form of two Swedish bikers who watched my bike for me and believe it or not a gang member who used to live in Miami, who could speak English.

If you can imagine a scene where about twenty people are roaring and shouting at you and me talking to this gang guy in English through the roaring, I really wished I'd that machine gun. This gang lad (Jordan was his name) eventually got me sorted out, you could see that when the other guys saw him with a dose of facial tattoos, showing gang membership of MS-13, they weren't going to mess with him.

Eventually I got out of there after about six hours, hating everyone in Honduras and anything to do with the country. For me the unforgiveable part is that the police and all the government officials let it happen. If you get into trouble there, you can't even call the police because they are taking bribes from the criminals who are extorting the money from you, so you're just completely FUBAR.

Honduras

I hooked up with the two Swedish bikers and we stayed in a motel in a town called Choluteca in Honduras near the border with Nicaragua. They were great lads and we shared stories from the road over a couple of beers and dinner. The waitress who was serving us was a dyed blond young girl who was about as friendly as a rattlesnake who you had just taken a piss on.

It was great to be in a semi-civilised situation again and not at a border.

I went to bed that night thinking that Honduras was the biggest shithole that was ever created anywhere, at any time, by anybody + 1. That night the thunder and lightning as if to mirror the days happenings was ferocious and it was accompanied by torrential rain.

The Swedes and I left the hotel a little after 6am to get to the Nicaraguan border as early as possible; we were expecting the worst. As we rode for the border the dawn sun burned off the mist which cloaked the hills either side of the road. The road surface was great quality and it twisted and turned through several mountains as we made our way through the evaporating mist; what a great way to start the day.

We got to the border and were met by six or seven guys who had a rope across the road. These were not border officials, it was the usual story of thugs trying to extort money; thankfully there were three of us so they just let us pass. As I drove through the makeshift border it served to cement the feeling I had in my head that Honduras really was a complete shithole.

We got to the official border and went about stamping out of Honduras. To our complete surprise, it was painless. We walked into an official and she stamped the passports, easy as pie.

From there we went onto Nicaraguan immigration, which was also painless, the whole process taking less than an hour. The whole thing immediately set the scene for a very different experience in the country, almost as if the first impression you get tends to set the tone for the rest of the country.

Nicaragua

I said goodbye to the lads, their road was taking them in a different direction and I thanked them for their help the previous day. I hoped we´d meet again on the road. The goodbyes didn't seem to hurt so much anymore, maybe I was getting used to them, or maybe it was that I wasn't "leaving it all out there" only for the door to be slammed when you don't get to see people again.

The roads, scenery and people I met along the way in Nicaragua were great. The police stopped me several times, but each time it was just a chat.

These were just guys around the age of thirty who just wanted to chat to someone to break up the day, and I was happy to oblige. I was having a fantastic time, the best since I'd got to Central American and I rode the two hundred miles to Granada before early afternoon.

Grenada was a beautiful town. I booked myself into a gorgeous hotel, time for a few well-earned comforts after a shit forty-eight hours. The guy behind the counter took a real shine to me, he was one of the most overtly gay guys I've met but in fairness to him, he was great fun.

That evening I was sitting in the Cafe Europe sipping some freshly brewed coffee looking out on the town square as several fine women were passing, I just couldn't believe that it was only twenty four hours since I was in that steaming cesspool at the border with Honduras.

From there I headed out into the town and hooked up with a black Nicaraguan from the Caribbean coast. His name was John Oliver (something something) and he was a street poet and artist, which essentially meant that he didn't have a pot to piss in. I said that I'd buy him his dinner and a couple of beers in exchange for the company and if he'd write me a poem about my journey, he was great fun.

This is the poem he wrote...

30000 miles of road
30,000 miles of road, all the way from Alaska
through Mexico and Central America

It is sweet enough cos adventure is fun
Now here I am on the run

Sometimes things seem so far away,
That I just can't delay

Sometimes it seems so near
While I drive and drive without no fear

I know I must be there cos now I'm here with the
Nicaraguan eastern poet John Oliver having some
cold beers

Still I´ve got another 15000 miles to go
Just let it flow

So I'll drive and drive through forest, up hills, and
down valleys, across bridges
Nonstop until I hit Buenos Aires, Argentina in South
America

Then I fly home back to Ireland
don't worry loved ones, cos Oisin is going to stand

I thought it was great. When I got back to the hotel the gay guy who worked in reception was in his civilians, and saw me coming in and we'd the following conversation:

Concierge : oh I luv ur ayre, eets Bonita... so blond... eets golden! ... tu esta Bonita senor

Oisin: sorry horse... I don't putt from the rough

Concierge (Confused look)

Oisin: I kick with the other foot.. Not gay.... you know what I mean.... prefer the senoritas

Concierge: ah u prefer... but you like men also? Si?

Oisin: nope.... just the senoritas I'm afraid, but listen, thanks anyway

Concierge: (looked really sad, and a bit hurt)

Oisin: listen if it's any consolation... if I was gay....y'know

Concierge (starting to beam)

Oisin: ok where's the feckin JCB, I'm outta here.

I was having such a good time I decided to stay a second night. I got up and went out for breakfast the next morning and tucked into a delicious round of coffee and pancakes.

There's plenty of tours running out of the town and I burned an afternoon on a tour of the lake looking at monkeys and small forested islands. I wandered back to the hotel where I bumped into a couple from the US and Britain, David and Ellie who lived in Costa Rica and were up in Grenada on holidays. We had a great chat by the hotel in the pool and were joined later by a girl called Miriam and later by her mother, both from Slovakia.

I was sitting by the pool as Miriam stripped off into her Bikini and got into the water. After picking my tongue up off the ground, we all introduced ourselves and talked for about an hour.

We met for dinner that evening and Miriam and I ended up snogging, the first girl I had kissed on the trip, and it had only taken 19,000 miles. If I'm honest I was desperate for a shag but the gentleman in me didn't want to get involved, actually the last thing I wanted to do was fall for someone and then have to carry the parting with me for the next 12,000 miles.

I bailed out for a walk later around the square, with the temperature so high during the day the night-time is really the only time you get to feel cool. I was walking down the cobbled streets when a song popped into my head which made me smile and think of home.

Top to toe in tailbacks, Oh, I got red lights on the run
I'm driving home for Christmas, yea
Get my feet on holy ground

So I sing for you, Though you can't hear me
When I get trough, And feel you near me
Driving in my car, Driving home for Christmas
Driving home for Christmas
With a thousand memories

I left Granada the next morning feeling very blue. I had met some great people there and as always on a trip like this, you always have to say goodbye. It was the most people I had met in one place and saying goodbye to John Oliver, David, Ellie, Moses, and Miriam made me feel very sad and lonely.

Costa Rica

I didn't have long to dwell on it as the stress in my system began to rise again at the thought of another border crossing that morning; from Nicaragua into Costa Rica. Costa Rica is the most modern country in Central America and after only about two hours I got through and pushed on to Lake Arenal, situated beside the Arenal Volcano, one of the ten most active Volcanoes in the world.

I stayed in the town near the lake that night, and everywhere I went all I could see was couples. My mind drifted back to Miriam; why don't I just go back up to Grenada? I knew it was a bad idea; this was not the time or the place to be getting involved with anyone, so I just bottled it up and pushed on.

My abiding memory of Costa Rica is of a day I spent driving through rain forests. The noise of the birds, the smoking volcano and the unrelenting incessant pissing rain, are all etched in equal measure on my mind. The rain drove down all day and combined with savage humidity meant that you're either soaking wet from rain, or soaking wet from sweat, the only difference is that you don't draw any flies when it's raining.

The swings in fortune and as a consequence swings in mood on this trip were almost too hard to deal with. In just five days I went through 1) Close on most scared ever in El Salvador, 2) Angriest-maddest ever at the Honduras border 3) A magic time in Granada and 4) today the opposite of yesterday; feeling down in the dumps.

On the bad days I'd go into Star Wars mode, likening myself to Luke Skywalker heading off to the cloud city to save Han and Lela not forgetting oul hairy arse himself Chewbacca.

In the bright lights of the fighter, Oisin loads a heavy case into the belly of the ship. Artoo sits on top of the X-wing, settling down into his cubbyhole. Yoda stands nearby on a log.

YODA: Oisin! You must complete the training.
Oisin: I can't keep the vision out of my head. They're my friends. I've got to help them.
YODA: You must not go!
Oisin: But Han and Leia will die if I don't.
BEN'S VOICE: You don't know that.

Oisin looks toward the voice in amazement. Ben has materialized as a real, slightly shimmering image near Yoda. The power of his presence stops Oisin.

BEN: Even Yoda cannot see their fate.
Oisin is in great anguish. He struggles with the dilemma, a battle raging in his mind.
BEN: If you choose to face Vader, you will do it alone. I cannot interfere.
Oisin: I understand. (he moves to his X-wing) Artoo, fire up the converters.
Artoo whistles a happy reply.
BEN: Oisin, don't give in to hate -- that leads to the dark side.
Oisin nods and climbs into his ship.

YODA: Strong is Vader. Mind what you have learned. Save you it can.
Oisin : I will. And I'll return. I promise.
Artoo closes the cockpit. Ben and Yoda stand watching as the roar of the engines and the wind engulf them.
YODA: (sighs) Told you, I did. Reckless is he. Now matters are worse.
BEN: That boy is our last hope.
YODA: Yep, fuckin right he is

The rain cleared and I set off in the direction of San Jose finally ending up in a town called San Isidro. I drove down from Lake Arenal over the mountains and up until midday the clouds passing over the mountains were putting on a real show for me. The roads were great as they weaved and twisted with views of mountains and tropical forests all around me.

The noise from birds and monkeys and lord knows what else as you go through dense tropical foliage is exhilarating, the whole place is teaming with life. I hit San José the capital of Costa Rica at about two pm, and in keeping with every single large town that

I'd travelled through since crossing the border into Mexico; I got lost. There wasn't a sign to be had for going south in the country but I knew I was getting better at the whole "intrepid explorer" deal because after only about an hour I was back on track.

The journey south takes you over a mountain range and once I hit a certain altitude the rain came down like I was in a drive through car wash. For four hours, I drove through fog, lashing rain, flooding rivers and landslide residue. I'd started that day feeling really low but I guess your system only lets you feel like that for so long; eventually you hit a turning point, lord knows what triggers it. I just started having a great time, it was absolutely brilliant craic; the more inclement the weather conditions got, the better my mood got, at one point the rain got so heavy I was driving along breaking my arse laughing, there was nothing else you could do.

I think if you're in the right frame of mind you can take almost anything, if I'd been in a bad mood no doubt I would have been driving along cursing like a sailor in a storm at sea. I'm sure someone said a prayer for me somewhere to snap me out of the doldrums and that's why I was able to get through what otherwise would have been a terrible day. I think the hardship also helps keep you focused and stops your mind wallowing so in a way it's a good thing.

The plan I had was to hit one of the quieter border crossings into Panama the following day, I guessed I was less than two hundred miles to the Panama

Canal. I was imagining just sitting there having a tall frosty beer watching all these massive ships go by, saluting the distant figures standing on the decks waving at me and the bike.

Panama was going to present its own bunch of problems, the biggest of which being the fact that I'd have to ship the bike to Colombia. I kept thinking to myself, how the fuck am I going to be able to do this. I supposed that I'd just head for the airport nearest the city, and then find a Cargo company and just ask them to ship it, and do it all with very poor Spanish.

The day started for me before dawn as I set out for the Panama border. I got a lot of advice not to take the border on the Pan American highway and instead to detour over the mountains to a much smaller border post near a place called San Vito. The roads and the view the whole way were great but as I approached the border and had less than ten miles to go the road disintegrated into just rocks, not even gravel and I started to wonder had I taken the wrong way; surely this couldn't be it?

In any event it turned out that it was, and the people at the border were brilliant. I was through in less than thirty minutes and to thank the folks I went over to the supermarket and bought them seven or eight litres of fruit juice and we sipped and talked away for about an hour about all sorts of stuff.

Panama

From there I had to cross the mountains in Panama to get back to the Pan American highway. That journey took me through tropical forests that looked like something out of an adventure movie; I loved the fact that every day was so stuffed with so much variety. Seeing as things were going so well and God likes to equal things up, the next two hours the rain pelted down like I was stuck under a bull taking a piss. I had to stand up on the pegs several times to let a pool of water slide down my legs that had built up around the oul chestnuts.

Once I got to the Pan American highway, I realised I hadn't fully opened my map and had an extra two hundred and eighty miles of road to go to get to Panama city, which meant I had to knock out over four hundred miles total that day. As it turned out the roads in Panama are in great shape so I wasn't overly worried. My main concern was to get to Panama City before it got dark; the city had a reputation of having some serious no go areas.

About twenty miles outside Panama City, I got lost in the metropolis, so I pulled in to get some gas and get some directions.

A trucker pulled over and roared out the window: "what the fuck you doing here amigo!" I said that I was looking for the Holy Grail and did he know where I could find it? It turned out he was heading to Panama City downtown and I just followed him in, It was a big relief as by this stage it was completely dark and I was going around in circles.

I pulled off the freeway into the downtown only to pull into an area called the red zone or at least that's what one of the people said it was when I got there.

As I was driving along looking for a hotel three people beckoned to me that it wasn't safe there to get out of the area as fast as possible. As I was stuck at the lights, a woman about eighty said to me to hurry out of here and once again that it wasn't safe. I had the most eerie feeling that it was my mother talking to me, so spooky!

I did my usual trick, grabbed a taxi and motioned for him to drive to a hotel and that I'd follow. Then with marine efficiency we lashed through the city and found our way to the front of a hotel whereupon he helped me check in. The garage doors to the hotel were opened, my bags were taken to the hotel room and in what felt like five minutes since I talked to the old woman, I was safely tucked up in the hotel room and I lay on the bed thinking, "what the hell just happened?"

I'd officially reached the emotional halfway point of the journey, even though I was up over 20,000 miles at this stage. Everything from this point on would be South America.

The first order of business was to find a way to ship the bike to South America, note there's still no way through the Darien gap on a bike or a car, so even though there is a land link you can't get through what is impenetrable forest and swamp. You could get through on a horse by all accounts, but would be shot by one of several rebel groups or drug lords which control the area.

The next morning I drove the bike to Panama airport, armed with only the information that there were two companies out there who shipped bikes reasonably regularly. Now if you think this is a handy thing to do, you'd be mistaken.

Imagine you had a motorbike out your back garden and you wanted to ship it to England. Now remove your ability to speak the language and the only tool you have is the schillings in your arse pocket and a rough idea where the companies might be located, it's not easy.

I found the place after a while and parked the bike up, thoroughly impressed with myself. The bad news was that the first company Panavia had shut down, "nice one", I thought to myself. From there I talked to a really helpful security guard who took me to the Girag shipping company, my last option.

After a while talking to the folks there in broken Spanish and broken English, it turns out that that cost to ship to Quito in Ecuador was $1900 and the flight only left once a week (fuck that!). Alternatively, you could fly to Bogotá in Columbia for $900 dollars with the flights leaving daily, and the bike would be available to pick up that Monday. Bogotá it was. Before the bike could be shipped the mirrors had to be removed, battery disconnected and the fuel removed which is where I came unstuck.

I´m one of these guys who are about as good with his hands as a donkey is at making fine china, and I did not know where to start. Just then a Japanese lad who spoke ok'ish English and worse Spanish who was also looking to ship his bike to Colombia came over and helped me. My Spanish was better than his, and his motorbike knowledge was better than mine so between the two of us we got both bikes shipped.

The heat and humidity was so bad that I had to strip down to just a pair of shorts while getting the bike ready, I think the sight of my rotund frame walking around in a pair of shorts that you´d normally expect to see someone wearing in a porno movie helped to speed the whole process up. "Get that guy out of here before he takes off the togs, quick!!"

Hiro and I headed back to Panama City to book the flights to Colombia, however with all the mad countries showing up on my credit card there was a stop placed on it. I had to sort that out by talking down a payphone on a crowded Panama street with heaps of chicken buses and noisy trucks driving by at about a hundred decibels, it was manic.

I eventually got it all sorted and it was time for a treat. All the American chains are here and I needed a dessert. The best dessert I'd had so far since crossing into Mexico was a tin of peaches turned onto a plate with some nuts on it nowhere near enough for me to maintain my reputation as a fat bastard, so TGI Fridays had my name on it.

In Panama, all the yuppies go to TGI, so it's a totally different buzz than in Ireland or America. Hiro and I chatted away for a while that night, and his English was pox, so the conversation dried up rather quickly. He had travelled extensively at this stage in his trip all through Africa and the Middle East on his motorbike on the strength of, what could best be described as pigeon English. Just goes to show the world is a very helpful place after all.

I had another two days knocking around Panama before I was due to fly out to Bogotá. I was expecting a torrid time since those IRA lads went to Columbia and suddenly made their way home with the help of Gerry Adams. (I wondered if I could get his home number.) I could see it now, back home on the news "Irish man arrested in Colombia" and all the people back home going "Well, if he's in Colombia he must be guilty!, sure who in their right mind goes there?"

Panama for me just oozed sex. All the billboards were stuffed full of women wearing half nothing. As a result I was working my way to my right palm being fully covered in hair and being a fully fledged membership of the Stevie Wonder club. The women walked around the city almost naked, all of them wearing jeans and shorts, two to three sizes too small for them.

The typical outfit as far as I could make out was a vest and a pair of jeans borrowed from a ten-year-old child. The cultural mix in the town is wild. It was brought about when they brought in labourers from all over the world to work on the Panama Canal, when it was built most just stayed in the country.

I pottered off to see the Panama Canal, which was a surprise. If you go to "old" Panama City and look out to the ocean, you can see lots of huge boats all waiting to get in through the canal. Apparently, the backlog at that point was about four days so it was a complete surprise to find that I had to wait around drinking beer in the Mira Flores Cafe for about three hours before a boat showed up, something rotten in the state of Denmark methinks!

The canal is full of tourists, it's "the thing" to visit when you're in Panama City and it's a good opportunity to meet people. You have to force yourself to keep going through doors, in other words keep introducing yourself to people and saying hello and not be deterred from being the first person to say hello just because you think maybe the person won't reciprocate. I always told myself that I'd two choices either keep going through the door and introducing yourself to others or sit quietly alone by yourself for the rest of the trip. When you're in good form it's easy to be outgoing, when you're not in the best it takes a bit for work, but for the most part, it always pays off.

While I was there I met James and Kate a great couple from Camp in County Kerry in Ireland. James was over working on a start-up with Digicell and invited me along to a few drinks they were having in a place called the sky bar. From there we went onto a nightclub, which was heaving with people and we had a great oul night.

I spent the next day nursing a wicked hangover. They have a beer over here called "Panama" which is exactly like "Harp" in Ireland, and it seemed like they copied the recipe exactly. The headache from it is wicked, in Ireland it's served with two paracetamol. It was fantastic to meet up with some Irish folks for a chat; somehow, it felt like I wasn't so far away from home.

That night I managed to get caught in the hotel elevator for over an hour. One guy, six women and I were all lumped together in this mettle cage. As soon as the elevator stopped, two of the girls just started roaring crying. As time went on two more started so if you can imagine the scene, eight people in a roasting hot humid elevator, with four people whinging and snivelling, two more of them trying to console the others and myself and this other guy. No one spoke any English bar me. The Hispanics do nothing quietly and the noise in the elevator was like sticking your head into a blender.

Anyway, it was at that moment I realised that I'd never make a fireman, with all that whingeing I was ready to just start throwing people down the elevator shaft and this was after only about 45 minutes. I've no patience, I know, but many of us go through life not knowing who we are, I'm ok with me not having any patience.

Eventually we were hauled up to a home position, all drenched in sweat and as cranky as a bag of pit bulls. Later that night in an Internet cafe the Colombia prep went haywire over visas, I couldn't get any feedback on whether or not I needed one. Half of the websites reckon you need a visa, some didn't say and some said that you didn't. Those that said you did mentioned that the only way of getting one being to present yourself to the embassy. Ireland was the only EU country that has this restriction; it was as a result of the IRA lads who were over here training FARC rebels.

Eventually I got the whole thing sorted by going onto the department of foreign affairs website, and the visa restriction was changed in November 2007, so I was as high as a kite with the news. The next day I was going to Colombia, everyone back home just thought I was crazy. As I went into the hotel lobby to head up to my room for the night there was an American man giving out that he'd had no sleep in three days with the noise in the hotel; I just thought to myself "Welcome to Central America buddy!"

Chapter 10
Colombia

I met Hiro at the hotel and we got picked up by a taxi to head off to catch a plane to Bogota. The taxi was a complete banger and started to overheat about two miles into the journey. He didn't have any water with him so he just used a milk carton to collect water from the side of the road filling the radiator with the collected rain. In the end we made it to the airport with time to spare, but things like this leave you feeling that something a bit looney happens every day without fail.

Looking out the window of the plane, any land I saw was completely covered in dense rain forest. We got to Bogotá airport in a little over an hour. The decent into the airport is a wonderful experience owing to the fact that the plane flies in through a valley before it lands. The security was about as heavy as you´d expect for where you are in the world. Then we got a taxi and headed for a hotel, Hiro was on a tighter budget than I was so he was looking for a cheaper place, and I went a bit more upmarket. My cut was, "Fuck it, I'm in Columbia, its dangerous enough without staying in a shithole to boot".

The first problem that became obvious was that the taxi guy seemed to be ultra-concerned with our safety, we told him where we wanted to go based on information in the lonely planet and he just flat told us "no way!" it was too dangerous. I really got the impression that he was concerned for our safety so I was happy to go with the flow. The result was that I got to a lovely little family run hotel that was in the middle of nowhere.

Bogota

The next morning was going to be our first attempt to get the bike out of customs. I reckoned that it might take anything from one day to a week, "there was no point in trying to rush it, it will be ready when it's ready" was what I kept telling myself. It was such a relief to be in South America, I felt that the ugly part of the trip was over and from this point it would onwards and upwards. The plan was as soon as I got the bike, to head north and loop round to Cartagena; about a three-day journey all told.

We went straight off to customs to see if we could pry the bikes out and we used the taxi guy from the day before who spoke great English to help us. I had asked him how much would he earn normally for this amount of time and just paid him that amount for the duration he was helping us.

Two hours later we got the bikes, much quicker than we could have hoped for, even in our wildest dreams. I said goodbye to Hiro at the cargo terminal, his road went south whereas I was heading north; he was a good lad. At the point we said goodbye he had done 34,000miles hard miles, he was a hard-core young fella no doubt about it.

Colombia is bigger than you´d think, as big as the UK, France and Germany put together so I was expecting to clock on a lot of miles over the next few days, so this was as good a time as any to take a day off. Once I got the bike, I headed off into Bogotá for the day. The pavements are in a wicked state; anyone would think your drunk as you're walking along as your stride is constantly interrupted by the uneven pavement. It is also as dear as fuck, about 30% dearer than Ireland and that's saying something. Someone needs to tell em "hey you know this is Bogotá right?"

The city itself feels like an eastern European city, some nice areas with sprawling high-rise apartments in the suburbs. The city has a population of over seven million people so is absolutely chock a block. The people in the city are not that friendly, but that's the same in all cities I guess, but it's obvious that people don't seem to be happy. Hardly anyone smiles. Now before someone chimes in with "if you smile at the world it´ll smile back", I was in great form, I had the bike back so it wasn't me projecting a bad mood but I was sure it would be a lot better in the countryside.

After spending two days in Bogota I said to myself there's no way you´d ever come here if it wasn't because it's the only place in Colombia you can fly the bike into. My impression was that it's a Dark, depressing, miserable sort of place. The paranoia on safety was also bit off-putting, the taxi guy and another lad in the hotel had put the fear of god into me, both recommended calling into the police in various towns to let them know your there, no chance!

I even tried an Irish bar to see if there was any Craic but no joy. On top of serving crappy food with Irish names, it had all the cheer of a funeral. The last night I spent in the hotel, the fucker in the next room blared the TV into the wee hours, it was only drowned out when he started snoring like a rhinoceros. The lack of peace and quiet I think is one of the things Westerners find hardest to get used to about Latin American cities, compared to the northern hemisphere, its bedlam.

The night before I got on the road I looked at the gear I had for the remainder of the trip. Over the course of the last eighty days, I had kept throwing away gear that I didn't need. At every place I stopped for more than one night I would keep asking myself; "Ok, so you haven't used this piece of kit yet, so what makes you think you'll need it in the future?" The extent of the gear I carried now fitted comfortably into a tank bag, two panniers, and two hold all bags.

As the trip went on this trend continued until at the very end I flew home with just one bag whereas I left for Canada with three. If I ever end up going on another trip, I'll know better. On the upside it made travelling very easy, on the downside it would have been nice to pick up a few souvenirs but I had the consolation that I was on the trip of a lifetime, and that was a small price to pay.

The plan for the following day was to head to a city called Medellin and from there up to Cartagena a distance of about 1100 km, from there I would take a couple of days to complete the 2000km journey south to the border with Ecuador.

The following morning I was the proverbial scalded cat out of Bogotá, except Bogotá had other ideas. I spent the first two hours utterly lost and eventually decided to just head north, which was "kind of" in the general direction of Cartagena. As things turn out I found myself on the Venezuela side of Colombia, not the side you´d be hoping for from a safety perspective, based on what I'd read on the travel advisories.

The weather was shite all day, it just rained and rained and rained, but it didn't dampen my mood, the scenery was a mixture of dark green forests with mists of cloud moving through the tops of the forest canopy.

I knocked out about two hundred and fifty miles but due to the roads twisting and turning through mountains and the heavy traffic it took me all day to do it. As a comparison, you´d knock out the same distance before lunch in North America. The roads were full of soldiers, and in my first full day on the road, I comfortably passed fifteen checkpoints, but didn't get any grief.

It was the first time on the journey where I felt things coming to an end believe it or not. I had over 20,000 miles done and I knew I was on the last leg. It was a silly thing to be thinking reflecting on it now, I still had over eighty days of riding to do; you'd be amazed the pure horse shit that jumps in and out of your mind as you drive along on a motorcycle.

San Gil

I stopped in a small town for some grub and this Colombian guy came up to me and said "where are you from?" I said Ireland. The usual story followed as to how I got here, how many CCs the bike was, yada yada. It turns out this lad used to work for the tourist board of Colombia (yes there is one!) and towards the end of the conversation, he thanked me for visiting his town and Colombia with a vigorous handshake. I said to him "listen buddy, I'm no one special or anything like that." He followed with "when one comes, many will follow, I'm certain." I said goodbye and he left me feeling quite emotional. I was thinking about it for the rest of the day, and just couldn't put my finger on what the emotion I was feeling was.

Having headed north I decided to pull in at a small town called San Gil at about 4pm, normally I'd drive till about five but seeing as it was Colombia I said I'd pull in that bit earlier each day. The welcome I got at the hotel was very genuine, and I was stunned with all the smiling faces compared to Bogota. The girl working on reception was a knockout wearing a two-piece pink suit; I was foaming at the mouth. I had a shower and headed off into the centre of the town which was lovely and quiet centred about a lovely park.

Everyone you passed smiled and said hello and when I went into a restaurant for dinner, the people in there were just great and made me feel very welcome. I got the distinct impression that a couple of the senorita's were checking me out, I thought to myself maybe this is the place you'll get into the gratuitous sex part of the trip, where the women never having seen anything like me would all be harassing me for a lick of the cango (in my dreams!)

Very few of the towns on the way to Cartagena were either in the rough guide or the lonely planet for Colombia, so I'd be taking a lot of chances as I drove north on whether or not towns on the maps had places to stay in.

I sat in the restaurant sipping a beer and trying to work out a route to Cartagena, the big problem for me was that I was on the *wrong* side of the country; there were lots of mountain ranges with no roads through. The FARC were on the news tonight releasing a guy who they had captive for over a year.

I was preparing myself for plenty of heebie jeebies moments until I hit the coast. It wasn't only FARC I had to worry about, the power of drugs cartels in these areas is a major concern for would be tourists, but I comforted myself with the fact that I was now in Colombia and I must therefore be a hard core stud.

The next day I celebrated my birthday, the 8th of October. It was thirty-eight years since I was dragged out roaring and screaming and I have not stopped since. If easily offended skip down to the next page.

I hit the road early that morning and about an hour out of San Gil I had a minor/major emergency depending on how you look at it I guess. I'd had something a bit weird for breakfast, a Colombian dish of potatoes and sweet bread mixed into a watery soup.

Anyway, about an hour after I hit the road it felt like that scene in Alien where the yoke jumps out of yer man's chest, except this was making a B-line for my bum.

It was one of those situations where you get absolutely no warning apart from a couple of minor sloshes in your stomach. There was no place anywhere close with a toilet and I was driving on a mountain with sheer drops on one side and steep cliffs on the other side. I kept saying to myself "hold on ... hold on... hold on.... holy fuckin bollix hold on... Jaysus hold the fuck on"

I got the signal that there was about four seconds to detonation, I pulled the bike over to the side of the road, jumped off, dropped the tweeds and hung my arse over the metal barrier on the cliff, the bike hid at least some of me from the passing traffic.

I sat on my make shift throne for about ten minutes with all sorts of traffic beeping the horn at me. When I felt the fresh air on the back of my throat, the only true sign that the chamber was fully purged I was left with a bit of a conundrum.

Let's just say the words "clean break" were the furthest from the truth. With no bog paper handy, it was off with the motorbike boots; both socks met their waterloo and were subsequently donated to the Colombian cliff face.

From there I made my way, gingerly, north to a place called Aguachica (water girl I think it translates to), along the Ruta 45A. For the first time since I left Costa Rica the sun shone all day and I was having a ball soaking up the wonderful Colombian countryside. The amount of soldiers and police on the road was very high and I passed a checkpoint every ten miles or so.

I booked into a hotel and I was again taken aback by how friendly the people were, it really took me by surprise. How could a country with all these problems and such a bad reputation have so many wonderful people was the thought chiefly in my mind. The women in Colombia are knockouts, fantastic figures with long black hair but I go the distinct impression that they were a cranky bunch, sure why else would all the lads in the country all be out fighting. So far, the Colombians had completely blown my mind.

As I checked into the hotel I was met by an apparition. A girl with long wavy black hair, a pink vest and a pair of Jeans which were spray-painted onto a body that just wouldn't quit, man I'd a ploughed her till next July.

She showed me to my room, and it's these moments you pray that at least some of the stories in these porn movies could be true "Do you need some help undressing Mr Hughes". This hot tamale might fall for a tall gringo with interesting tales to tell from the road or "he's different he might be great company for tonight" and maybe the next hundred years, but no, off she went. I went in and had a cold shower, at this stage I was so horny I'd a got up on the crack of dawn.

I went out in the town that night and none of the restaurants had any menus so it was back to pointing in the air with one finger with a high pitched "Si" when I heard something I recognised. There were large amounts of soldiers everywhere I went and as I sat in a cafe looking out on the people passing up and down the road I got a sudden burst of homesickness, not surprising really, after all it was my birthday and I was a long long way from home.

The next day it was time to leave and it all started great. As I was checking out of the hotel the owner gave me a birthday present; you have to give you passport details in hotels here and sure enough they twigged my birth date and gave me a little bag of goodies; I was going to ask if there was any chance I could just marry their daughter.

I left and started to roll north. The countryside was a dreamy wonderland. The vast majority of the roads are lined with trees that grow over the road creating a tunnel for you and the bike to drive through. When you can see into the distance, the mountains are always there, with swirls of mist moving across them. I remember one stretch of road where on my right side clouds were passing up and over mountains so fast, it felt like I was fast forwarding through a dream.

There are over two million Motorcyclists in Colombia; most are of the smaller variety. When you stop for gas on a big 1150 invariably you draw a crowd of at least seven or eight kids all with the same questions: "Where are you from, where are you going., do you like Colombia, how much did the bike cost, how do they get the figs into the fig rolls." It's enough to give you an ego.

I hit the coast road near Santa Marta close to the very northern tip of Colombia and turned left for Cartagena. I pulled in for a bite on the road and had shrimp cocktail about ten yards from the beach. The shrimps, only caught a couple of hours earlier were mixed into a cocktail right in front of me, fresh lime, mixed with veggies and whatever else goes into a shrimp cocktail. It was so good I had to have a second one. Just sitting there supping a coke, eating shrimp cocktail with the sea at my back and a lovely cool sea breeze blowing all around me, I thought to myself "man ...these are good times!!!"

A kid by the side of the road tried to sell me a live rooster, or at least I think it was a rooster. Obviously, poultry is about as useful as ashtrays to motorcyclists so I said no and the kid looked like he was going to start crying. The rooster didn't seem to like the look of the deal either. I asked him how much it was, about eight dollars so I just gave him ten dollars and told him not to kill the rooster!

I fully expect forty gold bars in heaven for this one should God in fact turn out to be a rooster fan.

I rode all day and as light was fading, I arrived in Cartagena. On my right side the sun was setting in a blue grey sky as I swept into the City, it was incredible. That day was so good, I had every experience imaginable for a road trip; rain, sun, sunsets, wind, gorgeous scenery, mental drivers, gorgeous grub, roosters, presents!(yay), some really bad roads, and the best people in the whole world.

It took me a good while to find a place to stay in the city and I booked into an "ok" high-rise hotel. As a rule of thumb I'd tried to avoid big cities on this trip, and my advice to anyone is you get a better sense of a country by staying in the smaller towns and villages. By and large cities are the same the world over. If you want to avoid the bottom feeders of the world, staying away from the big population centres is a good idea.

Cartagena

Cartagena is an attractive city, reputed to be the best-looking city in South America with lots of colonial architecture and the old town is completely ringed by a massive wall that was built to defend the port from pirates. Many of the original cannons are still in the walls and it's very impressive to look at. Sir Francis Drake and the boys used to plunder Spanish gold from this port. The women were fantastic looking (Yeah I know I'm labouring that point) my final point on the matter is that hot pants were in fashion.

All over the town and I do mean all over, there are bakeries churning out roasting hot rolls, pasties, cakes, and every manner of pastry and bread. The smell creates one of those Scooby doo moments where you get the scent of all the freshly baked gear, it tastes great and it's cheap as hell. Most people eat on the streets as the restaurants are pricey, but you can get a good breakfast for about $3 as long as you don't mind chowing down on the kerb.

If your calorie conscious, it's not the best place to go as its all pastry, so you can feel yourself getting fatter by the second eating it. I tried out a Chinese restaurant when I was there, I saw the sign and thought to myself "Yes, nice round of sweet and sour chicken!" When I'd ordered I looked at the price and said to myself, "Jaysus that's expensive" but when the grub arrived I figured out why. The portion was so large it had to have been put on the plate with a spade; there was easily two kilos of grub on the plate.

On a down note, as a tourist in these places you're targeted as having plenty of cash and therefore fair game. For example that day I had about ten transactions where I was paying money, in at least seven of them I was ripped off straight to my face. There wasn't even a hint of trying to cover it up. Some examples were trying to give you the wrong change, charging you twenty dollars for a five-minute cab ride, pretending they had no change and leaving you waiting for twenty minutes in the hope you would just leave. In the hotel, they wouldn't give me a key so I had to keep going up to the room with the porter who was looking for a tip each time. You just handle these things but each time one of them happens your estimation of the place drops a notch.

On one occasion I felt like a complete dumb ass, I stopped a taxi and asked him to take me to a part of the old town, he looked at me kind of funny and we drove for about ten minutes and pulled up to the place I was looking for, I paid him and said Adios. As I closed the door and he pulled away, I looked across the street and about two hundred yards away was the back of my hotel, I could almost hear the guy saying as he drove up the road "dumb fuckin foreigners".

The women seemed as cranky as hell in this town, much like Bogota. Every time you order a drink, a coffee, or a cake or pay for anything they look at you like they just caught you rifling their purse. They may be hot tamales, but cranky is too high a price to pay; this lot make Irish red heads look like baby kittens. They can keep their tanned hot bodies, fake boobs and bountiful arses, give me a freckly set of Irish titties any day!

It was becoming more and more apparent since I'd left the US that nobody seems to really care about the countries natural treasures down south. The fort walls, which surround the city, doubled as the city latrine with lots of the feature stinking of piss. I saw at least ten lads all taking a leak up against the ruins of a wall that took two hundred and eight years to build. This fort is cool and is massive, but there's rubbish all over the place, the stink is brutal and there is no planning control and all sorts of out of place buildings surround it.

It's a shame; imagine you went down to the pyramids and the whole place banged of piss, or had a McDonalds parked right beside it. On top of that, the whole sea front and most of the other features are covered in garbage. There's lots of homeless people knocking around, and many folks missing limbs, apparently Colombia has one of the highest amounts of land mines in the world. Cartagena is definitely worth a visit but it has its warts, no doubt about it.

That night I headed out in Cartagena for a bite to a place called El Bistro, a German restaurant recommended by the lonely plant. While sipping a coke I met two Swiss girls, Vera and Annette who had been travelling in South America for the last two months and just got back from a seven-day cruise on the Amazon. We had dinner and a couple of drinks and shared stories from our trips. I had a great night, the Swiss are a cool bunch and guess what, English was the girl's fourth language, after, Swiss, German and Spanish. They would put you to shame.

I said goodnight around 10.30pm and headed back for the hotel.

When it gets a bit later things get quite a bit more seedy in the busy spots, and as I was walking back to the hotel, there were lots of prostitutes all flogging their sliced pan. Some of them were persistent and I summarised a quick conversation I had with one of the girls below. She was about forty-five years old, and had a set of choppers that could chew an apple through a letterbox.

Charlotte the harlot: Hey... u.... Hey... u.... where u go

Oisin(jedi): back to my hotel darling

Charlotte the harlot: ....which hotel my lova...which hotel...

Oisin(jedi): ...ummmm emmmm...dont remember the name... it's a long way...long long way

Charlotte the harlot: You wan fuckee fuckee?

Oisin(jedi): emmm no thanks darling....have a girlfriend...y´know..Going out with Brittney spears!

Charlotte the harlot: no u not..no u not.. You wan suckee suckee?

Oisin: I am.... she told me to swing up to Los Angeles earlier and not to forget my tooth brush!

Charlotte the harlot: you wan tug? (doing handjob motion, I was surprised she didn't call it tugee tugee)

Oisin: ..no thanks... I'm grand... sure I better go... Brittney will have the kettle on! (She better have some Banoffie pie too or there´ll be skin and hair flying!)

After about five more propositions, thankfully I was back in the hotel.

I set off the next day with my chief goal being to get as close to Medellin as possible, not a town you want to ride to in the dark, lest you become a statistic. I ended up riding about three hundred miles and in keeping with all the time I spent out of cities in Colombia it was brilliant. There was rolling green countryside, beautiful warm weather, and fantastic people on the road.

I was very quickly falling in love with Colombia, and I found it remarkable how much of it reminded me of Ireland. I stopped in a town called Caucasia and at first tried to check into a hotel that was actually a hospital, they never changed the sign outside. The girls at the reception were in fits of giggles with me trying to check in.

In Caucasia that night I had almost a perfect moment, a great steak with lovely chilled beer in an outdoor restaurant on a beautiful summers evening. There was a lovely warm breeze blowing up through the streets and the whole place had a carnival atmosphere as Colombia was playing in a World Cup qualifier that night.

I just sat back and watched the world go by, it was lovely. It was when I finished I realised I didn't remember the name of my hotel but thankfully remembered the general direction it was in and found it after about thirty minutes.

I kept thinking to myself that if I was to get into trouble in Colombia no one would believe that I was just here driving a motorcycle through the country. I could see it in my head being read out on the Irish news "In international news an Irish man was arrested by Colombian officials for smuggling drugs, he maintains he was just passing through", and everyone in Ireland thinking "Passing through me arse, sure who in their right mind would go to Columbia".

I was continuing the trend of avoiding any more big cities and just staying in the countryside and small towns, with that in mind I was going to make for a small town just south of Medellin. I thought it would be about three hours however I didn't realise the road to it went over the mountains.

Mountain roads with a good surface and lovely warm sunshine had my spirits absolutely soaring. The people I met along the way were all smiling and everyone I met was unbelievably enthusiastic to meet someone from Ireland on a motorbike trip. There were military all over the place, and it seems like their favourite mode of transport is on a motorbike, with one soldier driving and the other riding shotgun behind holding the gun in a menacing grip. I got stopped a couple of times, and they were a bit picky but let me go after a couple of minutes. It definitely did feel like the ante had been upped on the security front, the closer I got to Medellin.

Medellin is a city in a valley, completely surrounded by mountains so if I wanted to drive through it, it would mean making my way through two mountain ranges back to back, I waited to see how I felt closer to the time, if I liked the look of Medellin I would stay a night.

During the climb, the rain started to come down like it only does in the tropics and as I went higher and higher, the rain got heavier and heavier. There were rivers of water coming down the road and the whole mountainside seemed to be washing away. I drove through three separate landslides, and floods over a foot high, at one point, I was afraid I would draw water into the piston heads. For about ninety minutes, the rain was torrential and combined with lunatic truckers, landslides, floods, cows and horses on the road made the morning insane, high octane doesn't come close to describing it.

The mad thing is that you keeping coming face to face with your mortality. As these things happen on the road you keep saying to yourself "fuckkkkkkk that was close". As soon as I started to descend out of the mountains, the rain eased off and by the side of the road, people were funnelling the rain coming down off the mountains to wash trucks, have showers and wash clothes.

As you continue on the road to Medellin for about fifty miles by the side of the road there's one of the longest shanty towns in the world all hugging the space between the road and the river.

Medellin is a town of about two million people and you hit the sprawl a long time before the city so progress on the road was very slow. I made up my mind that I wasn't going to stay in the city. As it was, I was already wanking like a fourteen year old and looking at all these gorgeous women would only torment me.

As usual, in the big cities, I ended up getting lost and that's when the first problem happened. The scumbag element exists in every city; the difference is that down in South America driving a BMW with a BMW enduro suit you stand out with the word TOURIST written in Neon yellow all over you. The inevitable result is that these hombres are drawn to you. For the second time while stopped at traffic lights two muck birds showed up, although this time the outcome was different.

I had learned my lesson from the first encounter in Mexico, firstly I had left at least fifteen feet of room in front of me to give me somewhere to go, and I had a lump hammer in my tank bag. The first lad showed up under the guise of begging and approached me on my left side; I was watching his friend closer who was circling to the right. I had replayed this situation in my mind a thousand times since Mexico, what would I do if it happened again?

The guy on my right was carrying a big stick, nothing more. I wasn't overly worried about the stick, the enduro suit with gloves and helmet left me well protected. With the bike in neutral, I kicked down the stand in anticipation of the guy on the left pulling at my left side, and with my right hand whipped out the hammer and swung wildly, "Come fuckin near me and I'll fuckin do ya!" I roared to the guy on the left. The guy on the right then just cracked the stick off my shoulder. I jumped off the bike and ran about ten steps towards him with the hammer lofted above my head "Get the fuck away from me ya C#$T!"

No sooner had I roared it when four of the folks who were in traffic behind me jumped out of their cars and ran for the two muck birds, who promptly ran off. The people here are genuinely concerned about tourist's wellbeing and so, there we were; me and a bunch of lads from Colombia shaking hands saluting our victory with about half a mile of traffic stopped behind us, it's a moment I'll never forget.

As the horns started to go, we all jumped into and onto our motors and headed off. As I was driving up the road at least ten cars beeped the horn at me, I felt like Thor! From there I crossed the city and as it was only 1pm, I could easily make it to La Pinta, a town south of Medellin. The road took me back over the mountains and it was a case of rinse and repeat on the weather of earlier in the day although thankfully it didn't last for the whole journey.

I met a Canadian guy and his girlfriend from Colombia on the road on a motorbike, in fact the whole mountainside was covered with bikers; easily 70% of the traffic. On the way to La Pinta I came across an accident, you always know there's one ahead when you have to filter through a mile of backed up traffic.

The accident was between a biker and a trucker, with the bike in bits and the rider in the recovery position on the side of the road. There's an unwritten code that if you can at all you have to help bikers in distress so I went over and gave the people helping him anything they needed out of my first aid kit. The poor lad was white as a ghost and looked in a real bad way. Off I went again for La Pinta; only it turned out that day was a bank holiday Monday so the town, which is a river resort, was completely booked out. This was at 5:15pm in the evening and I'd about forty minutes of light left. The next city was over two hours away, Manizales so I just had to pucker up and hit the road with a night ride ahead.

Manizales

There's a network of roads near Manizales that were designed by a psycho so once more, in the pitch black, in the middle of nowhere I was lost in Colombia, no matter which road I took I was over two hours away from somewhere to stay. The rain started again and the next two hours were mental. Unable to see due to the rain on the visor I had to contend with horses and cattle on the road, masses of construction, people just walking out onto the road and every type of road hazard imaginable, but it wasn't my first time, I made it and booked into a motel.

The best way to deal with these situations is to use a truck as your battering ram. If you nestle up behind a truck you don't have to worry about hitting any animals or people on the road, and if its pitch black it's far safer to do this than go it alone.

The motels double as love hotels in Colombia as is the case in Mexico and Central America and you pay in four-hour instalments; I paid for three to get me twelve hours kip. Knackered tired, I was serenaded to sleep by the sound of couples shagging all round me. The only fringe benefit was that the TV programming was wall to wall porn; but that quickly turned sour as for some reason all the channels were showing women with very unusual looking front bottoms.

Things really went crazy the next day. As I was filling up with the usual hoard of kids around me a really shady character came over. I knew he was odd because he wouldn't look at me. He asked a bunch of questions of the kids that I had answered them earlier, "where is he from, how much is the bike worth" and then he just walked off, you didn't have to be Sherlock Holmes to figure out something was up.

He went back to his car and sat there making some phone calls as I talked to the kids. I waited until I saw him drive off before leaving.

I stopped for breakfast a short time later on the side of the road; these restaurants are just an area of the road with a canopy covering some tables and an area where you can cook some food. As I was eating, who drives by really slowly eyeballing the bike, none other than the guy with three other guys in the same car.

"Fuck me, what the fuck is going on?"

I took the Reg. of the car and said to myself "ok... go to the police...give them the details it can't hurt." I went and had a nightmare time explaining to them what I meant; there was ample use of the word bandito.

I told them I was headed for Popayan and would phone them by six this evening and if I didn't show, that car was the culprit. I drove off.

Bandits

Along the way, I thought, "so do they want me? ...nah don't think so, no room in the car, and they would have to butter me to get me into the boot...., the bike..... hmmm maybe?..., to rob me?" I'd no idea and then as I rounded a bend my heart instantly went to 199 beats per minute.

There on the road pretending to be broken down was the car; I could see it about four hundred yards ahead with two of the four guys standing out on the road. I had a truck behind me so couldn't easily pull over. My mind just went crazy, "What the fuck am I going to do!!!!!!!!???"

Well the right hand went back into the tank bag for the hammer, I moved it over to my left hand and with the right hand wound the accelerator back as far as it could go. Very quickly my speed was almost 100mph and in my mind's eye one of these lads was getting the hammer right in the head if they tried to stop me.

The engine roared. I roared "Me Bollllllllliiiiiiiiiiiixxxx" as I passed one of the guys who had moved into the middle of the road into a blocking position. He noticed the waving hammer and backed away from the bike as I screamed by at 100mph in fourth gear.

I switched the hammer back into the tank bag and looked into my rear view mirrors to notice the guys all getting into the car and pulling off and turning to follow me. At that moment I was petrified, I have never felt fear like it. My whole body was lathered in sweat and I was hyperventilating.

With sixty-five miles to go to Popayan I put the hammer down like nobody ever has before and few will ever do again. I kept telling myself "if you can't keep this bike at 5000rpm you are a fuck bag who deserves what he gets".

I screamed through army and police checkpoints, rounded bends on the ragged limit, rallied over ramps and overtook on the hard shoulder. You name it I did it.

My thinking was to try to get the Rozzers to follow me; If they did I'd be safe then. Thinking about it now I should have just stopped but with fuck all Spanish these guys could have made out like I had robbed them or at least that was how I reasoned. The reality is I could have just as easily been shot for rallying through the checkpoints.

I made it to Popayan in well under an hour, and with the manoeuvring I did on the road, no one in a car could have kept up with me; I never saw the car again. I pulled into a police station and spent an hour with the police explaining to them what happened. They have federal and local police here so I had to wait for the federal guys to show up. They even sent around a guy who spoke some English so that took a lot of the hassle out of things, the second guy in Colombia I met who could speak English and his name was also Carlos!

Anyway, he said that the number plate I gave him was Venezuelan and that he thought that most likely they were going to rob the bike and any valuables, but nothing more. We chatted for a good while about what I was doing in Colombia, where I'd come from and in his owns words "Man your fuckeeen crazy travelling alone in Colombia with no spaneesh, no phone! Alone!... no fuckeen clue"

When it came to giving descriptions I was brutal; average height, tanned, black hair, tache, the whole country looks like that! I told them I didn't want to take things any further and I was going to head south the next morning. Carlos gave me a route to take which took me off the beaten track in case they might be waiting, they knew from talking to the kids that I was heading south which could only mean Ecuador, the main road being the Ruta 25.

When I got back to the hotel I was laying on the bed thinking about all that had happened and kept running it over in my head, my mind was caught in a big loop. My heart was going like a jackhammer. I was taking my pulse and resting it was running at 140 and wasn't getting any slower. I think it was some sort of a reaction after having burned so much adrenaline of the sixty plus mile bull ride through the countryside.

This next part isn't particularly macho, but it's a wart's and all account so I said I would include it. I sat on the floor of the room in the corner taking really deep breaths to try and slow my system down but it wouldn't work.

The walls in the hotel started to close in on me and it felt like there was no air anywhere and although I´ve never suffered from claustrophobia, or had a panic attack (unless you count yesterday) I really felt like I was going to get crushed where I sat. I was certain I was going to have a heart attack at any minute. My chest felt like it was going to burst and I couldn't breathe.

Over the course of the next two hours slowly but surely I got myself back in order. I was a mile away from getting to sleep and just packed up my stuff and sat in the dark looking out the window of the hotel room waiting for the first sign of the dawn. As soon as I saw the first slivers of light I was going to leave. This sort of thing never happens to Indiana Jones.

The dawn came and I hit the road, the goal being to get to Pasto, about 140 miles from Popayan. On the map it looks less than an hour, but the roads twist through the mountains like nowhere else on earth and combined with terrible weather, it took almost five hours to get here.

I must have passed over five hundred soldiers, the average age being no more than twenty years old. There's something wrong about a young lad that age standing on the side of the road in all weathers carrying a loaded machine gun or rifle, when you talk to them you can tell their just kids and nervous as hell.

I was ragged leaving; I hadn't slept a wink, and felt like someone had let the air out of me. I ended up spilling the bike while trying to take a picture while driving by some mist covered mountains. I wasn't going very fast and neither the bike or me were damaged although my pride was severely dented. So by about 8am I was completely in the horrors.

When you're surrounded by the Colombian countryside it's hard to stay in bad form for long. The roads weaved their way through stunning valleys, up and down the side of mountains and as is seemingly always the case in Colombia, the distant mountains were always covered with a beautiful mist. The roads had sheer drops on one side; with steep cliffs on the other side and I spent quite a bit of time going through several tunnels.

I stopped for lunch at a small roadside restaurant in the mountains (four tables with a tin roof, definitely not the Ritz) and the family took me into the back, sat me down at their table and made me lunch. None of them had a word of English but we got along great.

The amazing thing is that these people survive on way less than fifty dollars a week and there they were sharing out the grub refusing to take any money from me. The Colombians are amazing.

Imagine that, you´re as poor as a church mouse and you´re still sharing with a complete stranger. I just had to do something to return the favour so made an excuse that I was meeting "mucho amigos" down the road and bought ten bottles of diet coke, crisps and chocolate bars from them. About twenty minutes down the road I met some folks on the side of the road and gave them the goodies, they looked as though all their birthdays had come together.

From there I went up over some more mountain passes, where you feel like you are on top of the world. At one point I just jumped off the bike and sat there on the side of the road, looking down at the valley and mountain range all around me, sipping a bottle of water. It was a perfect moment, you get them every other day and I was back on a high.

Most people who ride a motorcycle always say that they spend a lot of time looking at the sky. The main reason is to see whether or not you're about to get soaked, and in Columbia given it's in the tropics the cloud formations that dance across the sky have to be seen to be believed.

All through the journey I had become increasingly fascinated by the sky, I wondered whether or not it was always like this but because I normally drove a car, I just never noticed. When you're driving in very remote areas, sometimes a sliver of light appears through a huge bank of clouds and you imagine that the light is a beacon showing you the way home; that the light is just for you and it was made by your guardian angel.

Pasto

The next day I was supposed to cross into Ecuador, but I was worn out and did not have the heart to do a border crossing, so I said I would take a day off and scratch the arse off myself. I took the bike up for a spin around the mountains and volcanoes that surround the town. I took a bit of time out to reflect on how things had gone so far.

In ninety-five days I'd knocked out over 22,000 miles, which is 2000 miles longer than the total road, and air miles Charlie and Ewan did in the long way round in 115 days. By the time I would finish I´d have done more miles than the long way round and the long way down combined, which was always the intent anyway so no big surprise. I was in my tenth country (USA, Canada, Mexico, Guatemala, El Salvador, Honduras, Nicaragua, Costa Rica, Panama, Colombia) with the 11th to come, Ecuador, and the rest of South America coming soon.

I did what limited touristy stuff there is to do in Pasto, probably the most notable thing about the town is that it's surrounded with active Volcanoes and keeps being destroyed every now and then. The shops and people as a result have a fatalistic sort of attitude from what I could pick up e.g. the driving on the roads is suicidal.

It's almost as if the attitude is "Well it's better to die on the road than get scalded alive by molten lava from the volcano!" You cannot get diet coke, or diet anything in the whole town "sure what would you want to be on a diet for...don't you know we´re all going to die any minute! Fucks sake have a cream bun outta that!"

The beggars were as aggressive as hell, there not big on playing the pity card, putting on a sad face so you´ll feel bad and cough up some readies, nope not here. It's more like "hey you.... yeah you ya big rich gringo bollix...give me some money! Or I´ll breathe on ya!"

The people here are a mix of Indians, creoles, blacks, and some other stuff not necessarily walking on two legs. There was seriously not a looker in the whole town, when it comes to restocking the herd, they won't be coming down here for samples although I doubt they'll come my way either.

Anyway, Pasto was an ok place to go to sleep in, but not much more.

Chapter 11
Ecuador and Peru

Every time you have a border crossing you always plan to be there really early so you don't run the risk of getting caught there over night and also to avoid getting caught behind big busloads of tourists.

I had no idea what to expect but given it was the Colombia Ecuador border, I was not expecting a good time. The road there wound a path through massive mountains with sheer cliffs on one side, and huge drops on the other. This part of the world is raved about in the motorcycle overlander fraternity and it certainly lived up to its billing. I arrived at the border at 8am and parked up the bike and for the first time since I crossed into Central America it went like clockwork.

One of the border guards took me under his wing and the whole thing was over and done with within ninety minutes. Now, while in the western world a ninety-minute border crossing might have you penning a letter to your public representative let me assure you in this part of the world its cause for celebration! I was elated, and setting out for Quito at 9 30am, I said to myself "fat boy, you've earned yourself some nosebag!"

Quito
The chow never lasts long when I'm around and before too long I was back on the bike haring for Quito. The only difference between Ecuador and

Colombia is that Ecuador is completely deforested, near the border with Colombia at least. It's much poorer than Colombia too; many of the small towns on the way to Quito were in a terrible state.

The road was littered with checkpoints and there was a massive police presence. In Ibarra a town in the north of the country, I came across the aftermath of a mini riot with lots of debris on the ground, with lots of riot police wearing gas masks. They must have used tear gas to break it up and while there was no gas visible in the air it was there because in about two seconds flat my nose throat and eyes felt like someone and taken a garden rake to them.

That aside It was a fairly trouble free journey and along the way I stopped off to take some pictures as I passed the equator. I was giggling away to myself as I imagined that one of my balls was lying on the northern hemisphere and the other on the south with my mickey lying on the equator. Hey, I'm a guy, that's what we do.

Eventually I got to Quito. The main reason for going there was to get the bike (faithfully renamed to Sam Gamgee) serviced and tarted up after a gruelling time since Phoenix.

Quito is a big city and very spread out so I was pretty worried that it was going to take a long time to find the BMW service centre, but sure enough as I was driving into the town there was the dealer on my right hand side.

When I went in to the reception, they took the bike straight in, not only that; they said that they would have the bike ready for the following evening. They even paid for a taxi for me to a nearby hotel; they were awesome.

The hotel was very plush, for $38dollars you get some style down this part of the world, lovely soft and fluffy toilet paper not like the tracing paper I was used to in Colombia.

That afternoon I headed into Quito town, for what I promised myself, was my last ever look at colonial architecture, I had seen enough "colonial gems" to last me a lifetime.

That night I hooked up with a fellow biker, Steve Barnett from the USA who was also riding through South America. We met in Finn McCool's Irish bar, which is run by a girl from Ireland, Ursula. She was very friendly and introduced me to the whole bar when I got there. We had a heap of pints as one must when introducing oneself to a countries beer and I woke up the following morning not unexpectedly with a wicked hangover!

I went off to do all the touristy stuff in the city. Quito is vast and the traffic is insane, so I hired a taxi for the morning and got him to take me around all the hot spots. Doing this normally works out at well less than $20 and saves you having to figure it out for yourself, yes that's right; I´m a lazy bastard.

The taxi driver as soon as I got in put on leather gloves and proceeded to drive like Mario Andretti all over the town, when the traffic permitted it. The dude was a font of nervous energy, changing the radio station every two minutes, beeping the horn as if he was being paid for every beep and he was continuously fucking the whole world out of it.

There is a code to the beeping that goes on in South American Cities, and I think I´ve deciphered just a bit of it, some examples below translated into a slight Dublin accent!

Beep: Heads up der bosco!...that light will be green in a minute

Beeeeeep: its gone green...go ya slow bollix!!....go will ya!

Beeeeeeeeeeeeeeeeeeeeeeeeeeeeeeeeeeep: it's been green for a full second... move it Tonto!

Bep Bep: Nice arse love! (passing girl on the street)

Beep Beep Beep Beep Beep : Stop Beeping the feckin horn will ya... it's not me .... it's the oul one in front of me!

Beeeep Beeeep Beeep: Don't get thick with me hair oil! or I´ll burst ya!

Beep Beep: I´m behind ya... don't pull over I´ll plough your motor out of it

Bep Bep Bep Bep: Nice Jugs!

During the course of the tour, we came across two riots involving students. The basis for the rioting was that the city had put up the price of bus fares so much that it meant they were beyond the student's means to pay it. It was all turning to violence and on three separate occasions, we saw police running away from hundreds of students.

I've never been witness to a riot before but your first clue is the deafening whistles and shouting. There is definitely an undercurrent in the city for this sort of thing and I remember thinking that I would not be surprised if Quito makes the news at home soon, apparently several people had already been killed.

In Finn McCool's the night previous, a bunch of expats and myself talked about the things you never get used to once you leave the United States and head south. The one common denominator we all arrived at was the noise. A good example was the hotel I stayed in. It was right beside the airport and as the planes landed and took off; you could feel the vibrations, on top of that, it set off all the car alarms on the street. Sleep south of Tucson is fleeting at best.

Someone turned on the rain that night in Quito, turning the city into a parking lot. There were knee high floods everywhere. Despite the obstacles I collected Sam Gamgee from BMW and from there it was a quick dart back to the hotel and from there back to the touristy part of Quito for a couple of pints and a bite to celebrate my last night in the city.

On the way there, the taxi driver was blaring salsa music. Now I don't mind a bit of Salsa but it was all I'd heard now for nearly two months and after a while it just starts to sound like some bollix scraping out the ashes out of a fire. You know those fuckers who always scrape far more than they need to and you are just sitting there, clenching your teeth so your fillings don't drop out, Jaysus me nerves!

At the end of the second pint, the whole town had a power cut leaving the Mariscal area in total darkness. I bailed out with two fellow Dublin lads who were on their way to an all-night rave and jumped in a Taxi. Both lads had been on the lash solid for a couple of months since both breaking up with their girlfriends and going on a drugs and drink binge.

Ursula from Finn McCool's was telling me that a pub owner was shot dead the previous day. We had actually seen the shrine the night before and were wondering what it was all about. She was also saying that most of the expats who run businesses carry guns. Quito is definitely not a place to be bringing the kids, even though for the most part it was a good spot.

Steve had talked to me about riding together on a section of road as we both headed south. I explained to him that having come this far on my own I really wanted to complete the rest of the journey alone. To his credit, he completely understood, and we have kept in touch since.

I got a taxi back to the hotel early and when I got there, I knew something was up. The whole street was empty and there was two police cars making announcements. Apparently, there was a curfew in that area due to fears of more students rioting. The city had that vibe running through it, when you can feel that something bad is going to happen.

It was time to leave and under a cloudless sky, I drove out for a town called Banos. The first task was to find my way out of Quito. Trying to get out of Quito is an exercise in relative failure. I got lost as usual and was "F" ing and blinding like a bear with a sore mickey, but sixty minutes spent lost in Quito's urban sprawl was a massive victory compared to the two hours I'd regularly spend lost in the towns of Central America.

Banos

Along the way, the route runs parallel to huge mountains and volcanoes. One mountain in particular was snow-capped, and I was only a hundred or so miles from the equator, I found myself saying "Kilimanjaro my hole." I was armed with brand new set of intermediate tyres instead of knobblies and it was the smoothest ride I'd had since Arizona.

Banos was lovely. It's completely hemmed in with green mountains and a volcano. There's lots of hot springs knocking around, waterfalls and the ubiquitous colonial church. The town was full of back packers too, no problem as long as I didn't meet any gap year types, I secretly prayed that when it came time to trim the herd, they would be first.

In this area there seems to be quite a large Indian community, I'd seen at least five Indian women so far no bigger than hobbits, all wearing dead cool hats. Most have unbelievably crooked teeth, bad enough to make even a dentist reach for a brandy.

Using Banos as a base, I took Sam Gamgee up into the mountains to do a bit of exploring. This was the first time since Costa Rica that I'd taken the bike off the beaten track, up until now it had been a bit too dodgy. In total I covered about fifty miles on gravel roads which bended and twisted as they climbed their way through the Ecuadorian mountains and volcanoes.

I spent most of the time off the bike acting the maggot and generally just enjoying the countryside. The road was dirt for large portions but seeing as I'm now a 9th Dan black belt Biker (similar to a 9th Dan Karate type, except we tie our suits with our mickey and not a belt) it was no problem at all. The road initially cuts across a bridge over a river many hundreds of feet below; as I peered over the side of the bridge, several people were walking across a rope bridge way below me.

I met a Danish couple on the way up the mountain, Ryan and his girlfriend (can't remember her name for the life of me), from there they were heading over to the coast to do some diving. I would have done that too but I look too much like a bull elephant seal when I wear a wetsuit, it would only draw great white sharks, and it simply would not be fair on everyone else.

I found a spot to sit down on the side of the mountain and I can't describe how good it felt to be just sitting on soft ground with a beautiful cool breeze sweeping up from the valley below. This was all going on at about 10am in the morning where I was (-5hrs GMT) and my thoughts started to drift to friends and family all over the world. I wondered what they are doing now around the world as I sat and soaked up the moment for about two hours.

In Los Angeles, it would be 7am and Helmar the guy I met in Alaska would no doubt be still in bed hopefully nursing a hangover with vague memories of the night before. The folks I know in Portland, would be starting to get the first hour of their sleep-in over with, I hoped it went well. In Phoenix it was about 8am and the tens of people I know there would all be about to head out for Sunday morning breakfast, everyone does that in Phoenix.

In Atlanta, the same time as here, they're no doubt combing their way through the Sunday morning broadsheets. In New York my brother probably just has the kids up and washed and is about to head out the door with Shannon to do some family type stuff. Back in Ireland its 3pm and folks are no doubt all tucking into a Sunday dinner with gravy flowing left right and centre, the men all chasing the grub down their necks so they can go into the sitting room and watch the sports on television, the women all saying to themselves... "well he can go fuck himself if he thinks I'm cleaning all this shite up!" The lads who are under the thumb (modern men) will give a dig out the others are saying "sure didn't I go down for the Chinese takeaway last night?"

In Germany its 5pm, Twisted Robot is helping himself to a bit of dinner and will be in the shower soon, he's got a hot date tonight with a full-bosomed Fraulein and in Australia its already tomorrow and the Fosters are all fast asleep, its 4am. Wherever they were, I just hoped their Sunday was as good as mine!

Banos was turning out to be a trip highlight; it had a really relaxed buzz and was full of great people. That night I went out for pints with Carina (German) and James (English) a couple who met in Quito and were travelling their way through South America. While we were out eating dinner, we met Jake and Jemma from England who were off doing an epic two-year travelling spree all over the world. I had planned to leave the following day but Jake and Jemma talked me into going canyoning and bridge jumping.

Canyoning for the unenlightened (which included me until we started it!) is where you take a section of rain forest where there's a canyon and lots of fast flowing water and you hike, abseil, and repel down through a river. On the way, you're absolutely drowned by waterfalls and spend a good four hours just in the water. It's a brilliant experience, it lashed rain for large parts but as you're soaked anyway it just adds to the event. The whole day you're treated to beautiful butterflies flying all round you and with the steepness of some of the descents you really build up a lot of camaraderie with the folk's you´re out with. All day there was lots of moral support being given and gratefully received.

For the decent, you have to put on a wetsuit. These things never seem to fit me and the suit I was given for this adventure was no different. It was final proof if any was needed that you can get six pound of shite into a five-pound bag. Lots of male camel toe showing, not a flattering look for me.

A bridge jump is where there's a rope tied to the underneath of the bridge and you jump off and swing back and forward over a mountain stream. The last time I did something like this it was about ten years previous and the feeling as you initially jump is terrifying.

I stood there and the guy who was supervising says to you "on 3; 3......" Then through your mind flashes "Jesus these ropes look awful thin, will they hold my weight!" 2 "Is this buckle latched properly, holy fuck, holy fuck 1. Here is where you jump but instead today Jake started roaring "no don't jump...don't jump...not yet" I started roaring inside my head "is it the ropes are they broke?...what the fuck is going on!!!" Jake just turned around and said "Sorry about that mate...hadn't got the camera turned on mate...now you can go!"

"You Cu$t"... my heart was doing cart wheels and then once again it was ....3..... I'm not ready.... 2.... I'm not fuckin ready....1....go........ And as you initially free-fall it feels like your stomach is just going to pop out your arse, and then it's just like being Tarzan in a movie; that is as soon as you figure out you're not actually going to die.

When I came to Ecuador I really thought the highlights would be to get the bike serviced and pass through the equator, maybe a couple of mountains but it exceeded all my expectations.

In keeping with the trend of outrageous swings in future, the following day started crap, I woke up with eleven mosquito bites around my left ankle and the itch was brutal. At that moment, cutting my foot off with a spoon seemed a good alternative to the itch. The fucker must have invited his mates in to help him feast, let's face it I'm the best of stuff, so you can't blame him.

After that, as I was walking down the three stories in the place I was staying with my bags, I fell down the last four steps, about as graceful as a bull in wellington boots.

As I picked both myself and my dignity up the oul one working in reception, about 80 years old mutters "Mas despacio...no problemo", in summary slow down. I resisted the temptation to take out my hammer and took comfort in the fact that no doubt, she´d be dead soon.

I left Banos with a bit of knot in my stomach after having such a great time there. Jake and Jemma were first class. The British are the best swearers in the whole world, a great quote from Jake "Mate I´ve give my right bollock to be on this trip with ya!" it sounds so much better with a Bristol accent! Jake was a man's man, the son of a Vicar he had a mouth like a sewer. I asked him how long he'd been into motorcycles, to which he replied "Since I shot out the cunt mate"

From there I headed back to the Pan-American Highway to head south to Cuenca, another colonial gem "yawn", but it was as good a place to shoot for as any and it had been recommended a bunch of times to me. Up until midday, the road continued to cut through the Andes as it wound its way towards Cuenca. With about a hundred miles to go I stopped for petrol and the guy asked me where I was going. I told him and he said four hours more or less; I said, "For fucking 100 miles... you must be joking!"

Well he knew what he talking about, the road was awful and the weather turned crap. There was fog sprinkled with pissing rain and lunatic road users for mile after mile.

The whole country is addicted to over taking no matter where it is on the road. Say if the top speed of your car was sixty-five and you were an Ecuadorian and say you were driving at 64mph and there was a guy in front of you doing 64.9 mph. Well to not try and overtake for an Ecuadorian is like saying "would you not like an extra two inches onto the end of your John Thomas", they just can't resist.

When I got to the hotel, similar to a scene in the long way round, I asked do you have secure parking to which they replied, "Yep...bring her into the lobby"

The following day the plan was to cross into Peru, Ecuador was quite small, only about the size of the state of Nevada in the USA but seeing as I had to cross a border I set off very early hoping to be at the border for midday, and through to Peru for no later than 2pm. When I'd a border to cross I'd always wake up as grumpy as a red head on the rag and that day was no different.

The other part that was on my mind was that all the cool stuff to do in Peru was in the south, Nazca lines, Machu Pichu, Lake Titicaca, all of them, all in the south. Peru is over five times the size of Britain so there would be many miles to get through to get to the sexy stuff, but it still beat being at home working in Ireland.

During the last miles in Ecuador the countryside turned schizophrenic. One minute I was in lush green tropical mountains, and seven miles down the road, I was in a Mars like red desert landscape. The variety is all on account of the Andes, according to the guide books they block water ever getting to certain areas and that's where all the contrasts come from. At one point it was like someone found the green switch, you move from brown mountains to green in the space of three or four miles.

Not long after, as I approached the ocean the whole world turned into a massive banana tree plantation. All of the plantations seemed to be owned by large multinational fruit companies, with the brands you would normally see on a banana peel when you're out shopping.

As I approached the border with Peru, every gas station was dry and I mean every single one. Petrol is over twice as expensive in Peru as Ecuador, a fucker charged me $10 dollars for two gallons in Peru versus $1.79 a gallon in Ecuador, all the Peruvians not surprisingly head across the border to fill up their cars.

The best way of thinking about a border in these parts of the world is to think about a lovely lake, but at the sides, there's loads of pond froth and scum, well there you have it. The countries are lovely but the borders are full of scum bags and people of lower virtue than crocodile shit. These places are spilling over with muck birds, fuck bags, dingle berries, bastard holes, felchers, Snedgers, Sleeveens, not to mention bollixes.

Peru

In every country up until now, the process has been the same; stamp out of the country your leaving then stamp into the one you are going to and then import the motorcycle. Well in Peru, they like to do it differently. In Ireland's countryside, two hundred yards distance can mean anything from two hundred yards to five miles, well in Peru three kilometers has the same rough application.

I stamped out of Ecuador very easily even feeling confident enough to tell a few fixers to feck off. I should have gleaned something from the way they were smiling at me. Next I went down the road (3km) and instead of getting to Stamp into Peru first, you import the bike first, magic stuff, this was the hardest part done, woo-hoo I thought.

So I asked the chap where I stamped the passport into Peru. Note you can't get out of the country or into the next one without these stamps so it's a big deal. He told me 3km up the road on the right ok so that so that puts me right back at the start; I asked are you sure? "Si Si" he said.

Off I went feeling like a ping pong ball back to where I started "Senor?... where do I stamp into Peru?" "4km down the road" and I said "oh 4km down the road.... ok....must be just past where I was the last time." I went back down the road and this was the routine for the next hour, back and forward, back and forward.

Eventually I figured out I needed a stamp on one of the sheets which I got after four pongs on the tennis table, and then over to a bridge. There sat Jabba the Hutt with a moustache. If you asked someone how could you make Jabba the Hutt uglier? I would say give him a tache. Well there he sat delighting in his ugliness. I had watched a video of guys who did this border crossing a couple of years ago and it was the same bottom feeder doing the stamping through. No bigger bollix exists I can guarantee you.

From there you head off and stamp into Peru another 3km down the road. So like I said before, when I'm made king of the world which I'm sure will be any day now I will not only remove the borders of the world but then I'll to quote that shrinking violet in pulp fiction "Execute every last mother-f#$kin one of em!"

I started banging out the Hail Mary's so I wouldn't run out of gas. All the petrol stations on the Peru side of the border were closed down because everyone not surprisingly heads for Ecuador to fill up. On fumes, I arrived into a town called Mancora, a small coastal town beset with surfers. All the grub was seafood on the Menu's, which is great but as a result of yours truly Spanish IQ being 0.008 I ended up ordering octopus for dinner; it was like chewing a fucking tyre tube.

Peru started bad, I was ripped off several times and anytime I went near a city I got lost. Next time I see a charity box which says "buy sign posts for developing countries" I will gladly throw in a week's wages.

The Peruvians are a strange bunch, and my first two days travelling in the country left me thinking they were inhospitable, especially compared to the folks in Colombia and Ecuador.

I never really felt in the least bit welcome since I arrived and I had been doing the whole smile at the world and it will smile back at you routine. It's not like I'd been asking them to do much more than take my money. I didn't expect Peru to look the way it did, the early part being primarily desert and coast roads. There were lots of occasions where you'd pass a secluded beach with a couple of beach shacks standing empty on golden sand, and out at sea in the distance a couple of fishing boats busy hauling in their nets.

I left Mancora and drove south to a town called Pacasmayo. I decided to jump off the Pan-American Highway to go through the Peruvian desert; you would be amazed at what seems like a good idea when you are eating a nice breakfast.

The countryside slowly turned to yellow desert, first the trees thinned out, leaving just scrub and gradually that thinned out as well to leave just sand. The landscape was completely flat in all directions and not since Montana in the USA had so much of the horizon been visible. Given that, we do not see much of this sort of thing in Ireland and I had spent so much time in the tropics a desert was a welcome change in scenery.

In the afternoon, the wind picked up ferociously and for the last four hours of the day, I thought Mother Nature was trying to rip my head off. As the wind picks up it picks up the sand and it fills the entire sky making the world seem an off peach colour. Because the sand in the air blocks the glare of the sun, it appears as just a red disk in the distance.

I was ran off the road three times that day by oncoming trucks, they see a bike coming the other direction and say "fuck it, plenty of room for hair oil in the hard shoulder" but the hard shoulder is full of sand which gave rise to plenty of hair raising experiences.

I got to Pacasmayo as the sun was beginning to set and the world turned pink, a mix of a red sunset masked by the wind blowing the sand from the desert into the air. In my life, I never thought I'd live to see such a colourful sunset. As I got closer to the coast, I was treated to an orange sun dipping behind the horizon as I looked out onto the Pacific Ocean. I had a stroll down the pier and bought some necklaces and good luck charms from some stalls that were set up there. I had completed over five hundred miles in Peru so far, and in sexual terms, I hadn't even got the hand up the jumper yet.

Pacasmayo

The next morning I woke up and after all the fighting with the wind the previous day my body was in a heap. I decided to stay on the beach and read a book and just chillax for the day. The place I stayed in the town was right on the beach and as I was drifting off to sleep I remember thinking to myself that there is no better sleep aid than the sound of the sea lapping up against the shore; I'd still have swapped it for a good shag.

I spent the following day aimlessly wandering around Pacasmayo and it was quite an experience.

On the face of it, it's a lovely little sea side town on the North West coast of Peru. Elderly men meet for early morning coffee and discuss the comings and goings in the small town. On the pier, people drop lines into the water to catch crabs to bait their traps for bigger fish, and out in the distance you can see many small boats all fishing, albeit in crafts that look far too small for the height of the seas around them.

On the beach near the pier local fishermen work on repairing boats, it all feels very wholesome.

Along the beach front people sell ice cream as they do all over the world in similar locations, with stall sellers selling every manner of trinket imaginable. It seldom rains here; the town is on the edge of the Peruvian desert and the wind never let's up so there are decent size waves breaking onto the beach for most of the day, a surfer's paradise or so you would think.

As the day dragged on a thought grew in my mind until I found myself saying "Where the hell is everyone?" I know in these places they have siestas but the town felt completely empty. I went to a restaurant which was recommended by the locals as being the best fish restaurant around and for about $10, I got a whale sized portion of white fish, not sure what type of fish it was but it tasted mighty.

I walked down the beach and saw just one person, a young boy playing with his puppy, and started to see the reason why no one is attracted to the beach, it was full of rubbish. The further you walk you find that the towns sewage is running untreated via an open shore directly into the sea via the beach where people would be swimming. Still further on down the beach; a large gathering of vultures and gulls were feeding off the waste material from an abattoir where the effluent was pouring directly into the sea.

It is hard to believe that the folks there do not get the linkage between pumping raw sewage directly into the sea and people not coming there to swim in the water. As it is a fishing town, don't the fishermen know that fish prefer water that's shit free? You ask yourself why they don't do something about it.

As I walked from the beach along the sea front, kids were playing barefoot on the pavement. The children's park was empty; all the swings were long since broken. Its only when you look up the side streets where there's little more than rocks and mud for paving you see that, if barefoot is the way you have to play, the paved area is much more preferable.

I passed a guy who was catching crabs, if they were too small he didn't just throw them back, he threw them behind him on the pier where they quickly just died in the heat of the sun. It seemed like he didn't want to have to catch the same small crab again, better to let it die. He seemed to have no sense of tomorrow, just survive today, tomorrow's tomorrow.

I walked up to a statue of Jesus which most towns have overlooking them in these parts. Beside it was a graveyard; there was no one to be seen either up at the mirador looking down on the town or in the graveyard. Strolling around you see that the graves are above ground, and for a headstone some people just have their name scratched into the cement.

I stood there and thought about it for a long time. What if at the end, that is all there was to remember you? How would I feel? Or do people just live on in people's memories anyway and the headstone doesn't matter, I couldn't decide.

The sad thing was that Pacasmayo could be brilliant. It could be a Mecca for surfers, beach goers even just people who love fishing, or even just eating fish and it could be done very easily. How do you inject pride into people, or a sense of passing what they have now onto future generations? From a natural resource perspective the thought process on everything seemed to be, can I eat it? If not, can I sell it? That's where thinking about the consequences for future generation's stops and starts.

As the day dragged on it was hard not to feel that this town was doomed and that if folks in these countries don't imbibe some national pride in their natural treasures that there won't be any left, I couldn't help feeling that the clock was ticking.

Later a pair of dweeb surfers turfed out the environmentalist mood in me and replaced it with Machiavellian malice! I talked to these two lads for about five minutes and slowly felt the life force begin to ebb from my body. Two bigger Gobshites you would struggle to meet anywhere in the world. I finished up talking to them and was secretly glad now that the abattoir was pumping its gunge into the sea maybe it would draw in some sharks and trim the herd of these two shitkicker's.

That night in an internet cafe a girl the size of a hippopotamus chatted me up in Spanish. I was never happier that I knew the phrase "No Hablez Senorita"

I was glad to leave in the end and I tipped just a bit south. No sooner had I left the town than it was straight back into the desert and wind. It's such a strange feeling driving through this landscape. As with the previous ride, the wind picks up and throws the sand up for miles around. Mountains and any visible shape just become silhouettes of themselves and driving through it feels like driving in a black and white movie.

It goes without saying that you need to keep your wits about you and as I was driving along a truck which was carrying big sticks just started to shed its load stick by stick, it left me doing a slalom behind it to avoid the debris. The desert was full of rubbish, and the houses and buildings I passed were little more than shacks. I passed a desert town where all the houses had a strange looking receiver sticking out of the roofs; it looked like they were all dodgem cars parked together in the middle of the desert.

The vast majority of the shops serve out goods to you through iron bars, I guess most are worried that the place will be robbed, not too much spontaneous shopping done here then "oh I just went in for milk but passed the cookies and just had to buy them!" When your Spanish is as bad as mine you just do a lot of pointing "no up a little...no down a little.... yep that's it."

Out in the desert miles from anywhere some bastard had put up massive Pepsi and beer signs. So there you are driving through one of the driest landscapes in the world with your mouth feeling like a camels heel and what do you see; a sign for Pepsi.

My mind started to think about it "mmm, a nice cold Pepsi, mmm, the feel of the cold bubbles hitting the back of your throat, mmm and a lovely belch at the end of a long slug. But can you buy a fucking Pepsi in the desert? No. Are you even within fifty fucking miles of a Pepsi? No! These signs were pure torture.

I made it to Huanchaco, a surfer town which is famous for the weird crafts that the native folks surf out to get their fishnets in. It was a nice place with lots of backpackers. I went out to the beach and caught another gorgeous sunset.

I met a couple of really cool people, Andy from the states who let me know that you can't weld aluminium and Flo from France who was over my left shoulder eating a huge pastry as we watched the sun setting. I knew the next day would be very long, I was going to try to get from Huanchaco to *ANY* town past Lima, so it would be the longest day since I left the United States. In case you don't know; Lima is where they insert the enema for the world, its famous for having a crime committed every three minutes in the city.

I left Huanchaco at dawn with the plan to keep going south until I got past Lima, some four hundred miles away. Lima as I mentioned above has the reputation of being one place that no matter what you don't want to end up. However, if you want to go to Cuzco, Nazca, and Machu Pichu it's difficult without going this way.

As soon as I started it was straight into the desert except in a much grander way than previously. That day was in my mind anyway, somewhere between riding a bike on Mars, and taking a bike into the Sahara to chase down a couple of camels with Laurence of Arabia, all day it was drop dead deadly! The road stays very close to the coast so at regular intervals you get to see the desert run right up to the sea.

The weather started the same as it had for the last four days; high winds with loads of sand in the air with the mountains and oncoming traffic all just vague shadows of themselves. But as the day went on, the clouds burned off revealing more and more of the surrounding landscape and you would've had to be Stevie wonder not to utter a couple of "holy fuck's" along the way. The sand as it sweeps across the road can make driving conditions treacherous and with the wind blowing as hard as it was; at times you couldn't even see the tarmac.

In the desert you can feel completely alone, and you are; there is absolutely no one around for miles and when you drive through this your mind starts to wander in all sorts of directions. Things you´ve said and done, things you shouldn't have. It's weird how you have to force yourself to think of the good stuff, whereas the not so good stuff just floods in all by its lonesome.

Driving on the roads can also be like a turkey shoot in the busier sections, and guess who the turkey is. Two or three times a day I'd get run off the road due to trucks and continuing incidences of dropping debris from trucks carrying junk. All day horns are going, lights are flashing but I think one of the biggest pains in the arse is the fact that many of the buses have a horn that is very similar to a police siren so as you are dodging through traffic you constantly think you're getting pulled over. If that wasn't enough, Red lights seem to be just something to consider, not follow, on multiple occasions in small towns I had to swerve to avoid a guy who´d gone straight through a red light.

Eventually you just adopt a "fuck you" attitude and keep going until you feel the bite of steel entering your body from a bullet. En route I was stopped without reason by the police twice for speeding, completely bogus charges. These bucks don't even have speed cameras; they were just stopping me because I was a gringo with money.

On both occasions the routine is always the same "Mucho Rapido, blah blah, more shite more shite" and they leave you sit by the side of the road while they do their best to put on a concerned face. The other thing that became apparent is that they phone ahead to each other to let each other know there is a sucker coming "Get his ass to put out a twenty."

The annoying part about having to bribe these dipshits is not the money that you have to part with, it's that if something did happen where you needed their help; if the opposition drops a couple of Benjamin's you lose. The Police in Peru are pure scum.

I wasn't having a good time in the country so far. The Peruvians up to this point just were not in the least bit friendly. I'd stopped for gas three times, had three meals and say stopped for some water another three times and not once did I walk away with the impression that these guys were happy to even get the business.

There is an old saying when it comes to travelling and it is that its "people not places" well that's not true for Peru unless you're meeting other tourists there. The only sign of caring at all I´d seen in four days was when two lads helped me find my way to Chiclayo. The rest of the time was like selling rosary beads to Protestants.

What you try to do is not change who you are and always try and stay the same. I wondered when I'd meet the nice Peruvians. Most backpackers or normal tourists probably don't see this side as they go straight to the touristy spots which are well catered to.

Chincha

After over three hundred miles on the road that day, I arrived in Lima and as it was a Sunday getting through was straight forward. There's a three lane highway which runs through the city the whole way to reconnect with the Pan-American Highway to the south of the city. So as things turned out it was handy.

I got to a town called Chincha about three hours south of Lima and headed out for a steak. After almost five hundred miles on the road that day I earned it. I was the only one in the restaurant.

Half way through the steak I looked up and the movie Titanic was on the TV. It was the scene where Kate is letting poor oul Jack go and he sinks away into the abyss, not a dry eye at the table. I looked around and the two chefs were standing leaning over the counter with their chins on their left hand complete with big tuffty chef hats all glassy eyed, it was a lovely moment.

I was lying in bed the following morning and noticed that there were about twenty or thirty holes in the roof, not a problem when it never rains although when you forgot to put on deet the night before it's a big deal. I looked like a teenager after too many Easter eggs with all the Mossie bites. Thankfully, I didn't go to sleep in the buff and all was well with the frankfurter and town halls, so no major damage done.

I set off for Cuzco but gave up early, it was just too far away and I was knackered after the previous day's efforts. The road turned inland towards Nazca and all of a sudden it was like someone hit the heat switch. To be fair it wasn't a massive surprise given that the sun was directly over that part of the world when I was there but I was amazed at just how cool the coast was versus inland. I started to hit serious desert again, and it was so vast I just had to stop and try and take it all in. I pulled well off the road and followed a track a couple of miles out into the middle of nowhere. About five miles out I had an argument with myself; not something you'd like the lads in the white coats see you doing. The subject wasn't new.

For some reason the biker crowd of which I'm a member are a bit touched. I was in the middle of the desert, alone, with no mobile phone and not a soul for miles and miles. I'd about 250ml of water in my bag, a dozen sentences of Spanish and to cap it all was about 12000 miles from home. Like a lunatic, I was heading off into the desert on some track which was last trekked by some Inca with a dose of Rabies who was fucked out of the tribe for interfering with the village basset hound.

I won the argument as you'd expect and said to myself "dude just do the miles leave the trekking for the camels". Seeing as I was in a remote spot I decided to do a bit or roaring. The desert is unbelievably quiet and for some reason it just seemed that a good roar was an appropriate thing to do. I played Jack Nicholson and Tom Cruise in a few good men "You want me on that wall!" and finished off with a bit of Samuel L Jackson in pulp fiction "Listen man giving the Ho a foot massage, blah blah blah blah,holiest of the holies ain't even the same thing!" I fully recommend it; very therapeutic.

Nazca

I made my way to Nazca, where the famous lines are. The lines were made by removing the stones and rocks to leave just sand. It's the usual story; no one knows who or why they made them. Well I have a theory, they were bored. There's nothing else to do in the desert.

I headed into the town and stopped at a cool restaurant where they were playing traditional Peruvian music, lots of wind pipes and a lovely melodic music. At the next table a retired American lady from Dallas Texas introduced herself; her name was Grace.

Quick summary of the conversation below....

Oisin: So what brought you to Peru? you on holidays? or vacation as you´d call it

Grace: Oh I'm down here with my family showing them the sights I worked here for over twenty five years on and off as an archaeologist.

Oisin: Nice one!....wow... Nice one!....Indiana Jones what!.... plenty to keep you occupied here I´d say... Machu Pichu, Chan Chan....some nice gear alright....

Grace: Oh you don't know the half-of-it sunny!.... this place is just awash with history....

Oisin: Still they couldn't have been that great... a couple of Spaniards on horseback killed off the whole thing .....right?.... let's face it the Spaniards couldn't box eggs at the best of times...

Grace: Oh your just an ignorant son of a bitch ain't ya!.... laughing loudly

Oisin: Still... the people are very friendly though eh? ...both of us laughed

Grace: So how come your here...?

Oisin: Blah blah blah..motorbike trip ... blah blah...

Grace: wow sounds fun!....

Oisin: Yep.... having a ball....

Grace: So are you married?

Oisin: Why? you looking for a date?.... you're a bit old for me!.... (grace didnt laugh, I threw out a Hah!..just to say I was joking....)

Oisin: (bringing in the recovery JCB)...so how many of you are down here?

Grace: Don't think you can waltz round that "old" remark sonny! (thankfully smiling)

Oisin: Don't mind me.... I'm an ape at the best of times....

She went onto describe how Machu Pichu is sinking by 1cm a month (I made a joke..that's fairly slow eh? Another arrow that missed wildly) and how much was lost to conquistadores and private collectors. I got a heap of tips about where to go and what to see; but mostly it was brilliant to chat to someone in English again.

I left Nazca not bothering with the plane trip to see the lines. The place was too hot and my mossie bites were itching like I don't know what. My most vivid memory of the town is the incessant beeping of Taxi horns, they never stopped. If the taxi driver sees a foreigner he just beeps the horn so you see him and then you make eye contact and shake your head and so it continues for the duration of your walk around the town. I wondered if this is what if this is what it felt like to be wolf whistled at.

Cuzco

The next morning I headed for Cuzco and was on the road once more at dawn. The sign on the way out of Nazca says 561km which given the route was going to go over some mountain roads I knew I had at least nine hours of driving ahead of me. With 200km done, I passed a sign that said Cuzco 472km. What the fuck!, it meant riding nearly four hundred and eighty miles, whatever way they measure the distance here it doesn't work. The road had very few gasoline stations so I filled up at every opportunity. It was hard to get any gas above 84 octanes, which is basically baboon piss, but Sam Gamgee lapped it up and kept going.

The road gradually carved a path through the Andes changing from desert to rocky planes and finally into mountain farmland. All day I was treated to steep climbs and descents through the mountains, high mountain planes, deep canyons, rolling rivers, lakes, a stunning sunset, snow-capped peaks, I really thought I was going to burst, I didn't realise that anywhere in the world was so beautiful.

The most spectacular thing about it is that you're completely alone. The best way to look out into vast sweeping canyons is when it's completely quiet, so the less people the better.

I stopped for something to eat in a remote village and sat outside under a parasol chowing down on rice and chicken. As I was eating the grub, three pigs two sheep and a chicken walked by; I swore the chicken gave me a dirty look, "You're eating my brother you cunt!"

With the length of time it took me to do the drive, over twelve hours, I ended up out in the Andes with sixty miles still to drive in the dark. The hazards when it's dark are many and varied. The amount of cattle on the road made me think Noah was up around the corner, at one point I almost ploughed into a herd of cattle, I'm pretty sure my pannier caught a tail; my heart was all over the place. I was taking my life in my hands and I'd no one to blame but myself.

That night I tossed and turned all night in the bed, I just could not stop thinking about the Altiplano which I had seen that day. In my mind I'd seen the best scenery that I was ever going to see and I had an uncontrollable urge to see it again. The great thing about having such a long journey is you can do just that, so the next morning I set off at 5am to go back. It took a little over two hours to get there and then two hours back; I was afraid that it would look different or wouldn't be as good as yesterday but it was exactly the same.

The place is haunting. When you pull off the road and step out onto the trails it feels like your stepping out onto an endless plane. I said already that the silence is the most striking thing; the only audible sound is a cool breeze blowing in your face. In the far distance a grey blue lake sat motionless, and beyond that steep mountains. The roads stretch off into the distance without a bend, if there are any you're far too caught up in the moment to notice. The clouds paint shadows on the yellow plane, and as if to cap the experience you can see them drift across the sky and plane in unison.

I think it's only in the most remote and most quiet places of the world that a person really relaxes and unwinds, just sitting there thinking about things you never normally take the time to. Then as you drive on, the hills rise imperceptibly at first but before long you're shaken out of your trance by sweeping right and left hand bends which drive the pulse up into the 160's.

Cuzco is very touristy, and with that, expensive. You can't sit anywhere but you're beset by people either begging or selling something, so it's not a comfortable place to just go out and walk.

A lot of the bars sell T-shirts with the words "No Gracias" printed on them as a way of showing solidarity with the beleaguered tourist. The altitude has some interesting side effects. First of all, you do anything at all and you're out of breath, but the second one is that it gives you brutal wind, just for a while I was farting like an officer's horse. (Well it's either the altitude or someone put farting powder in my grub).

Thankfully, all the chambers equalised to the lower pressure and I booked up for Machu Pichu the following day. When I was done with Machu Pichu it would be time to head south to Puno and Lake Titicaca, but all of Cuzco was awash with stories that the road was blocked and you couldn't get through.

I met a great Irish couple, Fergal and Aoibhann in an internet cafe and we headed around to O' Flaherty's pub, a real Irish bar. Fergal was probably the biggest Liverpool fan in the world and we were both anxiously waiting to see if Liverpool held out against Portsmouth; thankfully they did and off we went for some grub and pints. Aoibhann was an archaeologist and liked football, a much weirder combination than Inca ruins on a mountaintop if you ask me.

There were lots of negative stories about Bolivia; if half the tales were true the country was starting to unravel, with civil war apparently a certainty in the next year. There were several horror stories on the news and others getting told by the backpacker crew, one was about people getting kidnapped and taken to an ATM every day to empty out their cards until they had no money left. Apparently three Irish folks were kidnapped and held in this way for over two weeks, and when they'd no money left in their accounts they were released.

In the south of Peru there was a farmers strike, and the roads are totally blocked with no way through. The same is apparently starting to happen in the north. At that moment everyone was just flying to La Paz bypassing the problem; however it wasn't an option open to me on a motorbike. So I decided to stay another day in Cuzco while I tried to plan a route which allowed me to get to Lake Titicaca and to the salt flats in Bolivia.

We met a dead on guy in the pub called Dayna (I know, he knows it's a girl's name too) who was a cousin of Fergal's and slowly but surely the amount of pints in the system kept climbing. As I went out to draw on the porcelain, I met Sam from Australia who I met in Antigua in Guatemala. He came to join us and the crack was mighty.

More and more folks kept showing up and at one stage there were Germans, Canadians, English, Ozzies, Irish and Dubs all swinging out of pints at the table. We went to a nightclub, and got absolutely hammered, it was a great night. I got back to the hostel at 4am, and was getting collected at 6am to go to Machu Pichu. Man it felt like I just blinked and the door was getting hammered down by the tour guide. I just had time for a wing wash (can't beat the Boots Cucumber wipes!) and off we went, with me still drunk.

The only thing I can say about Machu Pichu is that it exceeded my expectations and with everything I'd heard about it I really thought that would be impossible.

Even though the place is full of tourists it's still possible to find places where you can be alone and just soak up the whole experience. As I was sitting there looking off the side of the mountain into the yawning chasm below, a girl from Slovenia came along and started eating a sandwich while sitting up against a rock about five yards away from me. She was a cracker and was working as a tour guide. We chatted for about two hours and really hit it off but we were both heading dramatically different directions; who knows in another place and time we might have been something.

On the way back to Cuzco on the train I met a couple from Uruguay who I took an instant liking to. They were always laughing and joking and telling stories, I wrote in my diary that a good sense of humour is one of the best qualities you can have; I think it just draws people to you. I guess no one wants to be hanging around a bunch of moaning Michael's.

In the main square in Cuzco I met a young lad of about eight years of age called Nino. He was a shoe cleaner, now normally I wouldn't get my shoes cleaned not because I'm a tight bastard but because I have a problem with kids cleaning shoes for people at such a young age, but in this case I told him to go ahead.

The care and attention he put into cleaning them was amazing. He carried a box about the size of a small dollhouse with him and it was full of little doors and presses. Every now and then, he would take out a little bottle of some potion or other and use it to clean off a blemish from the well broken in cross trainers. We ended up having the coolest of chats, which started with him saying to me "Do you like Snickers bars?"

I replied "yep but there not as nice as a Double Decker".

He said that he'd never heard of one so I described it to him in detail. I also said its best out of the fridge and served with a cup of tea, I said that I'd post one over to him. So it went for the next half an hour just chewing the cud about which type of chocolate bar was nicer and did they have this type of bar in Ireland, and did I prefer Mars to Milky way or Twix to Snickers.

The night before I left I met up with Sam again for a couple of beers in a local Irish bar. While we were there chatting we bumped into Vanessa from Belgium. She was touring South America on her own and she was a cracker. The other attractive thing about her was that she could nail a pint as quick as any guy.

We were in rounds and although she kept saying "just get me a glass" we kept getting her pints. She always was the first one to get near the end of the glass and look over with a look which said "Dudes! The tide is out, your twist".

We went back to a party in her hostel, I considered trying to slap the gob on her but decided against it, she was too hot, and too nice; I'd only end up pining my way through Bolivia thinking about her, better to be on my own. Of course, it was much more likely that if I did try and slap the gob on her that she'd respond by giving me a good kick in the nuts.

It was time to leave Cuzco, and it was harder than you might think. The previous night it was Halloween and the Peruvians really go on the slaughter. The car park where I had my bike parked didn't open till nearly 10am having supposed to be open at seven which is when I showed up to collect it. The lad who was working there, when he showed up was so hungover looking I didn't even bother to moan at him, he was suffering enough.

Before I'd got to the car park I'd woke up and one of my Mossie bites had become inflamed, or at least I thought it was a mossie bite and that maybe I'd scratched it during the night. Some people really flare up if they get a bite, I normally don't so I used the time I was waiting for the car park to open to pop down to the surgery off the square, and get them to have a look at it.

The attendant looked at the bite and started making a weird face, the sort of face you make when you think one of the lettuce leaves in your dinner salad just moved all by its lonesome. He took the arm under one of those magnifying glass platforms and then started a round of shaking his head with lots of tsk tsk tsk'ing.

Next thing I knew he had gotten a needle then popped the lump and sucked out the gunge. Then he said a word, a word which turned my face green in 1 second flat "blah blah blah Huevos". Fucking eggs, I nearly turned inside out.

There was an American guy there who spoke English and they were asking me was I trekking or camping in the desert? Some nasty beast had laid eggs into me so next thing the doctor got me to strip off, I hadn't had a shower so was cringing; the doctor did a full check from head to toe and there were no more around the place, thank Jaysus. "Unusual" was how he summed up.

I logged onto the Department of foreign affairs website to see if the roads had cleared to the south of Cuzco and it said the following:

Protesters are currently blocking the main road, near Sicuani, between Cuzco and Arequipa. Travellers should avoid this route. In recent weeks several political and labour-related strikes have been occurring across the country. These demonstrations may lead to violent outbreaks at any time, especially in the departments of Apurímac, Ayacucho, Arequipa, Cuzco, Huancavelica, Huanuco, Junin, Lambayeque, Piura, Puno and San Martín. The armed forces and the national police were recently deployed nationwide in an effort to control civil unrest. Roadblocks may occur on main roads and cause traffic disruptions. Irish citizens should not attempt to cross blockades, even if they appear unattended. Curfews may also be in effect and airports may be closed in response to further unrest.

If I did manage to get through the protests in Southern Peru it said the following of Bolivia:

Currently the situation within the country is very tense and there is potential for social unrest, particularly in the eastern provinces. It is possible that flights to these areas may be cancelled. It is recommended that travellers exercise caution and monitor the media for developments. We are advising against travel to Tarija and Santa Cruz regions for the present. There is also the risk of violent protests in Pando and Beni regions

Fuck em! I went anyway.

I set out with a bit of a knot in the stomach, I'd met a lot of people there and it was time for goodbyes again, but the road cured my mood of any doldrums very quickly. The initial part of the journey followed the course of a river through green valley's hemmed in by massive brown mountains. Slowly but surely the roads started to climb and I was back onto another section of Altiplano.

I've never felt as at home in any landscape in my life. For me this was a mirror image of Rohan in the Lord of the Rings and instead of riding a horse it was me and Sam Gamgee the bike.

I like an old ruin as much as the next guy but it just raises a couple of hmmmmsss's, interesting's, really's and ok's, for me anyway. Whereas natural beauty is what I really love. It was like my feel good meter was absolutely maxed out. The only thing that could have made it better would be watching Liverpool win the European cup while getting fed marshmallows by a nude Brittney spears.

By the time I got to the blockaded area, the road was clear bar a lot of rubble, but you could tell things had got nasty as the area was heaving with police. I continued down the road and got to Puno, the last town I would visit in Peru. I went out for dinner in a lovely restaurant on the square and just above the church you could see the moon and a very bright star, it was all very romantic but it was just me and Sam; Man I needed a woman.

The tour bus collected me at the hotel at 6am to head to Lake Titicaca. To be honest I wasn't really expecting much, a big lake at high altitude with some people living on funny islands, not really my bag but you can't come to this part of the world without doing it, and so off I went.

The trip started bad, the boat that was taking us stunk of a mixture of crap and diesel fumes so there was a scramble to get up top. They only let ten up there at a time so with ten hours to go on the trip the atmosphere on the boat was going downhill quick.

Early on in the trip before everyone was either barfing from the smell of crap or unconscious from diesel fumes; we pulled into one of the reed islands. The islands are built on the roots of these reeds that float like corks. They then pile lots of reeds and stuff over it; it's squishy to walk on and it was all very different from anything I'd encountered so far. The initial part felt unbelievably touristy as the family on the island sang a couple of songs, so a bit naff, but cool at the same time.

As it went on it got a lot better. Apparently the people who live there suffer terribly with rheumatism and after the age of fifty most can't walk. You can't help but notice that the people's faces are etched with hard work; all have unbelievably deep wrinkles on their faces with most people very bent over. They took us out on a reed boats which was paddled by only one guy, carrying twenty tourists, he still managed to keep up a good gallop.

We then went to an island where with the altitude was over 4000m above sea level; I was out of breath just tying my shoe laces. The island was touristy as hell but nice at the same time. We had a trout lunch and the locals put on a couple of dances and stuff, it's the sort of place you'd bring visiting aunties and uncles really. As the air is so thin you can see for miles and the sun is unbelievably strong, and because of that the lake is unbelievably blue.

On the way back the sun was setting through a storm, I felt so calm I could have given Buddha a run for his money. I went out for dinner in the square and ended up talking to a girl from Russia who was travelling as well. Her English was about as good as my Russian so the conversation was mainly taken up with polite nodding.

I thought to myself which nationality of women have a penchant for hairy arsed Irish bikers out on a world trip with a beard that Jesus would be proud of? The answer was no more apparent than on any of the previous 114 days of the trip through 25,000 miles.

The next day I was going to Boliva.

Chapter 12
Bolivia and Chile

Have you ever had a near miss in a car? Most people have and it's enough to keep them talking for about a week afterwards, "oh you just wouldn't believe it, I really thought I was a gonner". I can see a caring partner sitting beside you with the arm around the shoulder saying something comforting like "Oh you've had a lucky escape, really makes you think about how lucky you are to be alive". Then you'd reply "Oh your right, now make me a cup of tea and get me a couple of chocolate biscuits, I've had a hard day".

Well, driving in second and third world countries you end up having as many as four or five of these moments a day, eventually you just stop thinking about them, you expect them and if they don't happen it almost seems like the day was a bit of a bore. It must be the same thing that kicks in for adrenaline junkies; when they feel the need to get into increasingly dangerous situations.

I left Puno and drove towards the border keeping Lake Titicaca on my left side as I circled round for the town of Copacabana in Bolivia. All morning I was spoilt with views of the lake and a mixture of Altiplano with distant snow-capped peaks.

Along the road, old Indian women tended small flocks of cattle and sheep. The main reason for this is that no one appears to own the land by the side of the road, so it's free to pasture. All they do is drive the cattle up and down the roadside and it struck me how simple a life it was. I didn't see any guys doing any work; in fact it seemed that the vast majority of labour in these countries was carried out by women.

As I drove along an old man who was walking along the road was throwing lots of bricks and stones out onto the tarmac and I happened to be driving by him as he threw out another causing me to swerve while uttering "What the fuck was his problem?"

Further along the road just in front of me a truck just went straight off the road for some reason, it didn't hit anything, and I guessed the driver fell asleep. The incident seem to happen in slow motion, I could see the truck on down the road about half a mile in the distance, then there was a shattering of glass and then the truck went off the road, I can't tell you how many times I said "Holy fuck" in that couple of minutes, but it was enough to send me straight to hell.

Bolivia

The last couple of days were some of the best of the trip and I even found time to meet some lovely Peruvians. I have to say overall it's a great country, and I really enjoyed it. I hit the Bolivian border at what I thought was 11am, plenty of time to get the whole importing the bike routine done before the lads go on lunch but forgot about the time difference, once you cross the border you lose an hour. In fairness the customs guy was great and got me through; in fact the whole border routine took less than half an hour. The whole thing put me in great form about Bolivia, I found myself saying "What a great country! I love it!"

Soon after the border I got to Copacabana, a town on Lake Titicaca and a really nice place. The Virgin Mary appeared there and it's been a place of pilgrimage since. There's a really cool tunnel where you go in and light a candle and graffiti the wall with candle wax. At the end of the tunnel is a statue of Mary and given the tunnel is only lit with candle light and you're surrounded with candle graffiti it's pretty eerie. Somehow writing "Oisin was here" just didn't seem appropriate.

That night I had a dose of the "itchies" in bed. I got up and turned on the light to figure out what the fuck was going on. The bed had about two hundred ants rummaging around in it. The only thing to try and get rid of the little blaggard's was to get some damp soap so as you give them a smack, they stick to it. After about two hours I thought I'd got them all, maybe I did but spent the night scratching either way. The next morning I went in for a shower and it was an alleluia moment; the water was not only hot but was high pressure, I must have washed my balls twenty times to celebrate. (Ball washing isn't masturbation, I think)

My second day in Bolivia turned out to be one of the toughest of the trip. I crashed the bike four times and ended up in hospital again. It was like someone upstairs said "Yer man has been having too much of a good time, let's throw him a couple of kicks in the bollix and see if we can rise any Craic out of him"

I left Copacabana early, I knew it was a short run to La Paz and I wanted to get there early and do a bit of sightseeing. As I was leaving the town I was "clothes lined" by a police chain. I saw the check point but normally they just wave you through. It was cloudy and I was wearing sun glasses and as I hit the check point the chain hit the wind shield, then popped off it and lamped the shit out of my chest throwing me off the bike. I wasn't going too fast but it hurt like a mother!

I did my usual systems check, wriggle toes, ok, wriggle fingers, ok, put hand on Mickey, I can feel it. I got up and felt like someone had dropped a cavity block on my chest. Sam Gamgee was fine as usual despite falling over on its side about eight yards down the road. After catching my breath and agreeing to go "Mas Despacio", I set off none the worse for wear, but there would be no cuddling of any women tonight, no change there so.

The road continued to hug Lake Titicaca and I couldn't help thinking the whole place has a magical quality. When I first saw it, I wasn't overly impressed but the blueness of the water and how it sparkles in the sunshine starts to grow in your mind the more you look at it. The second big surprise of the day was that to get to La Paz you had to take a ferry. The ferries are tiny and don't look in the slightest bit lake worthy. The floor of the ferry was missing lots of timber, so much so you could see the lake water and to top it all off, the only way off the ferry is to reverse and there was no metal plate to act as a ramp to the shore. Luckily, there was a heap of Finnish bikers on the other side so they gave me a hand getting the bike off.

On the way to La Paz, you get back into the Altiplano and in the distance; you can see massive white capped mountains. The city however, is a massive ugly sprawl, with only one main thorough fare, which on the plus side makes it difficult to get lost. The city reeks of car fumes and is wedged with people so I just kept the hammer down and burned right through it, heading for the next biggish town called Oruro, on the way passing a statue of Che Guevara.

On the way from La Paz to Oruro, every single gas station was out of gasoline, and I do mean every one. I didn't know the reason why but I tried at least ten of them over a hundred-mile distance with no joy. All along the highway there were cars parked up which had run out of gas. The implications to my trip were huge, if I couldn't get gas I risked being stranded or at best I'd have to cut across to the Chilean border and miss out on the salt flats in Uyuni. As it turned out there was a strike which was going to last the next four days, you could only get gas in major cities and towns, not a disaster but meant that I'd have to plan my miles carefully through the country.

I eventually got to Oruro on a mixture of prayers and fumes and filled her up until there was petrol flowing out the overflow tube, I was pretty sure I'd need ever millilitre. It was still early so I had another idea that I wish I could take back "Sure fuck it Ois, its only 320km to Uyuni, let's go!" Uyuni is famous for its massive salt lake and it was the main reason I came to Bolivia.

Uyuni

Either I took a wrong turn or this Bolivian bollix gave me the wrong directions but I ended up in the middle of nowhere. The road ended, which wasn't initially a concern because it had been crap before and had turned to autopista before too long, so I was ok with struggling on.

After forty miles of sandy gravelly shite, the road turned to just sandy shite, and I can't ride an 1150 on that much sand. At times, it was so deep I had to strip the bike of all the gear and panniers just to make any progress. Three times I fell off the bike, each time hurting a different part of my body.

The first time I was doing about 30mph and the front wheel just washed out, the bike just went straight over on its left side on top of me. My left wrist was the only area that took any impact but I was sure it wasn't broken. It took a massive effort to get the bike back up off the ground; one more time having to completely strip it before lifting it.

The bigger problem came because of where I'd fallen; there was nowhere to stand the bike as the whole area was deep sand. Eventually I just rode the bike over to some scrub about thirty yards away and then carried the gear over to the bike and then rode on again. It's worth bearing in mind that all of this was done at serious altitude so any effort at all and it feels like your lungs are bursting.

The second time I fell, I hit a deep patch of sand and the bike just slid out from under me. This time it was straight down on my left hip. I took about ten minutes to get myself back up off the ground and then began to start to strip the bike again, find a hard patch of ground to stand the bike up in and they carry all the gear over to the bike and start all over.

I was in a bad place mentally at this stage and was really starting to descend into a terrible mood. I was completely and utterly lost. I had no idea where the road was supposed to be but was certain that I was in the wrong place. I was too far out. I had a choice to either go on or go back. The choice was seventy miles of shite to go back, and then a further sixty miles to go back to Oruro, or hope that the track turned to road further on. I had only about 200ml of water left so said to myself, "better the devil you know, turn around." The thought of having to refight a battle I'd lost was a crushing blow.

Just then, I saw a truck in the distance. I went cross country over the desert to see if he was on a road and could see that one was in construction about a half mile off. I managed to keep the bike up and got to the edge of the road without crashing again.

As I tried to go up the bank of the road to get onto the gravel the whole bike went into a wheelie and threw me off the back of it, the bike then proceeded to slide down the bank clobbering the leg I'd already hurt in Mexico. I lay there in the blackest mood of all time fucking the whole of Bolivia out of it. The gravel was too soft and too thick; I couldn't get the bike up onto the road and was killing myself trying, and burning the back tyre in the gravel to try and get some traction.

By this stage I had stripped the bike and taken off the panniers; I'd done everything and I just couldn't get it up onto the gravel. I was starting to panic. No one used this road, and anyone who might do would not have any gas in their cars because of the strike. I was seventy miles from a town which I only thought I knew the direction of, I was completely out of water and for the first time on the trip I genuinely thought "this is it, you are fucked."

I sat down on the side of the road; sore all over, dying of the thirst as the sun was setting behind me. I told myself "you´ve 2 choices, walk towards the town and hope you meet someone on the road, get some water and get some help to get the bike out" I really didn't like the sound of it, because it gets dark in a heartbeat here, in all likelihood I'd end up just walking aimlessly in the dark, or "try again to get the bike out".

Then I really started to give myself a hard time...."why the fuck can't you get the bike out of there?" "It's fully stripped, so it's a 250kg weight, why can't you drag it up onto the gravel?" When I was younger, I once dead lifted 220kg, so I used this as the spur to tell myself that it was possible to get the bike out of the hole. I allowed myself to go completely berserk with the bike and slowly but surely, dragging and pulling for all I was worth I got the bike up onto the gravel surface. I nearly collapsed panting for air, I was sure my lungs were going to explode and I spent about ten minutes just sitting on the ground trying to catch my breath.

I loaded up the bike, jumped back on and rode like a man possessed through the gravel and finally back up onto the autopista to get back to Oruro. As I drove up the road, and I guess as the adrenaline wore off, the parts of my body which had been clobbered gradually got sorer and sorer. By the time I was thirty miles from Oruro I could no long change the gear on the bike, both because my left wrist was so sore, and my left ankle was fucked. I booked into a hotel and the guy at reception looked at me like I was a ghost and I caught a glimpse of myself in the mirror, I was destroyed with sand, with my face caked in a mixture of sand and sweat. My lips were so chapped and burnt from the sun that it looked like someone had stuck green cornflakes all over them.

The guy helped me up the stairs to the room and I went in for a shower; my body was fucked. I felt my back and I'd a lump where I shouldn't have had one so I said fuck it, I need to go to a doctor. The guy in the hotel drove me to the emergency area in the local hospital where they told me to come back tomorrow after strapping up my wrist, there was me making sure I had a clean pair of underpants on me before I left; what a waste.

Things didn't improve the next day either.

I went to the hospital and things checked out ok. The only thing that was bothering me was my chest, so I said "fuck it, get back on the road."

I looked at the map and tried to figure out what was the best way to get to Uyuni from where I was without having to double back on myself again. I could get within a hundred and twenty miles of Uyuni if I went back to the route I tried yesterday before I hit sand.

Looking at the map I judged that if I headed southeast to Potosi, the highest city in the world, at over 4000m, that I could then head south west to Uyuni on what looked like road on the map. It was two hundred miles away so I hit the bricks. The road to Potosi was very much like the Grand Canyon, everything was orange, with vast canyons but the difference is the road is cutting a path through the Andean Altiplano so it's got a more "in the middle of nowhere" feel to it.

With the gas shortages there was hardly a soul on the road so you could throw yourself into the bends and take up both lanes, at times I was really putting the bike through its paces and loving every minute of it. I think it was God's way of giving me a break after the torment of the previous day.

When I got to Potosi my first task was to find out about the road to Uyuni. The total distance was about a hundred and sixty miles, which was less than a tank of gas which took away the risk of running out of petrol. But here comes the doozy, it's not paved, none of it! I think the taxi driver who was explaining it to me thought I was going to kill him "What the fuck are you talking about, not fucking paved, you fuckin kidding me, for fucks sake!" (Only Robert de Nero can get more fucks into a sentence than that!)

So the net result of that days two hundred miles was to move me over thirty miles further away in "sand road miles" from the target, yesterday I was a hundred and twenty five miles away, now I was a hundred and fifty five.

I said the word fuck for every atom in the Universe over the course of the next couple of hours. After I'd finished cursing I sat down and thought it through. I totally stripped the bike and went through my gear with a rapier "Do I need it today why do I think I'll need it tomorrow" the whole goal was to drop the weight on the bike by a huge total. I knew I could expect to be picking it all up off the sand a lot the following day.

Why was I so stressed?

Riding on sand is a huge mind fuck because if you go slowly you definitely come off, but if you go fast and you come off you'll injure yourself so in your mind you're trading that all the time. Instinct says slow, what you know says go fast; that sweet spot in the middle is managed by your nervous energy.

If I was to make it, I promised myself that tomorrow evening I was going to have a three course meal, all deserts and woe to the restaurant that didn't have a nice desert when the conquering hero darkens the door.

All joking aside I was very afraid and I was certain that I'd bitten off more than I could chew. I really didn't know what to expect but as Sam Gamgee's gaffer used to say "it's the job that's not started is always the hardest." I needed some inspiration to get me through what would no doubt be the biggest physical test of my life so far. (Apart from the time I won a bet to drink 12 500ml cans of fosters in an hour, the last 2 cans were being recycled from my nose to the can as I finished them)

I left Potosi around 7am with about a hundred and fifty five miles of "who knows what!" ahead of me. The one thing I knew for certain, there wasn't a millimetre of asphalt along the way, the road would be terrible and I was pushing myself well beyond my limits.

As I was getting ready, I prepared my gear with great care. I took extra special attention to the boots, taking time to really fasten the buckles and pull all the straps as tight as was comfortable. I put each ankle into an ankle strap which I had from the accident in Mexico. I tied each wrist up tight in Buffs, double buffed my neck and zipped the suit jacket top and bottoms together so if I slid the jacket wouldn't slide up my back or if going the other way so my trousers didn't slide off and destroy my pristine arse, already the proud bearer of mucho blisters. I was ready and roasting hot.

I just had to find the road to Uyuni, sounds easy eh? Me hole. The Bolivians are a very polite bunch and tend to give you the answer they think you want to hear so when you say in Spanish "Excuse me... is Uyuni this way?" You´ll nearly always get a yes. So every two hundred meters you double check with the next person you meet on the road so you don't trek off into the middle of nowhere.

I stopped for a heap of water on the outskirts of town knowing today I'd need it and asked for the last time "Is this the road Uyuni?", to which the woman replied "No the bridge is bad" you need to take a diversion and meet the road a couple of miles out the road, so off I set. (Obviously this all happened in Spanish with lots of hand waving and pointing)

The first mile of the road was in terrible condition, six to eight inches of sand everywhere. I just ploughed along in first gear with my two legs outstretched like stabilisers, and kept this up for about four miles. The road then started to climb into the mountains and thankfully the sand had for the most part been blown off the road so I was left negotiating a route through a gnarly rock and gravel landscape. Gravel and rock is infinitely more doable than sand so my wellbeing took a major shot in the arm straight away.

I started the countdown at 155 miles, and broke the journey up into six twenty five mile stretches allowing myself a break after every twenty five miles. With the first twenty five done, it had taken almost two hours and I knew it would be dark by the time I got to Uyuni if I kept this pace up. It probably goes without saying but there's one thing you don't want to do and that's drive on a terrible road after dark, so for the next twenty five miles I took a lot more risk keeping the hammer down; it only took me one hour.

The road alternated between deep sand, deep gravel, corrugated gravel, heavy riveting and bent and swept through red, brown and yellow mountains like a snake. I took over five hundred pictures of the scenery along the way. It was all just so out there, and so different to anywhere I'd ever been before. On many occasions the road was only a car width wide with sheer drops at your side, and with the surface as unpredictable as the Irish weather at times; it was at times terrifying.

With almost seventy five miles gone in four hours I hadn't fallen off and was starting to feel good. Coming over a hill, I met a bike going the other way driven by an Australian couple. I had only passed a couple of 4X4's all day and it was surreal to be out in the middle of the Bolivian desert having a chat with a guy from Australia. They had some great news for me; first of all it was only another seventy five miles to go, and second that the next fifty miles weren't too bad. The other thing that gave me heart was that there were two of them on the one bike, if they could do it with two on the bike and not come off, I should be fine, or at least that's what I reckoned.

I headed up the road brimming with confidence, and sure enough about five miles after leaving them I had my first spill of the day. I took the wrong line going round a bend and the front end of the bike swept out, as far as falls go it was a good one, I didn't hurt myself or damage Sam Gamgee. Sand was the culprit and for me at least, the word sand was quickly becoming a byword for all that was evil in the world.

To go through a road with sand on a bike is very hazardous, much more so than in a car. The critical differences are 1) A bike has only "1 wheel" drive; the back wheel does all the work, 2) the wheels are round at the road contact point so you've a lot less contact area with the road 3) If you hit the brakes at anytime other than when your perfectly straight up you'll come off. When you hit sand with a road tire, on a bend with a small contact area, made even smaller because you're leaning to turn, you're off the bike before you know it.

The biggest problem with my first spill was picking the bike up; it was facing the wrong way down a hill so I was foaming at the mouth from exertion trying to get it back upright.

Everyone always says "Practice makes perfect" or the other molten bronze droplet " You learn from your mistakes" but when you come off you don't learn till the next day, when you've had a bit of time to think about it. On the day that it happens in it just etches away your confidence. You start to look at every bend as having hidden peril and you start to vividly imagine that you back tyre is washing all around the place.

I set off again gingerly and after about another eighteen miles I came upon a construction zone. Over here there's absolutely no organisation to it, the work crews just drop heaps of shite on the road and flatten it. You can't drive on it till it's flattened because you just sink into the gunge.

There was a path up the side of the road where they were working and I burned off up this stretch. About halfway up there was a dip in the road full of really deep muck created by the work crews, as I went through it my front tire stuck deep and threw me over the handle bars. Out of pure instinct I had retracted my hands in time, as typically when this happens you catch your hands or fingers under the break or clutch and break the bones in your hands, "luckily" I was just thrown off and landed on the flat of my back after somersaulting through the air.

I was lying on the flat of my back on the ground looking up into the blue sky and went through the usual routine "wiggle wiggle" toes etc. I picked myself up of the ground and I've never been so winded, just standing not to mind breathing was done with huge difficulty. I looked at the bike perched in the muck like a stick in a toffee apple and said to myself "fuck this".

A work crew came along and gave me a hand getting the bike out of the mud. For the next fifteen miles or so it was on and off construction, the whole thing had become a complete and total nightmare. I had lots of little monologues with myself "you'd think the fuck heads would finish one part of the road before starting another!"

I was driving up the road like an oul one with piles and then as if a present from heaven the road straightened out and hardened up for about twelve miles or so.

After I was over nine hours on the road, with about twenty miles to go, I was doing about 40mph and again the bike washed out. As it was washing I pushed myself out of the saddle to avoid getting hit by the bike, but as myself and Sam Gamgee impacted on the road, the right pannier clobbered my right calf.

I was lying on the ground with the bike a mixture of beside me and on top of me at the point of despairing when my camera fell out of the side pocket of the tank bag and hit me right on the schnozz, the second time it happened on the trip. I just started roaring laughing and had a mini conversation with the man above "ah yeah as if I'm not bad enough! Throw the fuckin camera at my beak! Any kitchen sinks up there!!"

I couldn't get the bike up off the road, I was too tired and any time I tried, as it was sand on gravel, when I tried to push the bike up my feet just kept sliding. I just lay down at the side of the road; I said I'd wait till someone comes along. That plan was scuppered when I noticed petrol coming out the overflow line of the bike, the angle of the bike on the road was causing it to pour out onto the road. I didn't have any spare juice and not getting to Uyuni wasn't an option. So with the last piece of energy in my body and with a roar heard for many miles I pushed and pulled till the bike was back up. I was panting like a dog on a roasting day after a run, sore all over and overall just feeling like a bag of shit when I jumped back on the bike to tackle the last twenty five miles.

I was determined not to come off again, I couldn't take it. There was no way I could have lifted the bike again and I was certain that if I fell one more time that I'd do serious damage to myself.

Every mile felt like a week, the first fifteen miles of the twenty five took over an hour. When I was just five miles from Uyuni I came up what I judged would be the final mountain pass before my decent to the salt flats. I reached the summit of the mountain and looked down onto the most eerie sight I've ever seen. The town of Uyuni sat on the edge of a red lake, the salt lake looked like a red sea, and all through the red lake mountains appeared to be floating as the sun set in the distance.

I kicked down the side stand, got off the bike, took off the helmet and gloves and walked over the mountain edge, and while looking out onto the vast valley, with the road I'd just driven behind me roared at the top of my voice with a mixture of joy, relief, and above all exhaustion:

"WHO'S YOUR DADDY!!!!!?" "HUH" "WHO'S YOUR FUCKIN DADDY!!!!!?"

As I drove into the town the noise of millions of plastic bags rustling in the wind all caught up in rocks and various desert plants was the first thing that struck me; there was rubbish everywhere.

The town exists to bring tourists out onto the salt flats and that's it. The whole place feels like it just shouldn't be there, it's a horrible place really. People arrive, go on the tours and leave, the last time I got a feeling like this place gives off; I was signing on for social welfare! When the lake went, this town should have gone also.

The next day I decided to go out on the salt flats by myself, another in a long line of bad decisions. Unlike the salt flats in Utah which have layer upon layer of compacted salt built up, this lake has only about 3 or 4 inches and in the wet season it actually gets a bit of rain. I drove out and got stuck out in the middle of nowhere with the bike having gone through the salt into the mud. It took me three hours to go one mile, constantly having to push the bike over onto its side, lift it back up and then try and start again, whereupon I'd get about twenty metres before I was stuck again.

After about four hours struggling I stripped the bike fully down(again), and walked it out of the muck and shite for about a mile then had to walk back to get my gear, then obviously walk back to the bike again. All told I'd walked about three miles at altitude in motorcycle boots and an enduro suit, across pure muck. Then I'd have to load up the bike again. I gave up, totally knackered I headed back to town to see if I could catch one of the organised tours; they were all gone.

I keep a bag of "I told you so" just for myself "I told you it was a bad idea to go south in Bolivia","I told you to go on a tour and not go by yourself into the salt","I told you not to use carbolic soap to wash yourself" and worst of all "I told you she'd say no if you asked her out for a dance!"

In the end I just arsed around Uyuni, which is pretty much all there is to do in the town and got ready for the run to Chile. The run from Uyuni is one hundred and sixty five miles to the border with Chile and it's all unpaved. In my mind it couldn't be worse than the day before, as it turned out I was only marginally right.

Ollangue

The next day followed the previous day's trend, incredible rocky desert and brutal roads but that day I stayed upright. A new vector to deal with in tandem with the sand and gravel arrived in the shape of savage wind. It kept blowing sand in my face; even with the visor down it was coming up under the helmet at a savage rate. The stickler came when I had to lean the bike into the wind and also try and maintain as much of the tyre on the ground as possible, all day I battled to keep the bike out of the ditch.

On gravel roads there is typically only one or two good lines through, normally the track made by a big truck so if your pushed out of your line which is easy with bad wind the chances of you coming off, go up exponentially. At either side of your line is a build-up of gravel and sand; depending on the traffic and wind it can vary greatly in height. If you have to cross out of your good line you have two choices, either be going like the hammers of hell in which case you just blow through it, or slow down to a crawl and just bump through it.

All day I drove in constant fear that by leaning into the wind to keep your direction straight that I wouldn't have enough thread on the road and I'd just slide off.

Having started at 7am I arrived at the Bolivia Chile border at 6:49pm. The Bolivian side of the house was crazy. You have to first stamp your exit out of the country as normal, but have to climb through trains and walk across three train lines to get to the office. From there you have to go back across the trains and the train tracks to another office to complete the paperwork.

From there it's up to the "efficient" Chile side. I was knocking on the window to try and stamp into the country. I pushed in a door and said "Hola, Buenos Tardez" (hello good evening) to which I head a huge chorus of banging of knives and forks off plates as if to say: "Fuck off and wait, Were having a bit of grub."

After a bit of a wait I was through and was in the town of Ollangue, a town without a gas station and one of the most windswept and godforsaken places on earth. I'd about sixty miles of gas in the tank, and it was about a hundred and sixty miles to the nearest gas station, so I was stranded. Even If I did get gas it was almost another one hundred and sixty miles of unpaved road to a town called Calama in Chile which is when the asphalt would also start again.

That night I stayed in a hotel in the town which was as humble a lodging as I've stayed in. I had a bed and a door between me and the night which was the main thing. I went to the dining room for a bit of grub, and asked what they had; the reply was comida de la casa (food of the house) which turned out to be a shin of mutton and rice (think of a sheep, now look at one of its legs, more meat on a budgies wing!)

I had first tried the one and only hostel in the town which had two bunk beds in the dorm where everyone slept. When I walked into the room there were three dudes all lying on their beds with hefty bellies and bald heads with their shirts off. It all seemed very "midnight express" so I fucked off to the hotel, I didn't fancy having an eight ball strapped in my mouth that night.

The hotel lost electricity at around 9pm and didn't come back before I left, but not a bother on anyone in the place. Cooking still went on over the open heart, and it seemed like it was a daily occurrence

The plan the next morning was to try and bum some gas, maybe go down to the customs station or see if anyone passing had some. I'd work to do; it was time to make myself a sign.

I solved the no gas problem pretty early in the day; I just kept knocking on doors in the town and eventually found someone with some. I went around the back of these two old ladies house and there it was; a big fifty gallon drum of Texaco. I bought three gallons off them at war time prices but was delighted to be back on the road so I wasn't complaining. I must have asked them five times "Gasoline Si?" to which they always replied "Si" If it wasn't; this was going to be a short trip.

I was determined to conquer my fear of the sand, so I just kept remembering all the things I knew about how to drive in it and kept repeating it back to myself as I was driving along. One of the most important things to do is to stay loose in your arms and let the bike sway underneath you. Now the feeling of a bike swaying under you is enough to send the heart beating up into the 200+ range but you have to get over it. So stay loose and here's the rhyme I told myself...

Stay Loosey Goosey...Loosey Goosey...

Look at Hughsey staying Loosey Goosey

Up in Canada drove 10000 miles saw only 1 Moosie

Loosey Goosey....Loosey Goosey

The whole trip havent met one Flusie

Loosey Goosey .... Loosey Goosey

Very naff I know, but it worked and I just repeated it over and over for hours on end; a number one its unlikely to be, but it's all about staying in the zone and keeping yourself there, it worked a treat.

The last eighty miles of sand were the worst because the wind picked up where instead of just doing the loosey goosey routine I just kept saying "Fuck off wind, fuck off wind, fuck off wind". After over six hundred miles of gravel and sand, the asphalt was back, the most gorgeous, beautiful and sexy substance in the whole world. And when it came, if you had offered me a steam room with a nude Brittney Spears in it with Sharon stone on the way over with a tub of Ben and Gerry's ice cream, rum and raisin flavour, I would have taken the asphalt.

Once I got to Calama it was a short run to San Pedro de Atacama, through part of the Atacama Desert. I was going to hold up there for a couple of days to recharge my batteries. The town is an oasis in the desert and has the feel of a town on another planet.

The road descends to the town from the mountains and Altiplano and the scenery as you descend is like riding on Mars, which is how almost everyone who's been there describes it. The town itself is a little white washed village stuck in the middle of mountains and valleys of orange and yellow rock. It was the first time I noticed the difference in price, everything just hiked up incredibly. For example it's about five times as expensive in Chile for a room, for comparable places than Bolivia.

On top of that, because you've dropped from high altitude the heat is brutal. The following day I got up at the crack of dawn to head out to the Valley of the Moon near San Pedro. It's so hot here that if you don't go early, you'll boil alive.

No sooner had I finished with the fantasy of black asphalt, I was off-road knee deep in more sand and gravel. This was slightly different though, it was like a day trip, which was fun. The difference for me was that when you don't absolutely have to get through it; if you don't like it you can just turn back and head into the town and have a cup of coffee (and a bun)

The only trouble I had was that the back wheel got trapped in deep sand (again) and had to tilt it out and pull it to good ground (twice), but given it was a day trip I'd no luggage so it was much easier to deal with. After beating around the desert and the valley of the moon I went out for some grub.

I met two Irish girls who were joined by another; Laura, Orla and Sarah. They were all about twenty six and all off dossing around South America for six months. I hadn't talked with anyone really since Cuzco and the conversation felt awkward at first, I think conversation is an art that you need to practice, I think maybe you forget how to do it.

In the end we'd a good oul laugh, nothing like a few pints to get the chins wagging. In a bar later a guy gave me Cocaine for me and the girls, which I gave back to him. I'm sure the average Chilean living in San Pedro handing out free cocaine is an alright sort but I decided not to take any chances.

For the last three nights I'd been having a recurring nightmare about the desert. Every time it was the same: I crash the bike and break a bone and am stuck out there and I always wake up with a jump and in a sweat and it's hard to get back to sleep. In my reckoning the cause of it was that I was terrible on the sand and used to get myself all worked up about it, the only way to cure the dream was, yep you guessed it to go back out onto the sand.

I went about forty miles outside of San Pedro where I spotted a track through the desert, and I said to myself "Ok, time to conquer your fear." There's no point in having one of these recurring dreams back in Ireland, it'll be too far to go the desert, so fix it now."

I´d really no clue how I was going to do it but I found the track and just said to myself "ok Oisin, just keep riding till you fall off."

The whole time I stood on the pegs and did my whole "Lucy goosey" routine and just let the bike move around under me. I kept driving and driving and when an hour had passed, I´d rode about forty miles and then I stopped. "Ok, not bad, a full hour out in the desert and you didn't come off! Nice one". For the way back I just used a slightly different line and again made it the whole way back to the road without coming off, I wondered whether or not I was cured.

I'm asked a lot if this sort of journey is lonely or if being in these sorts of locations is lonely and I always give the same answer. If you are in the middle of the desert on your own, you feel completely and utterly alone but surprisingly not lonely. I think it's because you don't expect anyone to be there. However if you're in a city and maybe go to a restaurant, then you do feel lonely. It's no different than when I used to go on business trips, there's nothing worse than being in a strange country sitting down to a bit of grub with no one to talk to especially because all around you are people with their partners and family.

Mejillones

I left the desert and headed south for a town called Mejillones on the coast. On the way, I passed the Tropic of Capricorn, for the second time in my life. I passed the Tropic of Capricorn previously in Australia; somehow, I felt a whole lot "lower" in the world when I was in Australia than I did in Chile. When I think of Australia I think of "down under" but here I was, at the same point, it didn't seem that long ago that I passed the equator. After taking some time to digest the moment, I felt very far away from home and I really felt that the journey was starting to come to an end.

I got to Mejillones and thought it was a dump. However, I just wanted to get a room and go for a kip, the hangover from being out with the three Irish girls the night before exacerbated by the dry desert air left my mouth feeling like an old sock.

Even though the town appeared to be empty of people, there were no hotel rooms. I drove further south to Antofagasta to find the same thing, no hotel rooms. I looked at the map and it meant a two hundred mile drive south to Tal Tal, a fishing town on the coast. The time was 5pm, and I was hungover as hell with 200 miles to go, I groaned loudly with an audible fuck as the carrier wave, and proceeded to burn south. Would there be somewhere to stay in Tal Tal?

The memory of driving through that terracotta desert as the sun was setting from a clear blue sky will stay with me forever. On my left side, the moon started to rise and I felt my senses bursting. Despite it getting dark I had to pull over to try and take it all in. I took over fifty pictures of just that location and when I look at them now I can feel the warm desert wind blowing in my face as I watched the moon rise over a distant hill. It was dark by the time I got to Tal Tal but the twenty decades of the rosary said in hope that there would be somewhere to stay there worked and by 9pm, I had found a place to stay.

I didn't bother with a shower, just popped on the jeans and a beaney cap and paced off out for some freshly caught fish. After over five hundred miles I thought I´d sleep like the dead, I didn't. I had the same dream about the desert where I crash and injure myself, so I made up my mind to head back to the desert for one last swing on the tail of the dog that bit me.

I stripped the bike completely, no panniers, no backpacks, no water, no extra weight, nothing but the bike and me. I left about three gallons of petrol in the tank, "keep her nice and light" was the motto and I burned off to the desert around midday. The plan was to keep it short and sweet and just burn around for a while.

At times it was like being in the Paris Dakar rally; except that I'm a fat bollix from Dublin, and I wasn't in Africa. You don't have to go very far to find desert as the Atacama dominates this part of northern Chile. I had no nerves and just burned around for an hour or two and went back to the hotel feeling sexy. If I was made of chocolate I'd have eaten myself, but I settled for a hand shandy.

I finished the day off eating seafood watching the sun setting in a restaurant right on the sea front "a few well earned comforts, the spoils of war" I told myself as I downed half a bottle of cold beer in one slug. I'd completed my first five hundred miles in Chile and it started to dawn on me that, something other than the prices was very different.

There's no cattle grazing at the side of the road, no potholes, or cars or trucks coming for me on the wrong side of the road, no one running red lights; everyone pretty much obeys the rules. When I went to the ATM there was no friendly security guard armed with an AK47 or a sawn off shotgun, I missed those guys!

There's no incessant beeping of horns in fact I was beginning to think my hearing was damaged because in an entire day there was not so much as the smallest beep. There are no plumes of blue smoke behind every truck and bus, and I didn't have to bribe any police officers in fact I hadn't even been stopped by one. There were no military checkpoints to drive through, no hidden ramps to smash your goolies into next week, no guessing and hoping for hot water in the shower, it was always hot. On the news the previous night, it didn't catalogue about a hundred murders and finally there were no beggars putting on mealy mouthed expressions to help you rid yourself of your loose change. I guess it's the "little" things that let you know your back in the first world.

Santiago

I pushed to within two hundred and fifty miles of Santiago to a place called San Lorenzo. I was supposed to try to go to the space observatory but it was as cloudy as hell so no joy. I had finally passed through the Atacama, the driest desert in the world, pretty much everything since Uyuni had been part of it and it had taken well over a week. As you drive south towards Santiago you come to a valley near San Lorenzo. It's one of the places where the Andes stops the moisture from heading north to the Atacama, and there is such a dense build-up of cloud overhead, it feels like you could put your hand up and grab a fistful.

For the first time Sam Gamgee was starting to suffer. I'd a small oil leak ever since I left Ecuador and it was becoming a big one, not really a surprise when you consider the bike had been down ten times so far on the trip. There would be a BMW dealer in Santiago so it was only a matter of nursing it home.

I arrived in Santiago after slicing through the Chilean countryside like a knife through butter in a hot dish. To be honest it was too easy, I never thought I'd miss the hardship. I know it sounds a bit mental but I relish the test; doing something because it's hard. If it's handy and I know I can do it I say "What's the point?"

The last three days had seen me cover almost twelve hundred miles without a moment's difficulty. There was however one massive barrier still to cross on the trip, The Ruta 40. This is renowned as one of the toughest roads in the world for two reasons, 1) it's mostly gravel and 2) the winds seldom drop below 40mph as they roar across the Argentinean plane. It would be the last big test of the trip but it was still a long way off.

I was up to 28750 miles and after almost five months on the road I thought that I had most travellers pigeon holed pretty well. There are four basic types of people who were out here travelling; Attackers, Midfielders, defenders and goal keepers, all have their sub categories but for now I'll just hit the big buckets. (C'mon I'd rode over 28,000 miles by this point indulge me!)

Attackers (First Hello'ers)

These people are first hello'ers. These are the people who no matter where they go at any time they always end up talking to someone. They have no problem walking up to complete strangers and just saying hello. They are normally the second child in a household and strive for attention. Everything about them is a talking point, a reason to ask them a question, a reason for them to run their gob. If anyone was ever to wear a necklace with the mickey bone of a Mouse hanging off it, it would be an attacker.

The people who attackers most love is midfielders, they quickly grow weary of other attackers as they can't get a word in edge ways with them. They can't stand to be on their own, and eat lots of salads. Most don't admit to owning a television "sure I'm too busy to be watching TV!", but all love porn. These people read books to learn things so they can talk about it, not for their own enjoyment. Everyone knows a first hello'er, and the most common sentence used when describing them by defenders is "yeah they're ok in small doses". Midfielders really like attackers.

Midfielders (Reciprocators)

These people always reciprocate what they are given, so if a first hello'er comes up to them they'll always give exactly what they get and more back in the conversation. If a Midfielder is pretty lonely they'll jump state and become a first hello'er, but risk coming across like a transsexual as they are behaving in an adapted way.

In their natural state a midfielder is pretty balanced and doesn't actually crave attention the way a first hello'er does, so will sit quietly in a restaurant no problem at all. Midfielders love attackers, it's how they are introduced to most of the people they know in the world in fact nearly every midfielder gets married to someone who was introduced to them by a first hello'er. If it wasn't for first hello'er most midfielders would be blind and hairy palmed from masturbation. A midfielder loves midfielders but would never meet any because they only reciprocate, first hello'ers move the world.

Defenders (Civil servants)

A defender is very close to their family, and if you're on a holiday with a defender they'll normally be the one crying because they miss home and their family, especially their mum. If you know a defender well, it's because you married their sister or you're friendly with their parents or their husband. They only accept people who are introduced with a common frame of reference. People often say of these people. "Yep they are a bit cold, but once you get to know them they are grand!"

You can see piles of defenders on holiday where about twenty people from the one family all go together. Shagging first cousins isn't deemed a bad thing by defenders. Defenders never do things which are their own idea. Everything is a debate with their kin. Normally a female defender has a really hot sister you'd like to give a good seeing to!

Goal Keepers (Snedges)

These are the enemies of the attackers. Goal keepers are the world's leeches. You always know a goal keeper because they latch onto someone, normally a defender who has a family attachment which they can be manipulated from. They end up being the person who comes on your trip who you end up saying to your friend about "what the fuck did you brink that dick with you for!"The person who they leeched to says "I know but I just couldn't leave them behind, she's my cousin!" You can always spot a goal keeper because around 4am they'll slink off to the bike shed and sniff bicycle saddles. (Snedger)

Moving between states....

A first hello'er is incapable of being in any other state than that of an attacker. Only massive trauma like the loss of a limb or their entire country sank to the bottom of the ocean can move a first hello'er to a midfielder, but in all likelihood it will just give them something else to talk about.

A midfielder as already mentioned can adjust to a first hello'er but will be sensitive to knock backs. They don't have the skills of a first hello'er e.g.: they don't have a neck like a jockey's bollix or really bad hearing. They can, when depressed or incessantly nagged to, by their partner, move down to a defender; people often say of them when in this state "Your man is grand when he's not with that witch he's married to!"

A defender is too busy talking to their family on the phone to ever move up or down a notch. Most nights they dream of going to be with their parents. A goal keeper can at times move to a defender status, but only when they've a really bad cold and can't smell the saddles. So there you go, and it only took 28,000 miles to figure it all out!

Final point how do you know if you're a Snedger? Well, do you have the saddle off a bicycle which you robbed beside you in the room? Yes? That's right Snedgie! You're it!

For the next two days have I did the whole Santiago thing. I met my cousin Eileen (if right now you're breaking into a round of c'mon Eileen by Dexy's Midnight Runners, might I suggest a brandy?) the previous morning and she took me round lots of good spots in the city.

So how come I have a cousin in Chile? Well my uncle Vincent met a Spanish lady here in 1973 and the rest is history. I never met my uncle Vincent, he died in 2003 and I had never met any of the Chilean branch of the Hughes household, so really the reason I came here in the first place was to say hello.

We went for a great sea food lunch to the central market in Santiago; in your mind's eye picture every manner of fish from mermaids to squid for sale and then being cooked in restaurants right in the centre of the market, with lots of lads walking around playing the guitar and singing, a great way to spend an afternoon!

We then went out to a place near Santiago on the coast called Valparaiso and met two friends of hers there who have an apartment with the most spectacular view of the bay you could possibly imagine. Eileen missed her calling, she should have been driving formula 1 cars, the one litre vroom vroom we drove out in seldom dropped below 100mph the whole way, and the rosary beads never left my fingers till we stopped.

We sat in the apartment talking till about midnight and outside the moon seemed to be larger than I've noticed before as it cast a yellow highway across the bay. The lights from the buildings arced around the bay to the right; the scene was definitely filed under "Top moon moment" apart from when yer one showed her bum in the film "Clash of the titans".

That evening I headed out and around Santiago and went to see James Bond and I got a total boner because it was set in Bolivia, Bond was in Bolivia, I was too, that makes me Bond, follow my logic?

On the way back to the hotel a guy walked up to me and introduced himself. This guy was about sixty I guess and was missing every second tooth, with the rest clinging on for dear life to dodgy looking gums. He had a Bee Gees hair do, except it was black and grey, and had a serious moustache. He wore a grey pin stripe suit (Oxfam vintage), with a blue tie, and a shirt which looked yellow, but no doubt had at one stage been white, and a pair of black shoes with more mileage on them than Sam Gamgee.

He walked straight up to me and said hello in a very gentlemanly way, I said hello back he smiled which is when I caught a glimpse of the choppers, or a mixture of his choppers and the dumbbell at the back of his throat through the gaps in his teeth. I thought to myself "weirdo". It's not that I attract them I don't think, I think it's that they just see a foreigner and walk straight up to them, most people are better at telling them to fuck off than me, I think.

Anyway, he said to me straight up, "you're from Ireland", blown away I said to him "well spotted"(You got that from a hello!) and then he said to me that I was an engineer (which I used to be). Then he said to me that he knew my face. I was quite taken aback, but not stunned it wasn't like he'd given me a slip with that night's lotto numbers yet.

He then went on to tell me that he was schizophrenic and that he was trying to get to a town called Antofagasta which is north of San Tiago and that he didn't have any money and could I give him the fare. He showed me his wrists as if to prove he was sick, both had huge amounts of scar tissue on them where it was obvious he'd tried many times to commit suicide.

Now this guy was a very gentle mannerly man, so I asked him why he needed to get to Antofagasta. He said that he would be admitted to a "unit" there, but that he had slept of the streets of Santiago for the last eight nights while he tried to get into a place in Santiago or beg for the fare back to Antofagasta.

I asked him how much he was looking for and he said 40,000 pesos, which is about $80. I told him "listen buddy, no chance I'm giving you that much money". He then said to me "its ok I understand", he shook my hand and went to say goodbye and then I asked him was he hungry?

He said he was so I told him to wait. I popped into burger king and got him a double whopper with Cheese meal and as I stood there tucking into one myself chatting to him, this old man dressed as Santa was playing a haunting tune on a tin whistle funnelled through a megaphone. I thought I was in a Roman Polanski movie.

I popped over and dropped the change from the burgers into his mug at which point he stopped playing and came over and started talking to me and Mr. Wilkinson sword. I offered him my fries, which he gratefully accepted. There I was chowing down on fast-food with quite probably the two craziest guys in Santiago, like I was saying, something mental happens every day.

I put Sam Gamgee into the BMW dealers to get his final service before taking on the Ruta 40, with the usual story; I told them anything that looks even close to marginal swop it out. There was no point skimping now and then being stuck out in the middle of Patagonia broken down for the want of a couple of hundred dollars.

As I was sitting on a park bench writing up some post cards a huge ruckus broke out behind me. I turned around to see a bunch of police on motorbikes swarming onto a guy and hand cuffing him. As they were leading him off he kept kicking out at some dude in a suit, although he was only wearing flip flops so was probably hurting himself more than the other dude.

That afternoon I found the best internet cafe ever. Why I hear you ask? Was it because it had new PC's with rip-roaring bandwidth, flat screen monitors, ergo keyboards, comfortable seats, air conditioning, nice aromatic plants sporadically placed around the building or just the right lighting?

No, it's none of these things! It's because it was built next door to a strip club and although I'm not one to visit such dens of iniquity, there was a window right beside my screen and every now and then women clad in nought but a G string would walk by waving.

Obviously I'd be reporting this to the police and the Catholic Church, after a couple of hours. I also thought it was a good time to reread every email I'd ever received. Someone needed to stand guard at this window lest a child walk by and be forever damaged by such wanton debauchery. The Chilean people could sleep safe in their bed knowing Oisin was manning the wall tonight and maybe for a good portion of the next day.

I spent the rest of the day walking around Santiago people watching. There is more VPL in San Tiago than there are arses. On my road where I grew up when I was young; a woman complained that the tinkers were robbing her knickers off the line. I now know these types of jocks to be called roll-ons, and I can testify that the entire "stolen or lost" roll-on underpants have all made it to Santiago where they are being sported by women between the ages of thirty and forty.

At least the Chilean army is sure to never run out of tents. When does a pair of knickers become a roll on?, when it takes three pegs to hang them up on the line. Now how would I know about this VPL if I wasn't staring? Well I was staring, and as we lone travellers of the lonely planes say, staring is caring!

Large portions of Santiago spend the whole day kissing, I never saw anything like it. I was going to get a t-shift which said "Get a room already!" It wouldn't have been so bad I guess If I wasn't on the biggest barren patch since Robinson Crusoe got left on the Island, I was dying for a bit of woman Friday.

Benny socialists had a couple of the parks and visitor attractions shut down with protests so there were limited enough places to go and see. I can just see Che Guevara now rolling in his grave "Nice one ya pack of bennies, you shut down parks! "Ze favourite hangout of ze capitalist dogs!...... NOT"

I was starting to get a bit lonely in Santiago. If you want to talk to people in cities there's a lot of mistrust knocking around with good reason I suppose. The only people you can be guaranteed a chinwag with, are fellow bikers, nothing like something in common or Irish people who are always up for a chat.

On top of that, I'd spent so much time on the road on my own and had talked to so few people that when I did meet someone, I was like a fire hydrant and didn't stop talking, so people ran to the hills pretty quickly. However, maybe I bring it on myself. It's not like when you go up talking to people that you pick out that mad bitch from Misery, no doubt that mob would talk and talk and talk.

It's always people who kind of look like you might have something in common with, fellow tourists, who if they're early into their travels are so full of urban legends about them having to be "so careful in South America or they'll have their kidneys cut out" that they get their skates on pretty quickly.

Similarly, many folks travel in their own groups with three or four pals and likewise aren't receptive to a fifth beetle. Woe is me! Fuck em, I'll be Yoko Ono and start telling them that the other one robbed her roll-on and sold it to a Chilean girl.

There it was, Hughes, once counted amongst the mightiest of conversationalists in Christendom reduced to chatting politics with Mr Fluffykins (my toy rabbit); I really wanted Sam Gamgee to get well soon and bare me to the wilds!

I went off to some vineyards. It was the usual story lots of tasting all the different types, no spitting back with the big fella and I ended up having about three bottles of wine. They offered a lunch and all the wine you can drink for thirty-five dollars and as always when you bring the big fella to a buffet, they made no money.

I'd beef for lunch and was drinking white wine with it. This French bollix says to me "white wine with meat?" I gulped the glass of wine down in one, turned, looked at him, and said "Wines wine, it's all the same oul shite". He looked at me like I was taking a piss on the Arc de triumph.

Sam Gamgee was returned none the worse for wear and Merrie and Pippen arrived from Ireland. They were two college buddies and were great friends so it was pretty much wall to wall gargle for a couple of day, flying is thirsty work apparently. The next day I headed out to Valparaiso again to meet the lads, who because they were on the first days of their holidays were simply mad to go sightseeing.

After kicking it for a day I said goodbye to Merrie and Pippen, we were meeting again in Chiloe. I trekked off south to a town called Chillan, about seven hours south of Valparaiso. There was no real reason for me to go there other than it was about half way between where I was and the island of Chiloe. The road is called the Ruta 5 and it carves a path through the Chilean wine growing region. In the distance, you can see the snow-capped Andes, not a bad way to spend an afternoon.

However it made for a pretty boring ride, the road was too easy, too straight, and too predictable and the only battle you have to fight is against falling asleep, I can hear you now "you can't keep that bollix happy, it's too hard, it's too easy, I wish someone would cut his throat in six places!"

Chiloe

I crossed the 30000-mile barrier just as I got to the ferry to the island of Chiloe. The first impression I got of Chiloe was "wow this could be Ireland". It was springtime there so the roads were awash with colour and a wonderful spring freshness was in the air, it was a real tonic. The place was full of "mad as fuck" dogs, easy to get the impression that no dog on the island has ever seen a motorbike; every single one went Hezbollah as I passed them.

The bikes oil leak was back, BMW in Santiago just succeeded in moving the leak, and making it worse. When I looked down at my boots and pants they were covered in oil. I pulled over and started checking where the leak was coming from and how bad it was. All told I reckoned I was losing about a litre of oil for every six hundred miles, so not a disaster yet but there were definitely clouds on the horizon.

In Chiloe, it rains a lot, "so what" I hear you say? It rains everywhere." Well in Chiloe it really really really rains a lot, and that's three really's.

This place took rain to all new levels, it comes down in sheets, and it was as if an elephant was pissing right into your face at times. However the locals are used to it and no one seems to mind. Outside the hostel window that night, there were people outside talking until 4am, and it pissed rain the whole time, they weren't even bothering to shelter. No doubt, whiskey played some small role.

I hooked back up with Merrie and Pippen and we headed off on a mixture of sightseeing and hiking, which chiefly involved being involved in a human experiment for how much rain water can you take getting fired at you before you turn into a fish. The lads were mad to do stuff which suited me grand and we'd a good chat about whether or not doing nothing counts as doing something from a holiday perspective, know what I mean?

At this stage hiking up a Volcano for sixteen hours was about as appealing as a couple of hours in the scratcher with a skunk so I left the lads off and had a late morning.

At breakfast I talked to a nice American couple who told me to make sure to go to the penguin colony, Merrie and Pippen were taking the bus to Puerto Varas so wouldn't be able to see it, but me and Sam Gamgee with no such constraints decided to head off in search of the wee cuties.

The road takes you north and then west looping around the north end of the island. This part of the world is battered by the pacific and looked just like the west coast of Ireland with the notable difference that today it was sunny. Once you get about twenty miles west of Ancud, the most northerly town in Chiloe the asphalt stops abruptly and it was back to gravel, muck and shite but I'd had a good break from it so I was lapping it up.

Along the way there were plenty of cows (4 legged ones) and general farm animals and I asked a couple of farmers for directions to the penguin colony, let's just say there was much pumping of the right hand in the direction of where I was going "Guess it's this way huh?"

Every time I'd come to what looked like a beach I'd get off the bike and go for a quick walk in search of the elusive colony. I wondered if it was not that big or maybe it had moved. I stood there listening half expecting to hear the sound of millions of the little fellas roaring for nose bag, but nope, all that was to heard was the sound of the waves.

I gave up and headed off the Island in the direction of Puerta Varas. On the ferry I had my photo taken with about twenty kids who were on a school tour. They all wanted to get on the bike and put on the helmet which I hadn't washed the inside of for five months, no doubt their mothers would be delousing their heads when they got home.

I got to Puerto Varas, which is an old German Colony built on a gorgeous lake, and right at the end of the lake sit two Volcanoes. We were now officially in Patagonia and whatever you've heard, its better. Snow-capped peaks, gorgeous blue lakes, wonderful plant life; it's hard to imagine any place nicer.

We hired a car and headed off exploring the Volcanoes. When you head to an area that has had "recent" volcanic activity, it's a strange experience. First, you can see where the activity just cleaved a path through the mountains and the vegetation. It's like someone just spilled a bucket of light black paint on the landscape. Little by little, you can see where plants are starting to grow again. It starts with lichen turning the mountainside red, and then weeds can get a foothold and from there the trees come back. It's magic to be able to see all the phases of recovery happening at the same time in different parts of the mountain.

We hiked up several hills and kept working our way up the mountain. The view above kept changing as the wind either blew new clouds in, or the ones that were there away. It was like the top of the mountain was playing hide and seek, one minute it was there, the next it was hidden.

On the way back the exhaust fell off the car, Peugeot, say no more. A bigger bag of shite has never been built and we ended up having to tie it up with shoe laces. By the time we were done, all three of us were burnt alive, our faces glowing like a two bar electric heater.

It was nearly time for the Ruta 40. The road has several names. In Europe, we call it "The Ruta 40", In the USA they call it "the 40", in Yemen, they call it "Ruta Fuck story", and in Poland, they call it "Ruta Wherethefuck?"

The following passage was found in the pocket of a biker who was found in the middle of a hysterical fit lying by his bike on the Ruta 40:

Woe to You O Earth and Sea; For the Devil Sends his Road with Wrath

Because He knows that the big fellas Time is short

Let Him Who Hath Understanding ReckonThe Number of the Road

For it is a Human Number Its Number is 40

I said goodbye to Merrie and Pippen the next morning. The original plan was to take a four day ferry south but I couldn't for two reasons, firstly the thoughts of being cooked up in a boat for that length of time was getting to me and secondly it would short circuit about three hundred miles off the Ruta 40.

So what's bad about that I hear you say?

Well first of all if you're a girl you won't understand, it's a guy thing. It goes something like this. When I'm asked "So Oisin, did you do the whole thing on a motorbike?" I can't say yes because of the ferry. Yeah yeah I know, no one cares about that but secretly every guy in the world knows exactly what I'm talking about. You either did or did not go the whole way on the bike and are therefore "a big girls blouse or not a big girls blouse"

Moreover, there's a sublevel to that which is if I'm ever invited to the hard-core bikers Christmas ball, the question will come "So Oisin, Did you do all of the Ruta 40?" again I can't say yes. I will have to answer "well except for the bit..." and I'll get all those derisory "Harrumphs!" and let's face it nobody needs that.

At this moment I didn't realise that the Ruta 40 actually starts at the border with Bolivia, and not at Bariloche so riding all of the Ruta 40 would have to wait for another trip.

For my last night in Chile I was treated to a terrible dream. I was in college and I got a paper back from a lecturer with the assessment written on it "You are dumb, dumb, dumb". In the dream I reacted terribly.

It was one of those dreams that long after you wake you just can't get it out of your head. When you're driving a motorcycle there's nowhere to hide from your thoughts. Your head is stuck inside the helmet without a radio to turn on to drown it all out. I figured out a bit about myself while thinking about it over the hundreds of miles that passed.

It was important to me that people respected me and that I was thought highly of. I started to wonder if the only reason I came on the trip was so people would think I was cool. Even while I'm writing this I'm doing it I guess, I could put some shit down here that I'm doing it to inspire others, to show people what's possible; the reality is that I'm doing it to tell everyone how cool I was by doing the trip. It's one thing being a prick, but when you know your one too; now that is hard!

The other point I realised was that I talked too much, especially about the journey. I realised that I wanted to talk about it more than people wanted to hear about it. I couldn't believe that people didn't want to know every detail and that there wasn't a queue of hot birds lined up around the corner waiting to give me a blo job.

Stuck with that realisation, I headed off on my own for Argentina, not happy with the people I was with, not happy on my own wondering if I'd ever find peace.

I was pretty sure this was one of those moments where you find yourself only to find that you weren't really worth finding in the first place.

Chapter 13
Argentina

I drove north from Puerto Varas in Chile and cut east towards Bariloche in Argentina. I had reached my fifteenth and last country and the border crossing was a doddle. The drive towards Bariloche would make you want to leave Ireland and just move there instantly; the people living in this part of the world were spoilt rotten.

Mountains, rivers, blue crystal clear lakes, blue skies; no matter which way I looked I was confronted with an awesome display of nature at its finest. I was feeling like everything I'd done up to this point was merely "existing", at last I was living, and I wished this day would never end.

Sure, I was on my own, but I was happy. I then started to wonder how was it possible to be so down in the morning and so up by the afternoon. Do the Ups always follow the downs? The darkest hour is just before dawn I suppose, but I wondered if I wasn't just a bit mental.

I made it to Bariloche, which sits on a lake and is completely hemmed in by craggy snow-capped mountains. The day was full of colour; everything seemed so bright be it shimmering lakes or the ridiculously colourful hedgerows; it was like a garden show along the side of the road.

By the end of the day I was maxed out on scenery and beautiful landscapes so I was planning a big miles day the next day.

The forecast for the coming days was good; It's one thing to take on these gravel roads in dry and windy conditions, but in the wet it would be brutal, so as the old saying goes "get the fuck down the road before it starts raining."

I talked to one biker who said he drove through 70-80mph side winds on the Ruta 40 a couple of weeks back, he said his neck was like a coat hanger after it.

I was hoping to make it to Ushuaia in five days assuming Sam Gamgee and I could stand up to the battering by the wind and gravel. At this stage, I felt like I'd seen everything I wanted to see and now I just wanted to get to Ushuaia, I was itching to finish.

When I look back now I wish I could go back, smack myself in the head, and say "Dude! Cop the fuck on, when you go home it's all doom and gloom and there's a fucking recession, enjoy every second of it."

The 40 takes you through lots of one-horse towns so for a while it was back to cold water and no TV. I wrote in my diary that night "nothing like a bit of old, to make you appreciate the new, good oul days me bollix."

The four things I had consistently heard about Argentina were that 1) the women are gorgeous, 2) the steaks are unbelievable, 3) Its dear as fuck and 4) The Patagonia area is great.

My buddies back home had sent me a couple of emails threaded along the lines of "what are the women like in Argentina?" The answer is; it is very like the relationship I have with the average Robin Red Breast (it's a bird!). Namely, they´re lovely to look at, I can't understand a word they´re saying (either), they fly away if you get too close to them and finally they have no knockers!

The Argentineans in general were a very friendly bunch, mad into Soccer and Rugby. The place is really expensive though, marginally cheaper than Chile but still way more expensive than the rest of South America.

I did three hundred miles on the Ruta Diablo (40) on my second day and was still around to tell the tale. I knew what was ahead wouldn't be so easy; the further south you go, the more remote the areas and the less maintained the road would be.

This area stood out for me because it was all in bloom, given it was mid spring early summer. The average ditch had more flowers than fifty gardens put together back home. It all smelt similar to something between vanilla and honeydew and as it rolled up under the helmet I couldn't help thinking "man you could drive forever in this place!"

I saw lakes with perfect mirror reflections of the mountains that lay on their banks and while I was parked up taking it all in, a yacht with a huge white sail passed me by as it moved from right to left; it was paradise.

As I drove further and further south on the Ruta 40, lakes and mountains were gradually replaced with rolling hills as you start to arrive on the Andean Foothills and just like Alaska and the Yukon, there was absolutely nobody there.

I drove the last seventy miles without seeing a single car. Most of the tourist traffic takes a right into Chile at a town called Esquel and heads south on the Caretera Austral and then hooks back into Argentina later on, thus bypassing some of the shittier windswept sections of Ruta 40.

If I was to get my hard-core biker merit badge I'd have to do every mile so there was no "handy number" for me. At this stage I was under the impression that the Ruta 40 started in Bariloche and was about 2000km long, I since found out it starts at the Bolivian border, running for over 5000km right down to Rio Gallegos on the Atlantic coast.

The road to start with was ok; actually only about fifty miles or so was gravel. I had a mad experience while whoreing through the countryside. The wind was about 50mph or so (how I know that will become apparent) but I noticed when I rounded a bend the noise of the bike seemed to get a lot louder, almost like the bike was "chokeing" itself only louder. It took me a while to figure out that it was the wind.

What had happened was that the wind had become a tail wind and when the speed of the bike matched the speed of the wind the only sound was the engine of the motorbike, eerie stuff and one of those "you'd have to be there" moments.

Gobnorado

On the road I passed a good few what I think were Gauchos herding thousands of sheep. The noise was manic. When I got to Gobnorado (not making the name up) on the Ruta 40 I asked the service guy was there any nice hotels in the town, he replied "Mas o menos", which means "more or less" in English. Well let me tell you there was a whole lot of Menos and not a whole pile of Mas, the hotel was ming.

The town was quiet, all you could hear was the odd bird chirping, and even the noise my feet made in the gravel seemed an intrusion. Everywhere was closed; I guess the whole place was doing the whole siesta thing. As I walked around wondering if everyone had been kidnapped the only thing I encountered was a chicken, but by 6pm things had livened up a bit. I wondered if they were off having a secret meeting to decide how they were going to cook the gringo.

That night I lay on the bed looking up at a fan spinning on the ragged edge above me while it teemed down with rain outside. That's Patagonia for you, the weather changes like a whore's bastard, but I couldn't complain, the last two days were amazing so I was due some hardship, and I was nervous as hell about what lay in store for me out on the 40.

Many years after being here, Charles Darwin said of this area in his memoirs of the Beagle voyages "Why is it that this place so haunts my dreams and every waking hour", well Charlie a big Ditto from me to you.

The following day I rode over three hundred miles, this time all of it on gravel, muck, shite, sand with a hefty helping of brutal wind and driving rain. The only respite was that I saw some Emu's and road runners, Emu's are fast, road runners are, well I don't have to tell you.

I saw three trucks and cars out on the road in all those miles; the only time I came in contact with people was in the tiny towns to get some gas and grub. Finally I made it to a town called Perito Moreno. Halfway there I went through a town called Rio Mayo which happened to be paved for about five miles either side of it. It got my hopes up that maybe the Argies had spent a few bob and finally threw down some asphalt between there and Perito Moreno, my hopes were dashed as soon as I left the town; it was back to gravel.

Perito Moreno also happened to be the first town on the last page of all my maps. If you can imagine I left Ireland with over twenty different maps of all the different countries, and to be on the last page of the last map felt pretty good, not as good as a good shag mind, but in the wilds one has to take what little pleasures one can get.

Argentina is quite a poor country. Most of the shop shelves were empty or half stocked at best, a combination of low demand with a sparsely populated countryside but most of all the really shite infrastructure. None of the remote restaurants have Menus, the lady just rhymes off what they have and you say "Si", for some reason always accompanied with a finger in the air. Then it's on to drinks and you really hope you recognise something she says. For breakfast every day, no matter where you stay, its bread, jam and tea or Coffee.

My mother had two words for tea or coffee that was either too strong (Moonlach) or too week (Sulach). If you have coffee here you get Moonlach, if you have tea you get Sulach. I've been opting for Sulach, the Ruta 40 is no place for a dose of heartburn.

I left the next morning at about 8am very apprehensive about the road, not overly nervous or afraid more just a pain in my hole that I'd so much gravel ahead, about 1100 miles.

Every gravel road has lines. A line is a place you can drive your motorbike on, I touched on this before but it's worth spending a bit of time on.

What happens is the accumulation of traffic moves gravel around the place on the road and over time tracks appear. Most roads have three, one of the left, middle and right of the road and every car or truck follows these tracks. The tracks only disappear when you come to bridges, which they have a lot of or when two trucks meet and have to pull over to let each other by, thus destroying the lines in a section of the road.

So as long as you have a line, you can go along at a good clip, the problem is keeping your line. The line sometimes just runs out into the ditch, or the wind constantly pushes you across the road making it really difficult to keep to a line. If you go out of a line you have to cross what may be a gravel build-up of ten inches or more which is easily enough to make your front wheel wash out and put you on your arse. Note falling on gravel and rocks is much more risky than on sand, every time you go down your "gonna lose some meat".

The rules of the game are simple enough, for an amateur biker at least, or for someone who hasn't ridden that much off road.

1) If you use the breaks and you're not going straight you are pretty much guaranteed to come off so you have to break with the engine i.e. pop her down a gear and only go up a gear when the bike goes over 4000rpm

2) If you go too slow you'll definitely come off, anything under 30mph and your pissing against the wind. At speeds that slow you're just not hiding the obstacles in the road hard enough so you'll end up washing the front or back wheel. Anything over 70mph and you'll kill yourself if you do come off.

3) If you drive in the wrong gear and the engine idles, chugs or free wheels you won't be able to react if

something happens, the bike will be too sluggish. The engine has to be hauling ass the whole time, 3500 to 4000rpm.

4) If you tightly grip the handle bars and don't stay loose, you won't be able to compensate as the bikes rolls around on the gravel and you'll end up overcompensating, pulling the bike back too hard. Loosey Goosey is the name of the game, it's good to wobble, it should feel like you're riding a jet ski when on this junk, or that's what you keep telling yourself as you constantly fear a run off.

5) Accelerate is your only way out of any problem, hit the obstacle hard and burst your way through it. The bike wants to go straight so more gas will give it the best chance of getting through whatever it is on the road.

6) If it's raining it's impossible to see your line so you're pretty much fucked so better to just stop and wait for the rain to pass.

7) Do not put your feet down to act as stabilisers; if you're travelling too fast when your leg impacts the ground there's only one thing that's going to happen, you'll break it.

So as you're driving along you constantly have conversations with yourself an excerpt below"

"Keep the line Ois, Keep the line......nice one...nice one...Keep the line...going pretty good here....nice one....fuck! me line....where's it gone...fuck it..fuck it..fuck it..there it is....nice one.... get back on it ...get back on it... nice one...."

Or

"too slow fat boy...too slow...move it ..move it...move it.....(bike wobbling as front wheel in deeper gravel) fuuuuuuuccccccccccckkkkkkkkkk.. hold it .....no stay loose....stay loose.....(rode through it)....nice one ya big ride ya!...nice one..... stay loose ...stay loose....

And

"(quick song)...the loose...the loose....the loose is on fire...we don't need the loose so let the mother fucker burn...... bollix....the line the line the line...c'mon ya fat fuck...stay on line......nice .... nice....fuck off wind...fuck off wind...fuck off wind...accelerate ya big fuckin cardigan...gowan....gowan....ah there it is..... very nice....very nice.....

Also

"ah jaysus there's a bridge coming......uh oh...lines gone...lines gone..fuck off wind fuck off wind fuck off wind......(instinct says slow down!!!!)...mind says.....put the hammer down now!!....(acellerate and burst through the accumulation)............yeeee hawww....... made another one!.....nice one back on the line....."

(Rinse and repeat every two minutes for eight hours solid!)

By this stage I'd moved into a part of the world that has one of the most unchanging flat landscapes anywhere. My whole world had become flat barren pampas. The road seldom changes; the only thing that did change was the sky.

Rio Gallegos

I ended up doing over six hundred miles the following day, leaving at 5am and not getting to Rio Gallegos until 8:30pm. I didn't make up my mind to go that direction until that morning, I had originally planned to go to Calafate and from there onto the Perito Moreno Glacier and Torres Del Paine, but I was tired and really just wanted to get to Ushuaia. If I felt good I'd go and see them on the way back up from Ushuaia to Buenos Aires.

I had completed 2000km of the Ruta 40. The only answer one expects from a fellow biker upon telling them that you did this is as follows "here is my wife, please pleasure yourself with her", that is the sort of street cred you get.

I burst three blisters on my arse before I got into the shower that night only to discover I'd no clean jocks and went out and about in Rio Gallegos commando.

Apart from the length of the ride, the wind was terrible at times feeling like pure torture. For a guy the best way to describe dealing with the wind would be to imagine you were lying in bed asleep and your next door neighbour came into the bedroom and kicked you straight into the bollix with a pair of hob nail boots. If you're a girl obviously the above doesn't sound so bad so just imagine someone pulled your top lip up over your head till it was touching your shoulder blades.

At times I was just driving along uttering the same sentence over and over again "Fuck of Wind, fuck off wind, fuck off wind."

The only way to deal with the wind is to lean into it; you end up taking a position on the bike to compensate which is about as ergonomically friendly as someone hanging a nine inch cavity block off your left nut. I went to bed that night never realising it was possible to be so tired. I thought I had a chance at getting to Ushuaia tomorrow and wondered if they'd have a parade for me.

I thought to myself that I'd send a note to the owner of the website "9-birds-for-those-who-complete-the-ruta40.com", it would be the same guy who'll be organising the parade for me in Ushuaia.

I told him the women I wanted were as follows;

1) Brittney in the red latex suit

2) Kylie in the gold hot pants

3) Kyle in the white outfit from the "nah na nah" song (Saving you a bird there!)

4) Sharon stone minus the ice pick, and also minus the trolleys

5) Yer one from the club orange add with the nice arse

6) My secondary school female Irish teacher (wearing the tartan mini)

7) Yer one from Porkies who they called lassie (same outfit)

8) Yer one who worked in the cafe in Taxco in Mexico with the white trousers

9) Nell McCafferty, I know she's a lezzer but I just want to see if she can resist 240lbs of Jedi meat!

I knew it would all come true.

The next day was frustrating; suffice to say I didn't make it Ushuaia. The amount of border crossings was always going to make it difficult. Assuming no problems I had to cross from Argentina into Chile and then from Chile back into Argentina to get to Ushuaia, stamping in and out of each country.

When I got to the first border it was closed, it turned out that for the first time in thirty years the Argentinean Prime Minister and the Chilean Prime minister were meeting to shake hands and guess where they were doing it; at my fucking border crossing. It meant having to wait from 10:30 to 2:30, by which time a huge Queue had built up making the crossing even slower. It took away any chance of making Ushuaia that day. There would always be tomorrow.

Even though the sun shone brilliantly all day, the wind was appalling. It was so bad I nearly met my waterloo. I was overtaking a truck, with another truck a good distance up the road on the other side, the sort of manoeuvre you would do twenty times a day out on the road, and even in the wind it wouldn't normally be a problem. As I passed the truck on the left side and was coming round to go back into my "lane" the wind picked up a massive gale and I couldn't get myself back into the right lane with the other truck coming right for me with the air horn blaring.

There was nothing else I could do but gun the bike into the ditch on the left. Normally putting the bike in the ditch would be followed quickly by a ride in an ambulance, but the ditch on a gravel road is a gravel hollow (lots of spare gravel knocking around).

Acting purely on instinct I just rode the bike down the ditch at about 50mph, scooted along the bottom of the ditch gunning the bike down to second gear in the process, and steered it back up onto the road even taking the time to indicate and continued down the road.

About a mile up the road, I pulled over and kicked down the side stand. I took off the helmet, glasses and gloves and as the realisation of what had just happened came to me, it was all I could do to not throw up.

Terra Del Fuego

I made it to the Magellan straights and took the ferry over to Terra del Fuego. The seas were so high I was certain the ferry would be cancelled, but they're used to it down here. Black and white porpoises followed the ferry over but I was too busy being petrified to take any pictures. I've never been so close to so much violent water. If you fell in you wouldn't last a minute and the ferry was rocking about so much that the bike off its stand.

The northerly part of the Island of Terra del Fuego is very flat and you can see forever. With the delay at the border earlier in the day, combined with the fact that the entire Chilean side of the Island is all gravel roads it was late in the evening by the time I made it to Rio Grande.

The whole way into the town the sun was setting on my right side as you'd expect if you're driving due south, it would have been a very special moment if mother nature didn't have my head in a vice grips with the wind. If the wind can do that to a fat bastard like me driving a 250kg BMW I'd hate to think what it would do to people driving lighter machines who were a little less rotund.

I hung out there for the night and then pushed on to Ushuaia the following day. I was so worn out from battling the elements that I was really looking forward to the end.

It was a 230km run on the last morning from Rio Grande to get to Ushuaia. I felt so weird the whole way. I kept replaying Brothers in Arms by Dire Straits on my iPod, it seemed to fit the mood.

For some reason best known to God as you reach Ushuaia you leave the flat lands behind and once again you're back into the mountains. As you get closer to the town, the forests start to return; in places, whole sections were decimated by the wind.

The closer I got to Ushuaia I kept expecting that the excitement levels in me would grow and grow and grow and that any moment I'd be punching the air with excitement and roaring crying with happiness having completed my goal; it never happened.

Along the way I bumped into Graham, a Scottish biker also headed for Ushuaia, but I was anxious not to ride into the town together, in my head I was saying "No fuckin way; I've driven all this way alone, I'm going to finish it on my own."

When you get to Ushuaia it's not clear where to go to get to the end of world, or the "Fin del Mundo" as it's called. I thought to myself "you'd think they'd have a fucking sign!"

I asked many people did they know where it was, they all said they weren't sure what I meant. Worn out from travelling and very tired, I was starting to get annoyed and was saying in my head "how the fuck can you not know where the sign is, it's what every fucker comes here for. Every fucker in the world who comes here wants to have their picture taken up against this sign, how can it be no one knows where the fuck it is!"

I eventually got to the end of the Ruta 3, which had merged with the Ruta 40 in Rio Gallegos. Just two miles from the end of the road I came within an inch of being killed by a Taxi overtaking on the wrong side of the road on a bend. He was so close I thought it was game over. I eventually got there in one piece, parked up the bike, and stood looking at the sign.

This sign is one of the biggest draws for the world's list ticker travellers of which I'm a member I guess otherwise I wouldn't have been there.

My camera had packed in one mile from the sign so I got a girl to take a picture of me and send it on. She was lovely and had the worst lisp I've ever encountered; eventually I figured out that she was saying her name was Isis. At moments like that I know God has a wicked sense of humor, to give a girl a lisp only for the Dad to call her Isis.

I waited till everyone left and sat up against one of the tree stumps. I stared blankly at the sign. The sun shone and the trees shook in the gale that was blowing into my back. I tried to take it all in.

I tried to remember the places I'd been, how many days and miles I'd travelled, how many times I'd nearly been killed on the road, the different conditions, the different landscapes; I was done. I was waiting for the sense of accomplishment to kick in but it never came.

I could not understand it. I emailed Rafael to tell him what I was feeling and he told me to chill out and take a couple of days in Ushuaia and most importantly to go for lots of long walks to set things straight in your head. I do think that in some ways I wanted to be treated a bit like a hero. When you watch the long way round when the guys made it to New York there was almost a carnival and a big party with all their friends and family waiting for them. For me there was no one, just me and Sam Gamgee.

I found a hotel and booked in for three nights. Something unusual happened to my psyche because in the three days I spent there, I couldn't even look at the motorbike. I don't understand it, because up until that point every waking hour was spent constantly either riding the bike or thinking about it.

I spent the next days arseing around Ushuaia. The town itself has many snow capped peaks nearby and the weather was very changeable; not altogether a surprise when you consider how close it is to Antarctica. It's very expensive and full to the brim of tourists; most of the ones I talked with were from Holland; much like the tourists I'd met in Alaska.

The first two days I was overcome with fatigue and spent the day just sitting in restaurants drinking coffee looking out the window at the world going by. If anything I felt worse the second day than the first, I really felt empty inside. I wondered what the fuck I did this for. Does anyone give a fuck? It was such a waste of time. Not hard to spot I was in a bad place.

As I was sitting there bluer than the ocean, Isis walked in. She looked completely different today, her hair was down and if possible, she looked even more gorgeous.

We had lunch together and chatted over a couple of coffees. The weather had taken a turn so it was a great excuse to stay chatting to a fine looking young one. Her lisp was hilarious, if anything it made her more attractive, but she was far too young for me.

I'd met an Aussie couple earlier in the day and we all arranged to hook up for a couple of pints that night. The whole town was talking about a ship that had run aground on an Antarctic voyage, everyone had to be rescued off it, and luckily, no one was killed.

I walked her back to her hostel. It turned out she was a high profile engineer with a Japanese company. I told her she could have been a model to which she replied that she used to be a model but left it behind her to become an Engineer. She wanted to be known for her brains and not her beauty. "Confident bitch" I thought to myself.

On my last full day in Ushuaia, I threw my copy of the Lord of the rings into the sea. I had read it three times on my trip and it had been my companion through many a dark moment, but it was time to say goodbye. The night before I left Ushuaia I sat in my room looking at the route to Buenos Aires gloomily. I knew it was going to be a killer on the ass, and most of it bar the early section would be mind numbingly boring.

I went in to brush my teeth and noticed that I was going bald at a savage rate, I put it down to the length of time my head was in the helmet each day; "Air not getting to the scalp" and all that crap. I thought I looked old as fuck too.

Leaving Ushuaia to head for Buenos Aires didn't feel good. I knew that I was capable of doing every mile between here and there; I knew the first part would be hard as it was all gravel and wind, and that the second part would flat straight roads combined with incessant gales. It's hard to motivate yourself when you know everything that's ahead and that no matter how hard I pushed it; I'd be on the road for at least four days.

The first day started well, I left a little before sunrise. As I swept down towards the marina in Ushuaia the sun was beginning to rise pouring a peach light all around the harbour.

I had set myself many little milestones to try and build up a sense of accomplishment as I was riding along. For some reason the wind always gets worse in the evening so it was important that I get as many miles as possible done before midday.

Puerto Julian

I burned off at a savage pace in the freezing cold with the town of Tolhuin in mind. It was to be my first gas stop of the day and I wanted to be there by 7am. It was the first and last place I could get gas, before I would cross in and out of Chilean Terra Del Fuego. I stopped on the Chilean border for two roasting hot cups of coffee and a couple of cheese sandwiches. Next stop was the straits of Magellan, and given the wind hadn't picked up yet I was making great time despite the gravel road.

When I went through the Argentinean border, I thought it was very noticeable how cheap looking the uniforms the soldiers had. It also struck me how young they all looked. I couldn't imagine that these were the same folks who would have been sent to the Malvinas to fight the Falkland's war with Britain.

I got to the ferry and boarded. The bike had fallen over when I crossed a couple of days previous so this time I just stayed with it. I sat down on a metal step holding the bike with one hand; unknowingly I had fallen asleep when I was woken by an Irish couple who had spotted the Irish registration. They had just got engaged and were about to finish travelling after two years and go home and get married.

I was starting to get very worried about my tires, the gravel had taken its toll and my back tire had very little thread left on it at all. I wondered whether or not I'd have enough to get me home, and if I didn't what town on the coast would I'd be able to change them in.

Once you leave Terra del fuego it's the end of the gravel riding for the whole trip, that was it, I had beaten my nemeses. I wondered after all these miles and all the experience how would I fare if I were to take on the Dalton highway again; I reckoned I'd kick its ass.

I made it to Rio Gallegos by lunchtime and already had three hundred miles under my belt. I just put the head down and kept the arse up and didn't stop till I came to the town of Puerto Julian. It's a lovely little sea side town with lots of touristy stuffs along the sea side promenade including penguin tours and a Spanish galleon; a lovely town to spend a night in.

When I went for dinner in one of the town's only open restaurants, I met Grahame from Scotland, the same guy I'd met driving into Ushuaia. Both of us were stunned at the odds of the two of us bumping into each other in this restaurant in this town at this time.

We'd a nice steak and a couple of beers and wished each other well for the remainder of our journeys. You might ask why you didn't continue the rest of the journey together; my fault, at this stage I was so accustomed to being on my own that I didn't want to ride with anyone else.

I had less than nine hundred miles to go till I got to Buenos Aires so I decided to shoot for Bahia Blanca which was more than halfway, just short of five hundred miles. My ass was so sore from the riding (motorcycle riding) I was certain I'd need an ass transplant in Buenos Aires.

All day I saw bikers going south, no doubt with Ushuaia as their destination, every year there's a major motorcycle party in the town for New years with lots of folks starting the Pan American Highway heading South to North.

For some reason the two bikers John and Rafeal who I met in Alaska came into my head as I was looking at all the passing traffic. I remembered how desperate I was to meet some kindred spirits, when I think back on it, I was very lonely, whereas at this moment in time I just wanted to be on my own; I think over the course of the last 33,000 miles my personality had completely changed.

Sometimes serious bullshit crosses your mind as you drive along in these ultra boring stages of a trip; I kept thinking that people would undermine the achievement; would say it was easy and that anyone could do it. The truth was that anyone could do it, and that I'd met far more hardcore people on the trip than me doing things in a much tougher way.

I comforted myself by saying to myself that when I started I never thought I'd get as far as I had, and it doesn't matter that other people had done it a harder way, that's not the point; it was about testing myself. I'd passed the test and it was time to allow myself to feel good about it.

I had to keep reminding myself that I did this trip for me; not for anyone else and therefore the glory or the lack of it would all have to come from within. The chances were that people who liked me before I left would continue to like me; and the people who didn't would continue to not like me; why was I so obsessed with people liking me in the first place?

So it went for every mile up the Ruta 3 that day, continually tormented by the raging wind.

Along the way, I'd see the occasional motorcyclist in a town or a small village and he might have his girl on the back or maybe even his son or daughter clinging on for dear life. Taking your girl for a ride on a bike is a very romantic and intimate way to travel I think. You're touching so much of each other's bodies that it adds a whole sexy vibe to it as a mode of transport.

Bahia Blanca

There's also such a huge trust component; you trust the driver completely and utterly with your safety. I remember thinking when I was very young, that guys who drove bikes were crazy but that the fringe benefit was that they always had nice birds with them.

I was headed for Puerto Madryn when my back tire finally wore right through to the canvas. There was no rubber left on it at all in places. I was just at the town of Caleta Olivia and asked for directions to any motorcycle repair shop.

The town had one, and not only that when I pulled up they stopped working on the bikes they had, brought me in and changed my back tyre there and then. I was so happy, it seemed like my back tyre had dominated my every waking thought for the last day or two so it was a great relief to have it changed. They didn't have a front tyre but I reckoned I'd have enough thread to get me home.

The guy who ran the shop was very friendly, as almost everyone was who I met in Argentina. While they worked on the bike, I nipped around to a bakery and bought the lads in the shop a big box of cakes. While we were eating them the owner's missus came in with her newborn baby, she was comfortably the most beautiful girl I'd ever seen. The guy, who owned the shop I thought was the most average looking guy I'd seen, so I reckoned he must have been carrying an ankle scratcher of a mickey.

The last days riding had come; I looked in the mirror before I got on the bike and I don't remember ever looking so tired. The road for three days had been flat, straight and boring with incessant gales, I was worn out. The last leg was over four hundred miles and part of what made the journey so tedious is the fact that every mile of the journey is counted down for you by the km marker poles. They counted down from 3200 in Ushuaia; talk about ten green bottles hanging on the wall.

My oil leak continued to spew oil out onto my left leg and boot and I was certain some of must have made it down into the clutch or at least was making its way to the back brakes, I really got the feeling I was limping across the finish line.

It was only when I'd about a hundred miles to go that I finally started to relax and just enjoy the ride. For the last two hours all I did was reflect on the entire journey trying to remember every town that I'd stayed in, the more I thought about it, the more I smiled.

A friend of mine was meeting me in Buenos Aires and I'd arranged to stay in the Wilton Hotel.

I pulled up to the hotel and parked the bike and proceeded to check in. I must have looked a state. Gone was the pristine blue enduro suit and brand spanking new boots; the freshly shaven corporate goon, he was replaced by a completely filthy bearded tinker who had just completed a trip of a life time.

Epilogue
Going home and getting back to normal

I thought my adventures were over as I took a taxi to the airport in Buenos Aires. I checked onto the flight and flew out for Miami on the 19th of December 2008 exactly one hundred and sixty days after I left Ireland.

I had a four-hour layover in Miami so treated myself to a western breakfast in the Airport hotel, my first since leaving Tucson over a hundred days earlier. After picking up some duty free, it was time to board for Chicago. In December flying in or out of Chicago is a lottery at the best of times due to the severe weather, and while we were landing the plane was getting blown side to side so much that the pilot got a round of applause from the passengers when we touched down. I'd only one more flight, Chicago to Dublin; it wouldn't be long now till I was tucking into a pint with the lads.

The snow was falling very heavily as I waited to get on an American Airlines flight, and it finally taxied down the runway eight hours late. As it went into takeoff mode the right engine failed and we had to taxi back to the terminal. After another three hour delay with babies roaring crying and stranded passengers roaring and shouting we were all sent to a hotel for the night. We all had to book onto an Aer Lingus flight scheduled for the same time the following evening.

The passengers were all chucked out of the hotel for about twelve and headed to the airport to wait for the flight which was supposed to leave at 5pm. At 10pm we were once again taxiing for the runway to take off when the most unusual thing happened; the wing of our plane hit the tail of another plane which had unexpectedly reversed or been pushed out. This flight was made up mainly of the people who had been stranded the previous night and another bunch that were scheduled to fly out on this night anyway. The dynamic on the plane was crazy, the folks who were already stranded 24hrs were all saying "I hope he chances it and just takes off", the folks for whom this was their first flight were saying "No way I'm staying in this plane". Once more it was off to a hotel to return the following evening to get an alternate flight.

It was getting on for sixty five hours since I'd left Buenos Aires but as people were getting stressed out all around me I didn't even feel remotely pissed off. It all felt in control, I knew I'd get home eventually; when you've gone through Central American Borders where so little is in control and you are at the mercy of bandits; getting delayed in a US city is a piece of cake.

I ended up making some great friends at the airport and myself and four of five folks who'd been stuck for the same length of time as me ended up having a great time. Joel, myself and a girl from Madison Wisconsin headed out for a walk in the Chicago weather, it was the first time in my life I felt my nostril hair actually freezing in my nose; the only way I can describe it is imagine if someone just stuck a whole pile of newspaper up your beak.

With eighty hours on the clock and at the third attempt the plane finally left for Dublin, I wondered if there would be anyone bar my Dad to meet me at the airport, I wondered if my friends would have a surprise party for me, the returning hero!

As the plane approached Ireland I looked below the plane to see a layer of grey black clouds as far as the eye could see in all directions; it contrasted dramatically with the blue sky all around and the dawn sun beaming on the horizon. We descended through the clouds and landed in Dublin on a misty wet day.

While we were waiting for the bags to arrive, a pink bag kept on going round and round the baggage claim track; I made a joke to Joel "Do you think the owner is waiting till everyone leaves before he picks it up?"

My Dad collected me and drove me home to Portarlington. I dropped my bags at the door and went up to bed to catch some Z's. I lay on the bed on the verge of sleep, my eyes held open by the realisation that it was all over.

About two weeks later, Sam Gamgee arrived at the airport; I unpacked him and drove home and put him in my conservatory never to be ridden again. Sitting on top of the motorbike as he was the whole way with me through the trip is my pet rabbit cuddly toy named Mr Fluffykins, a gentleman rabbit if ever there was one.

Adjusting to life back in Ireland was hellish, the economy was in turmoil and it seemed like the whole world was imploding at a rate of Knott's. I was back in the job and it was like I'd never left, I finally understood why people were telling me to enjoy every last second of the trip.

People's moods in Ireland seemed to be very low and lots of my friends had lost their job, in fact there were few if any whose jobs seemed to be safe. It all seemed a million miles away from the splendid isolation of the Ruta 40, in fact it seemed like a totally different existence.

All in all was it worth doing? Absolutely, I rate it as the best thing that's ever happened to me. As to whether or not I'd do it again, well, as it happens I did, but that story is for another time, a glimpse of that story is in the opening pages of the book on the Honduras border.

My strong advice to you If you are considering doing something like this; just do it, don't live your life saying "If Only".

I'm often asked whether or not the trip changed me, and the answer is definitely, although not in the way I was expecting. I have always been a very social animal, very outgoing and happier with groups of people than being on my own. After the amount of time I spent by myself on the trip often going weeks without having a conversation with anyone, I'm now completely comfortable with my own company, happier in my own skin I guess.

I look back now and realize that I was on that road searching for what were all searching for, happiness. I didn't find it, but I know now, you have to bring it with you.

I often wonder how I survived so many near death experiences on the trip; I can only guess that someone was looking after me and that friends and family were praying for me.

A final thought. Were you ever driving down the road and saw a guy on a bike and thought to yourself "Where's he off to I wonder?"?

Well maybe it was me, and now you know!

The End.

If I Could Tell You

Time will say nothing but I told you so,
Time only knows the price we have to pay;
If I could tell you I would let you know.

If we should weep when clowns put on their show,
If we should stumble when musicians play,
Time will say nothing but I told you so.

There are no fortunes to be told, although,
Because I love you more than I can say,
If I could tell you I would let you know.

The winds must come from somewhere when they blow,
There must be reasons why the leaves decay;
Time will say nothing but I told you so.

Perhaps the roses really want to grow,
The vision seriously intends to stay;
If I could tell you I would let you know.

Suppose all the lions get up and go,
And all the brooks and soldiers run away;
Will Time say nothing but I told you so?
If I could tell you I would let you know.

W.H. Auden

Made in the USA
Lexington, KY
09 February 2012